Praise for *Smart Love*

"*Smart Love* is a terrific book of practical tips, psychological insights, and wise childrearing philosophy. Everyone who is smart enough to read *Smart Love* will have a much better idea of why babies to adolescents do what they do and of how to steer a peaceful and loving course through the daily and sometimes perplexing challenges of parenting."
—**Joan Ganz Cooney,** cofounder of Children's Television Workshop and originator of "Sesame Street"

"Every parent is determined to be a good parent, perhaps even a better parent than his or her own parents. We enter this important phase in our life with good will but also with many preconceived ideas and with great trepidation. *Smart Love* is an invaluable guide for every moment of the exciting and awesome task of being a parent."
—**Elisabeth Bing,** cofounder of Lamaze International and author of *Laughter and Tears: The Emotional Life of New Mothers*

"Raising children is the most rewarding, demanding, and joyous high-stakes job in the world. The Piepers have written an important book, recognizing that different children have different needs. *Smart Love* combines research and common sense and gives us fresh perspectives upon which to reflect and act."
—**Sharon L. Kagan, Ed.D.,** Senior Associate, Bush Center in Child Development and Social Policy, Yale University

"This is a book with a warm and embracing feel and style. The Piepers advocate a positive parenting approach that encourages parents to enjoy their children."
—**Linda A. Braun,** Executive Director, FamiliesFirst Parenting Programs

"*Smart Love* offers up sound common sense and confident parenting. And it works!"
—**Sheila Kitzinger,** author of *Tough Questions: Talking Straight with Your Kids About the Real World* and *The Complete Book of Pregnancy and Childbirth*

"At last! A parenting book that tells dads and moms it's OK to follow their healthiest instincts. This definitely isn't tough love, but it isn't permissiveness either. Over decades of experience, the Piepers have developed and tested a positive approach that is successful with all kinds of kids. Whether you're a parent or a professional, you will welcome the good news in *Smart Love*. You can enjoy a relationship with children that's based on mutual respect. You don't have to get tough—you can get smart!"
—**David S. Liederman,** Executive Director, Child Welfare League of America

"Martha and William Pieper focus on every parent's desire: the happiness of their children. They recognize that the best thing parents can do to achieve that goal is to provide love and attention in ways their children can understand and use. They encourage the long-term view of development that speaks to children's deep feelings of worthiness rather than to the here-and-now of how the child is behaving. The Piepers' approach to parenting makes the process easier and more pleasurable for both children and parents. This book is a great overview as well as a resource for solving problems."
> —**Barbara T. Bowman,** Executive Director, Erikson Institute for
> Early Childhood Education

"This seminal book should be in the hands of all parents who wish to raise caring, responsible, and secure children. The Piepers bring much clarity to the debate on parenting for the twenty-first century."
> —**Marshall H. Klaus, M.D.,** and **Phyllis H. Klaus, M.Ed., C.S.W.,**
> authors of *Bonding* and *Your Amazing Newborn*

"Martha and William Pieper have performed a real service for parents, grandparents, and all who are entrusted with the care of children. The Piepers cut through the maze of conflicting and confusing advice offered to all of us about child development, and they offer practical, balanced guidance based on years of study and experience. I'm especially pleased with the long view the authors take, with a focus on preparing children to be successful in life. I wish I'd had this book when my children were small, but I'm delighted to have it now for a better understanding of my grandchildren."
> —**Horace B. Deets,** Executive Director, AARP

"*Smart Love* is sure to engage parents who are searching for healthy and challenging principles in raising children. The Piepers put first things first—for example, that growth springs from quantity time as well as quality time."
> —**William E. Swing,** Episcopal Bishop of the Diocese of California

"I wish I'd had *Smart Love* when my children were young, but I'm glad I have it now. A must-read for anyone trying to be a smart and loving parent."
> —**Susan R. Estrich,** Robert Kingsley Professor of Law and Political
> Science, University of Southern California

"Finally, a refreshing view of the realities of childrearing. *Smart Love* will be very helpful to parents who want to establish healthy attachments and a positive communication style early on with their children. If you are a parent who is committed to raising a responsible and compassionate child, you need to own a copy of this book."
> —**Kimberley Clayton Blaine, M.A., M.F.C.C.,** Children's
> Institute International

Smart Love

Smart Love

The Compassionate Alternative to Discipline
That Will Make You a Better Parent
and Your Child a Better Person

Martha Heineman Pieper, Ph.D.
William J. Pieper, M.D.

The Harvard Common Press
Boston, Massachusetts

The Harvard Common Press
535 Albany Street
Boston, Massachusetts 02118

Printed in the United States of America
Printed on acid-free paper

Library of Congress Cataloging-in-Publication Data
Pieper, Martha Heineman
    Smart love : the compassionate alternative to discipline that will make you a better parent and your child a better person / Martha Heineman Pieper and William J. Pieper.
        p. cm.
    Includes bibliographical references and index.
    ISBN 1-55832-182-9 (paperback alk. paper)
    ISBN 1-55832-142-X (hardcover alk. paper)
    1. Discipline of children. 2. Child rearing. 3. Parenting.
I. Pieper, William Joseph. II. Title.
HQ770.4.P54 1999
649'.64—dc21   98-32053
                                                         CIP

Special bulk-order discounts are available on this and other Harvard Common Press books. Companies and organizations may purchase books for premiums or resale, or may arrange a custom edition, by contacting the Marketing Director at the address above.

Text design by Joyce C. Weston

10 9 8 7 6 5 4 3 2

For our children

Contents

Preface

We all wish that parenthood could be filled exclusively with joy and fulfillment, but it is, for many, a period laced with doubt, guilt, and uncertainty. The underlying question that plagues most parents is, What is *good parenting* and how can we become *good parents?* Unfortunately, there has never been either a universally agreed upon or a satisfactory answer to this question.

In *Smart Love,* we share our own thinking about parenting in hopes that others will find it helpful. We have been developing and practicing this approach for more than thirty years. Our findings come from two different hands-on sources—parenting our own five children and clinical research done in the course of helping children, adolescents, parents, and other adults in our professional practices.

One of us, Martha, has a Ph.D. in clinical social work and maintains a private practice counseling parents, doing psychotherapy, and supervising other mental health professionals. She has also been a consultant to foster care and adoption agencies and has written and lectured extensively on research issues. The other of us, William, is a child and adult psychiatrist and psychoanalyst who has consulted with children's agencies and hospital clinics devoted to children with developmental problems and has taught in various professional schools. He also has a private practice in which he sees individuals, counsels parents, and supervises other mental health professionals.

For many decades both of us have enjoyed the opportunity to work and learn together as both parents and professionals. Even at the beginning, we found the prevailing theories of child development to be both unsatisfying and ineffective. In our judgment, no theory we have come across offers adequate answers to the important questions that every parent and every mental health professional must address. Not only do the existing theories seem inconsistent and ineffective; they also seem to be at odds with the natural tenderness parents feel toward their children. We wanted to learn more about issues such as

What is a baby's basic nature at birth? How much happiness can humans rightfully expect? When and why does happiness transform itself into unhappiness? What is a parent's most important task?

So we set out on our own to find answers that would allow us to be better parents and more effective professionals. We learned from the insights and dilemmas of the many parents we counseled, from our own clients, and from supervising the caseloads of other mental health professionals. We evaluated the results of the counsel we gave to parents and to foster care and adoption agencies. As another way of testing our ideas, we created and ran a successful treatment program for adolescent wards of the state who had been designated "untreatable." Our research and experience taught us that the emotional problems of children and adolescents couldn't be treated piecemeal or solely as individual behaviors that need to be modified. We found that troubled children are difficult to help because they have learned to need unhappiness. We saw that the real goal is to help troubled children turn away from needs for unhappiness as they rediscover the desires for positive relationship pleasure with which they were born.

Our work with unhappy and difficult children, our experience with children who were thriving, and our ongoing parenting responsibilities combined to show us how vital it is for children to see themselves as loving and lovable, and led us to a new understanding of the goals of childhood and how best to help children attain them.

With the benefit of this large pool of experience, we developed the concepts that fill *Smart Love*. Initially, we set forth our conclusions in *Intrapsychic Humanism*, a text written expressly for professionals and academics. As word about *Intrapsychic Humanism* began to spread within the professional and academic worlds, we were repeatedly asked whether we would write a book specifically for parents. That decision was the genesis of *Smart Love*.

In *Smart Love*, we have collected practical guidelines that will enable parents to give their children the specific kind of love they need to grow into happy, fulfilled adults. We've seen the effectiveness of smart love with children, adolescents, and parents from all walks of life and different racial, ethnic, economic, and cultural backgrounds. We hope that parents everywhere will find *Smart Love* an indispensable tool for sustaining and nurturing their children's emotional well-being.

We are hugely indebted to the many people who have believed in smart love and helped us to make this book a reality. First and foremost, we would like to recognize the parents, some of whom we know and some of whom we have never met, who took time from their busy lives to give us invaluable feedback. We intended to mention you by name, but by now there are so many of you that the list would stretch on for pages. You know who you are, and we hope you will accept this expression of gratitude.

Jane Jordan Browne saw the diamond-in-the-rough manuscript we brought her and stuck with *Smart Love* until it found a good home. Jeffie Pike Durham tirelessly worked to improve our communication to parents and somehow maintained her energy and interest through draft after draft. The "study group" also read numerous versions, and we benefited from their professional as well as their personal advice. Josef Blass combined precision and insight in his suggestions. Jessica Heineman-Pieper was, as always, a penetrating adviser. Victoria Heineman Stein unstintingly offered us her time and special expertise. Carol Fass managed to be professional, demanding, and reassuring all at once. Finally, we are grateful to The Harvard Common Press for being so skillful at what they do and so committed to this project.

Introduction

What Is Smart Love?

All parents want to raise a happy, successful child, but there is little agreement about how best to reach this goal. Over the years, parents have tried dramatically different recipes. They have put their baby on a schedule, or they have fed on demand; they have let their baby cry herself to sleep, or they have picked her up as soon as she cried; they have stayed home with their child, or they have entrusted her to day care and gone to work; they have taught their baby letters and numbers, or they have left her mind a clean slate for her teachers to write on; they have given their child whatever she wants, or they have made her earn what she gets; they have made their child do chores, or they have asked little of her around the house; they have demanded good grades, or they have let their child find her own level in school.

These contrasting parenting strategies arise from quite different views of the nature of children and childhood and the roles of parents. Some parents view their child as naturally social and their job as allowing her the space to thrive, while others think that their child is by nature out of control. Some parents are convinced that their child is morally innocent, while others believe she is wily and manipulative. Some parents see their child as inclined to be dependent and needing help to leave the nest, while others are convinced their child needs constant attention and guidance.

Whether you are the parent of a newborn or an adolescent, the parent of one child or five, you may worry about making the correct response to your child when she cries, makes demands, is frightened, wants constant cuddling and other attention, or won't do what is good for her (for example, she refuses to eat her vegetables, go to sleep, do her homework, or come in at curfew).

As parents and as mental health professionals we have lived and struggled with these same fundamental issues. The discoveries we made in the course of decades of researching the subject of the true nature of the child, as well as the question of the necessary ingredients for a child's healthy emotional development, have given us a new understanding of children and childhood, which, in turn, led us to create guidelines that all parents can use to parent lovingly but knowledgeably and effectively. Hence the term **smart love.**

In the first three chapters, we lay out the basic principles of the smart love approach to parenting—for example, that it is important to see the world and, especially, yourself, through your child's eyes; that sometimes it is best to accept your child's emotional immaturity, even when it is played out in behaviors like cheating at games or not wanting to share toys; that parents are not stuck with a choice between soft permissiveness and hard discipline because smart love makes possible an effective middle ground, called **loving regulation;** that children who are treated harshly come not only to expect unhappiness but to want it; that you cannot spoil your child with positive attention and, in fact, that lots of loving attention will make your child independent, not dependent; that quantity time is as important as quality time; that tantrums, nightmares, night terrors, habitual sibling quarrels, and many other conspicuous displays of childhood unhappiness are not inevitable; and that the best parenting involves using your head while trusting your heart.

In the later chapters, we focus on the developmental milestones from infancy through adolescence so that you will know for sure what behaviors are appropriate at what age. When your child's behavior needs regulation, we will show you why it is less important to wonder "How do I get Jill to behave herself right now?" than to ask yourself, "How can I help Jill develop into an adult who will want to, and be able to, take good care of herself and be caring toward others when I am not around?"

We return to the question Socrates asked almost twenty-five hundred years ago, "Can virtue be taught, and if so, how?" All parents face the question of the best way to help their child acquire a reliable capacity for self-regulation. What history has taught us is that we cannot rely on the four most common methods of trying to teach children self-discipline —moral instruction, disciplinary measures, permissiveness, and rewards. We will show you another way to think about guiding your child toward responsible adulthood. Loving regulation is a means of protecting children from the consequences of their immaturity while at the same time offering them your ongoing love and admiration. When you help your child make constructive choices in a context of an ongoing close relationship, your child will come to recognize that the deepest happiness results from loving and feeling lovable and loved rather than from satisfying particular desires or achieving specific goals. Your child will learn to govern herself better through the desire to feel happier and more competent than she ever would from fear of negative consequences.

You will learn how best to satisfy your child's developmental needs and how to use loving regulation to manage her immature behaviors. With the guidelines we provide, you can help your child to acquire a stable inner well-being that is unaffected by success, failure, or other ups and downs of daily life, and that will enable your child to reach her full potential.

∾

You will benefit from this book if

- you want to help your child reach her full potential and grow up to be a happy, loving adult;
- you want to understand childhood from your child's point of view;
- you want to improve and strengthen your relationship with your child;
- you are uncomfortable with the disciplinary measures advocated by most popular books but worry that offering children too much love and affection will "spoil" them;
- you aren't sure how to regulate your child's behavior without stifling her spirit;
- you are a busy working parent and want to ensure that you spend a maximum amount of pleasurable and meaningful time with your child;
- your child is unhappy (difficult, moody, or has nervous habits, trouble sleeping, school problems, trouble maintaining positive relationships); or
- you aren't actively parenting at the moment, but you work with children and/or you are interested in understanding why some children grow up happy and fulfilled while others become unhappy and difficult.

As parents ourselves, we have experienced firsthand the joys and the demands of parenthood. And because of our therapeutic efforts with hundreds of families from differing socio-economic, racial, ethnic, and cultural backgrounds, we also know that smart love guidelines are equally useful with all children and can be applied by any parent. The case examples we use throughout this book to illustrate the principles of smart love are all real-life instances of parents putting smart love into action.

Until now, smart love has been used and appreciated only by our clients and in academic and clinical settings.[1] This book is the fruit of our long-standing wish to present smart love to a wide readership so that all parents will have the tools they need to raise happy, fulfilled, loving children.

Chapter One

---〰️---

The Basics of
Smart Love

No matter what your child's age, with the help of smart love principles you can implement more effective and compassionate parenting strategies. Smart love gives you a relaxed and realistic timetable for your child's emotional development; identifies heretofore unrecognized developmental milestones and shows you how to help your child reach them; offers you a way to protect your child from missteps caused by her immaturity without resorting to the extremes of permissiveness or strict disciplinary measures (both of which are counterproductive); and makes it possible for you to raise a successful and truly happy child. Just as important, if your child is unhappy and difficult, the smart love principles will show you how to recapture her birthright of inner happiness.

Smart love offers a new understanding of the entire sweep of child development, allowing you to view the process of growing up through your child's eyes. With an awareness of how your child's experience of the parent-child relationship changes as she grows from infancy through adolescence, you will be better able to provide your child with a lasting conviction that she is loved and understood.

By reading this book, you will have a better understanding of your baby's cries, and why your two-year-old's favorite word is "no." You will discover why four-year-olds refuse to believe there is anything they cannot do by themselves, and you will learn that the best way to motivate children to do chores and homework is also the kindest and most gradual. With the help of smart love guidelines it will be possible for both you and your child to enjoy your child's adolescence.

We would like to mention here that although in these pages we sometimes assume the presence of two heterosexual parents, smart love methods are equally useful in any family arrangement. We wrote this book to help all parents, and we do not mean for any parent to feel excluded or overlooked.

Your Child's Inner Happiness

The fundamental viewpoint that informs our approach concerns your child's outlook at birth. Contrary to conventional wisdom, your new-born is not an undifferentiated blob who is aware only of himself. Instead, our research indicates that when your baby meets you he is an optimist with regard to human relationships. Unlike adults, infants are absolutely certain that whatever happens to them is for the best, because their beloved parents have caused or intended whatever happens. Your brand-new baby believes both that he is engaging your love, and also that the care he receives is ideal. When these inborn convictions are confirmed day after day, your child grows up to possess a lasting inner happiness. As we will describe, this unshakable inner happiness, in turn, will allow him to attain his highest potential.

Primary Happiness

Primary happiness originates in the conviction that all infants bring into the world that they are causing their parents, whom they adore more than life itself, to pay loving attention to their developmental needs. Your child's primary happiness becomes *unshakable* when he is certain that you love caring for him. As he matures, your child will increasingly use the knowledge that you are helping him to become happy and competent as the source of his primary happiness. Once his primary happiness is firmly in place, your child's day-to-day happiness will no longer depend on whether or not you are able to respond to any one particular need at a given moment.

We have found that children can acquire primary happiness that will not alter with life's ups and downs, and that this is the child's most important developmental achievement. Even though you may have been told that "healthy" doses of frustration build character, it is your caring responses that instill stable primary happiness in your child. As you will see, unnecessary frustration and deprivation actually interfere with your child's acquisition of stable primary happiness by causing him to develop needs to make himself unhappy.

Secondary Happiness

While primary happiness is generated within your child's relationship with you, **secondary happiness** is the pleasure generated by everyday activities (such as building with blocks, dressing a doll, solving a math problem, playing the violin, hitting a baseball). The process of developing **stable secondary happiness** begins in your child's second year and is completed only at the end of adolescence. With the same smart love guidelines you use to foster your child's unshakable primary happiness, you can help your child develop permanent secondary happiness.

In his first year, your baby uses the satisfaction generated by intellectual, social, and physical pursuits to supply himself with primary happiness. Being fed sustains your infant's primary happiness because it strengthens his belief that he is causing you to love caring for him. When you give food to your hungry preschooler, his primary happiness is nourished by your responsiveness and, in addition, he gains secondary happiness in the process of helping with food preparation (stirring, mixing, and pouring).

As with primary happiness, secondary happiness follows a developmental course. Initially secondary happiness is unreliable because it depends entirely on your child's ability to attain whatever satisfactions his heart desires. By the end of adolescence, however, your child's secondary happiness can become as stable as his primary happiness because he recognizes that making constructive choices and pursuing them well is more reliably satisfying than getting what he wants when he wants it. Stable secondary happiness is linked to the enjoyment of activities and pursuits, but because it is not outcome-dependent it is not shaken by the occasional setbacks or frustrations that are bound to occur.

The All-Powerful Self and the Competent Self

In the early years, your child's secondary happiness is bundled with her conviction that she is so powerful that she can do and have anything. This belief, made possible by your child's cognitive immaturity, is one of the main reasons that she will be vulnerable to self-caused physical injury. If left unattended, your young child might, for example, decide to turn on the stove to cook, to drive the family car, to swim in the pool, or to plug in a hair dryer without the slightest inkling that she might not be fully capable of handling these activities.

We call your child's compelling but unfounded belief in her ability to fulfill any and every wish the **all-powerful self**. The all-powerful self represents your child's first conscious pursuit of intellectual, social, or physical pleasure in and of itself. The influence of the all-powerful self can be seen in the two-year-old who is determined to carry Mommy's heavy briefcase and who becomes upset when Mommy suggests that she might need help.

We know a six-year-old who could barely dribble a basketball but who announced to his parents, "I can beat Michael Jordan at free throws!" Parents often feel uncertain about the best way to respond to children who are claiming extraordinary powers. Some parents try to introduce the child to reality as gently as possible ("You're very good for your age!"). Other parents worry that the child's "boasting" needs to be checked, so they respond with teasing, confrontation, or disapproval. The smart love guideline is that *since your child depends on your approval for inner well-being, and since the child's all-powerful self is an age-appropriate phenomenon that he will outgrow, the best help you can give your child is simply to respond with positive acceptance* ("That's amazing!").

As your child matures, the source of her secondary happiness will undergo a crucial transformation. As your child experiences your commitment to make her happy even when she can't have what she wants, her all-powerful self is gradually replaced by a radically different sense of self-governance we call the **competent self**. The competent self is qualitatively different from the all-powerful self because it is gratified by the process of choosing constructive goals and pursuing them well, regardless of whether these goals are achieved.

When we refer to the all-powerful self and the competent self, we do not mean that your child is inhabited by separate personalities. Rather, we mean that there are two very different sources of secondary happiness: your child's success at getting what she wants, and the pleasure of making good choices and pursuing them competently. If you facilitate as many of your child's desires as possible and respond to her with understanding when she is upset because her wishes cannot be met, the source of your child's secondary happiness will evolve from the all-powerful self's need to gratify everyday desires to the competent self's ability to make constructive choices and pursue them well. In other words, your child will increasingly feel competent and confident even when the tower she is building falls over, another child won't share a truck she covets, or she can't go to the playground because it is raining. For example, when told it is time for bed, a child whose competent self is gaining influence can usually interrupt her pursuits with equanimity and can enjoy the stories and good-night hugs and kisses that comprise the bedtime ritual. At an earlier age, the request that she interrupt an absorbing activity and head for bed might temporarily diminish her secondary happiness and bring on anger or tears.

By the end of adolescence, children whose developmental needs are adequately satisfied will possess an enduring secondary happiness produced by the ongoing satisfaction of making good choices and pursuing them well. In contrast, children whose developmental needs are not fully met will remain under the spell of their all-powerful selves — their secondary happiness will remain yoked to their success or failure at getting what they want.

Why Children Become Unhappy and Difficult

Contrary to popular belief, inborn temperament is not the reason that children become unhappy and develop problematic behavior. Through our extensive clinical experience we have come to the conclusion that children become unhappy because they have learned to desire unhappiness, which happens when they are regularly made to feel unhappy or their unhappiness is not responded to with understanding and caring.

As we have said, all babies meet their parents as optimists with regard to relationships. Each infant believes that his parents are perfect caregivers who are perfectly devoted to him. He has an inborn conviction that everything that happens to him is for the best because it is intended and approved by his parents. As a result, when for some reason parents are consistently unable to satisfy a child's developmental needs, the infant reacts by believing that his unhappy or alienated feelings are intended and approved of by his parents. *Out of love for their parents, and in an attempt to care for themselves exactly as their beloved parents care for them, such children unknowingly develop the desire to cause themselves exactly the same discomfort they believe their parents want for them.* These children believe that they are seeking happiness when they strive to re-create the feelings they experienced in their parents' presence or absence. This learned but unrecognized need to experience unhappiness explains why so many children (and adults) react to success with depression or self-defeating actions. Children who have acquired needs to make themselves unhappy may develop symptoms such as frequent temper tantrums, depression, difficulties concentrating, low self-esteem, and problems with drugs and alcohol.

The good news is that it is never too late to help unhappy and difficult children. Smart love guidelines help parents help their children to change in positive, lasting ways. By learning how to build on their children's inborn, enduring desires to have a positive and loving relationship with their parents, *all* parents can make significant and constructive changes in their parenting and thereby ease the misery experienced by problem children of any age.

No one looking at infants or small children would think they were ready to put in a full day on an assembly line or at a computer. Even so, parents and professionals often assume that young children's emotional and social responses should be the equivalent of adults'. But when children are forced to behave like grownups prematurely, their emotional development is compromised and they develop inner unhappiness. We cannot overemphasize that *infants and children should not be expected to have the moral sensibilities or self-control of adults.* Children will develop a genuine capacity to share and to care (to be good citizens) only if they are given the space and time to freely choose to be like those they love and admire.

Many caregivers frequently mistake behaviors that are appropriate for a child's age for negative character traits that must be stamped out immediately. For example, parents are often needlessly concerned about their infant's expressions of anxiety toward strangers, or his anxiety about being separated from his parents. Parents sometimes feel embarrassed or as though they have failed when their previously friendly, outgoing child cries in fright at the sight of Aunt Mary, or shrieks and clings to them when they are merely going into the other room to get a book. Parents who worry that their child has become permanently timid or clingy may try to induce him to behave like older children. The most helpful approach to helping your child with **stranger anxiety** and **separation anxiety** is relaxed comforting.

Other normal vulnerabilities are hard to accept because they manifest themselves in extreme assertiveness. An example is the phase in which young children grab for every desired object—whether or not it is attached to another child, or even a baby. Young children are grabby because they are going through a temporary phase in which obtaining what they want when they want it provides a secondary happiness that they can't get any other way. Parents who are unaware of the underlying reason for their child's grabbiness may become disapproving when he grabs, and they also may insist that he share his toys with other children. Unfortunately these responses simply add to the discomfort young children naturally feel when they can't have whatever they want, and in turn having what they want becomes even more imperative. If you are accepting of your young child's inability to share, he will feel loved and understood. The security of feeling cared for will make getting what he wants seem less urgent, and will hasten the day when he will want to be generous because friendships will seem more important to him than things.

Many conflicts with children, for example, around issues of sharing, "disobeying," toilet training, and chores, occur only because parents do not realize that they can trust their children to mature on their own timetables. By familiarizing yourself with the developmental milestones described in this book, you will feel more confident and derive more enjoyment from your relationship with your child.

Loving Regulation

All parents face the question of the best way to help their child acquire the capacity for self-regulation. Previously, **discipline** has seemed to be the only alternative to its polar opposite: **permissiveness**. For many years the consensus in this society has been that parents need to respond to children's failures at self-regulation with an array of measures designed to manage unwanted behavior by attaching unpleasant consequences to it, including punishment, disapproval, isolation (time-outs), forceful language ("No!"), or withholding of privileges. Parents have been told that by setting rigid limits and meting out significant consequences for breaking the rules they will raise well-behaved kids who will stay out of trouble and will not trouble their parents. We believe that discipline makes children miserable without offering them any genuine benefit, because punishing children whose behavior is out of control actually interferes with their ability to learn self-governance. We advocate the use of **loving regulation,** a way for parents to guide their children away from missteps without adding to their unhappiness or interfering with their development of inner happiness. In later chapters we look at the behaviors and struggles of children at different ages so that parents can know how to apply the principles of loving regulation as their child grows up.

Guiding Without Punishing

There is no question that young children need to be protected from their own immature understanding and kept out of harm's way. For example, a young child cannot be permitted to light matches or cross the street alone. But through our work we have learned that parents are most successful when they regulate their children's behavior with loving assistance rather than discipline.

Because you are bigger and stronger than your child, you have the power to apply discipline to stop out-of-control behavior, but when you do so you teach your child—albeit unknowingly—that your love and warmth are conditional and that you sometimes want to make her unhappy. The best way to respond to a child's harmful or dangerous behavior is to stop it without imposing added unpleasantness. If you discover that your ten-year-old has been breaking the rules and riding her bike in the street, it makes sense to tell her that since, at the moment, she doesn't seem able to stay on the sidewalk on her own, you will keep her safe by insisting that for a given period of time she may ride her bike only when you are with her. Although your child may protest, at the same time she will realize that you are trying to keep her safe, and her wish to be careful will be strengthened. On the other hand, if you respond to the child's breaking of the rules by adding unrelated consequences—for example, you withhold her allowance, tell her she has to wash the windows, or forbid her from riding her bike entirely—she will conclude that you want her to suffer for her error. Because she adores you and wants to be just like you, she will learn to adopt a severe attitude toward herself when things go wrong. Also, her ability to remain safe will actually be weakened.

Time-outs, restrictions, punishments, and other forms of discipline are based on the assumption that being too nice to children who are "misbehaving" will encourage and reward their bad behavior. But we would point out that discipline interferes with the most consistent and satisfying source of young children's inner well-being: their conviction that they are causing their parents to love caring for them. For this reason, disciplining children makes them more miserable and less able to forgo their wishes. In contrast, loving regulation shows children that although they may have to give up gratifying a particular wish, they can always count on the pleasure of the parent-child relationship.

Even when experts define discipline as "teaching," the teaching component of their disciplinary program always includes lectures, consequences, and, often, disapproval and time-outs. Because children adore their parents and believe they are ideal caregivers, when parents routinely impose unpleasant consequences for "misbehavior," children develop needs to treat themselves the same way.

A GIRL DISAPPROVES OF HERSELF

From the time that Janet[2] was two years old, whenever she became angry, demanding, or oppositional her parents told her they were "disappointed" in her. After her third birthday, if Janet did something she thought was wrong, like spilling her milk or yelling at her sister, she would exclaim, "I'm a naughty girl!" and run to her room and fling herself on her bed. Her parents had great difficulty in getting her to rejoin the family. When they perceived that Janet's periods of self-imposed isolation were increasing, her parents came to us for help. We discussed how they could use loving regulation rather than disapproval to address some of Janet's troublesome behaviors. They developed some new strategies for responding to Janet. For example, if Janet spilled her milk and looked stricken, her parents would give her a hug and reassure her: "It's just a mistake—we spill things sometimes, too. Let's just wipe it up."

When she yelled at her little sister at dinnertime, they would remark, "If you're tired of playing with Sarah, just tell us. Maybe you would like to help Dad set the table and then play some checkers with him?" Over the next few months, Janet gradually recognized the value of turning to her parents for comfort when she felt upset or out of control. Most important, taking her cue from her parents, she began to treat herself less harshly. As a result, her self-imposed periods of punitive isolation decreased dramatically.

Loving regulation is an alternative approach to handling children's out-of-control behavior. You stop the unwanted behavior immediately, but you do so without burdening the child with additional unhappiness or depriving her of parental warmth and admiration. Unlike discipline, loving regulation does not alienate children from parents or teach them to dislike themselves.

Smart love removes the punitive component, not the regulatory component, of governing children's behavior. Frustrating children and making them unhappy teach them nothing worthwhile. Your child will be better able to accept not getting or doing what she wants if she has your warm understanding to fall back on. The long-term goal is to help your child develop the ongoing capacity to make good choices and pursue them in an unconflicted and competent manner. Children learn to govern themselves effectively only by identifying with your kindness and helpfulness toward them, not by being made unhappy. Genuine self-discipline is generated by a love that is abundant and available, and not by "tough love," which is rationed and conditional.

When you must step in and regulate your child's behavior, try to show her that you remain concerned about how she feels about what is happening, and that you will not turn your back on her protests or unhappiness. If your toddler is determined to pull the cat's tail, you may have to put the cat out of reach for a time, but there is every reason to comfort your child and to try to engage her in an alternative project that is equally appealing. Over time, the child who is treated in this way realizes that even though you must refuse some of her wishes, you will never abandon your cherished goal of making her happy by responding to her true needs. When you guide your child to make constructive choices in a context of ongoing closeness with you, she will begin to realize that genuine happiness results from feeling lovable and loved rather than from gratifying particular desires.

If you use the smart love guidelines, like all children, your child will occasionally behave in ways that would be unacceptable in adults—for example, your eighteen-month-old will typically grab toys from other children—but this results from immaturity and will be temporary. Your young one will outgrow and abandon this behavior on her own as it becomes unnecessary or unattractive. She is too young to understand why she cannot have what she wants, so it is best to guide her gently to a more appropriate activity.

Avoid Denting Your Child's Primary Happiness

Loving regulation is superior to both disciplinary measures and permissiveness, because it is the *only* way to regulate your child's immature behavior without diminishing her primary happiness. When you consistently support the child's inborn belief that she is causing her parents to pay loving attention to her developmental needs, you guarantee your child's primary happiness forever.

You want to avoid causing your child to feel ashamed, bad, or as though you don't want her around when she is angry or upset. Parents are frequently advised to tell their child that her behavior makes them angry. But children cannot distinguish between their parents' anger at their *behavior* and their parents' feelings about *them*. This is true even of adolescents, who possess the intellectual maturity to understand the distinction their parents are making, but feel hurt nonetheless. When children repeatedly experience their parents as being angry at them, they copy their parents and develop needs to feel angry at themselves. If a child has already acquired inner unhappiness, the experience that her parents are angry with her will strengthen her needs to cause herself unhappiness.

Parents are also told to say to their child that, while they don't like her behavior, they still love her ("I am unhappy when you…"). Even this is too negative. What children hear at such a moment is that their parents are disappointed in them. Instead you need to focus on regulating the action that is dangerous or inappropriate. It is enough simply to say, "Please don't pound with the hammer on the table. I'll go get your pounding board." If the child doesn't respond, the matter-of-fact statement "If you don't stop, I'll have to take the hammer away for a while" is strong enough. If you have to take the hammer away from her, try to maintain a positive and friendly manner ("I have to put the hammer away for now, but we can bang spoons on this pot"). Your child will realize that the hammer may have to go, but your love and caring remain.

Your Child's Point of View: If You're Mad, I'm Bad

Disciplinary responses, such as counting to three, giving time-outs, saying a loud "no!", or revoking privileges, teach children that you choose to use your superior power coercively rather than compassionately. Disciplinary measures may or may not force your child to behave as you wish, but inevitably they will teach your child not only that disappointments are painful in themselves, but also that these circumstances cause her parents to become angry or rejecting. *Because your child's love of you drives her to emulate you, she will learn to use anger and self-rejection as a means of managing herself.*

A TIME-OUT TURNS A BOY INTO A TROLL

A mother whose children were constantly fighting came to see us because she was at her wits' end. She gave as an example an incident in which four-year-old Stephen rammed his plastic bike into his sister while she, the mother, was talking on the phone with a friend. The mother told Stephen that his behavior was unacceptable and made her feel angry and that he would have to have a five-minute time-out. After Stephen served his time and was set free, he began jumping out from behind the furniture making faces and growling, "I'm a horrible ugly troll."

Why did Stephen react this way? When Stephen's mother fell into her customary pattern and expressed anger and then isolated him with a time-out, Stephen reacted by feeling unattractive to her and, therefore, to himself and everyone else. He expressed this feeling of being repellent by assuming the identity of the monster in one of his stories.

The next time Stephen began to push his sister when his mother was on the phone, this mother tried to respond with loving regulation. She told her friend she had to get off the phone for a moment, looked after her daughter, and then said to Stephen, "Look, sweetheart, I know it can be hard to wait for me when I am on the phone, but you can't hurt your sister. I have to call my friend back now. Get a toy and sit next to me until I finish talking. Then I'll play with you and Clara. Why don't you think about what you would like the three of us to do together?" In this way she regulated Stephen's aggressive behavior without depriving him of the warmth of their relationship and thereby diminishing his positive feelings about himself.

All parents have moments when it feels as though they have been drained of their entire supply of patience, humor, and perspective. Certainly imposing time-outs is preferable to hitting children, and you may need to use an occasional time-out to avoid a more destructive response. We would emphasize, however, that it is important that you recognize that these time-outs are for your benefit rather than your child's. Time-outs should not be presented to the child either as "deserved" or as a means to self-improvement. There is another approach. If you feel you are about to blow your stack, you can simply say, "I need a moment to collect myself. I'll go to my room and be back in a moment when I feel calmer."

Redefining Independence

Parents sometimes express concern that if they consistently respond to their child's needs, their child will develop an unhealthy dependence on them. This worry is groundless because true **independence** is not measured by the extent of a child's emotional and physical distance from his parents. Children are not like fledglings who need to be pushed out of the parental nest. When you meet your child's emotional needs, you foster a *genuine* type of independence, which has its roots in your child's reservoir of stable inner happiness and is expressed as an unconflicted ability to make good choices and to pursue them enthusiastically and well. True independence means that your child's inner happiness is not dependent on his everyday experiences, such as success at getting what he wants.

Children, adolescents, and young adults whose emotional needs have been adequately met do not go on to widen their circle of interests, relationships, and pursuits because they are pushed away or feel shame at enjoying their parents' company. Rather, they are enthusiastic about pursuing new relationships and about trying out their academic and recreational talents. They broaden their horizons knowing that they can go home again, and that they will be welcomed when they do. Truly autonomous individuals move on to a full life, not away from their parents. They possess an abundance of confidence and good feelings that is evident in everything they do; they do not go out into the world with the need to prove something or to fill an inner void.

When a child of any age clings to his parents and is unable to enjoy activities or friendships that are appropriate for his age, parents are often told that they have made life too easy or pleasant for their child, thereby robbing him of all initiative. But this child is not unmotivated; he only lacks the benefit of enough focused, informed, responsive love. Attempts to pry the child away from his parents and to force him to mature will only cause him to become dependent on forms of pleasure that are less constructive than the closeness all children wish to experience with their parents.

Through our years of clinical research and work with parents we have learned that children whose fundamental needs are met grow into adults who possess a personal and social autonomy born of an unshakable inner happiness, which no longer depends either on their parents' continued presence or on any other kind of external satisfaction.

Chapter Two

∼

Smart Love in Action

All parents want to give their children the gift of lifelong happiness and fulfillment, but some combination of the demands of making a living, the stresses and strains of daily life, or emotional baggage parents carry from their own childhood can make it difficult for them as parents to be consistently effective with their children. Also, bad advice is spread far and wide, often causing parents either to abandon their good instincts or else to feel needlessly guilty when they follow their own loving impulses.

In the following pages you will learn how to make the best use of your time with your child, and, contrary to what you have heard elsewhere, you will see how you can parent most effectively when you heed your warmhearted inclinations. Because you will come to understand how and why children acquire inner unhappiness, you will be able to improve dramatically the quality of your responses to your child, no matter what the age of your child or the state of her inner well-being.

Balancing Parenting Aims and Personal Desires

Parents of newborns often tell us that they have difficulty adjusting to the experience of having their schedule almost entirely determined by their infant's needs. Parents can have varying reactions to being constantly on call. Some parents are generally pleased and proud to be needed and helpful; others feel burdened or trapped. With the smart love philosophy you can view the world through your child's eyes and come to see how responding positively and generously to your child's needs for your focused warmth and attention will make your child happy and functional and shield her from developing inner unhappiness and problem behavior. Smart love guidelines will also help you to distinguish parenting aims from personal desires.

Parenting aims are your intentions to respond to your child's developmental needs. When you act on your parenting aims, you give your child the special happiness that comes from knowing she has inspired you to respond in a consistent and caring manner to her needs for love and attention. As she grows to adulthood, this sustaining inner happiness will allow your child to become a good caregiver to herself, to be caring in relationships, and generally to be accomplished at living her life. Your love for your child and your parenting aims enable you to awaken in the middle of the night in response to your baby's cries or your child's request for a drink of water and retain a feeling of satisfaction at having responded, even though, before your child's birth, at times you could barely be awakened by an alarm clock.

Personal desires are intentions that are not in the service of responding to your child's developmental needs. Certainly you continue to have personal needs after you become a parent—these do not wither away when children arrive. Parents must keep the house clean, shop, talk on the phone, and generally manage the tasks of daily life. They also have romantic desires toward each other.

Parents who are not overpowered by their own inner unhappiness or by external pressures will be struck by the strength of the love they feel for their child and their general willingness to subordinate their personal desires to the goal of helping her become happy and functional. The daily life of parents is filled with such choices. When parents realize that the need to rearrange their schedules to accommodate their child will last only a few years, even if they previously enjoyed the freedom to act on spontaneous desires to work out, dine out, or pursue hobbies, they will become more willing to try to reschedule these activities to times when their baby is sleeping or to pursue these interests at home so they can be available to their child. By making these adjustments you sustain your child's inborn belief that she can cause your responsive caring, and you help her develop inner happiness. Your time and positive attention are the most important gifts you can give a child. This vital commitment will lay the foundation for a positive and loving lifetime relationship with your child and save you lots of time worrying about your child as she grows older.

While satisfying the emotional needs of children is time consuming, there is no good alternative to this commitment, and there is no room for shortcuts or half measures. Children whose needs are not adequately met can develop trouble sleeping, eating, learning, navigating the temptations of adolescence, and growing into autonomous, functional, happy adults. In the long run, any problems that children suffer if their emotional needs are not met are certain to soak up the time not only of parents but of teachers and helping professionals. The time you spend adequately satisfying your child's developmental needs will be filled with love and the joy of parenting successfully, but interactions with unhappy and difficult children, though no less time consuming, are rarely relaxed and are often upsetting and perplexing.

Parents of young children sometimes worry that responding to their children's developmental needs is so important that they cannot take time for themselves to have dinner together, do some work, attend to household chores, or go to a movie. Parenting aims and personal desires should not be mutually exclusive. You can usually find ways of meeting your personal responsibilities and desires in ways that do not interfere with offering your child focused and responsive caring. You can still be an effective parent if you occasionally hire a babysitter. If you have caring friends, relatives, or babysitters who can fill in for you, you can meet your child's emotional needs and still manage to carve out space to gratify your own personal needs and desires.

As your child grows older, you will have more time for meeting your own personal desires, such as reading, watching TV, exercising, or working on the family car, but even as your child gets older the same smart love principle still applies—namely, *to let your child's developmental needs strike the balance between your personal aims and your parenting desires.* Don't be thrown off balance when your teen suddenly requests nearly every moment of your free time. Although it may initially take some effort to refocus your priorities, as in earlier years, your child is expressing a developmentally appropriate need for your attention, and by responding you foster her emotional growth.

Understanding the Roots of Inner Unhappiness

Parents are often advised that allowing children to experience frustration builds character. Our research and experience working with parents and children have taught us that consistently causing children unnecessary unhappiness has negative long-term consequences. The smart love guideline is *before doing something that you know will make your child unhappy, ask yourself if it is truly necessary.*

Our research shows that children who acquire inner unhappiness do so out of the same love for their parents that enables children whose developmental needs are adequately satisfied to develop an unshakable inner happiness. Infants experience their world in a unique way. The most important difference between infants' and adults' minds is that infants are absolutely certain that whatever happens to them is intended by their parents and represents the fruits of ideal parenting. In *Candide*, Voltaire portrayed this worldview through the character of the tutor, Pangloss, who greeted every new misfortune with the attitude, "Since everything was made for a purpose, it follows that everything is for the best in this best of all possible worlds."

Young children whose developmental needs are not adequately satisfied unknowingly misidentify the discomfort they feel as an ideal state intended by their beloved parents. Like all of us, they want more of what they perceive to be a good thing. That is why infants and young children who are routinely made to feel unhappy come not only to expect unhappiness, but seek it out as a way to feel completely loved. Some examples are the infant who pulls out her hair as a way of comforting herself and the young child who hits his baby sister as a way of eliciting his parents' anger.

Of course, all parents want their children to be happy, and no parent would intentionally act in such a way as to cause a child distress. Children fail to develop lasting inner happiness because their developmental needs are not adequately responded to, not because their parents do not wish to gratify their needs.

A TWO-YEAR-OLD REACTS TO HER MOTHER'S DEATH

Two-year-old Jill was brought to us for counseling after her mother was killed in an auto accident. Although before the accident she had been a happy child whose parents were paying attention to her developmental needs, after her mother's death she developed the need to suffer. Because children under the age of three believe that all of their parents' behaviors are freely chosen and represent perfect caregiving, Jill concluded that the deep unhappiness she felt when her mother failed to come home was the perfect love her mother intended for her to have. As a result, Jill unknowingly began to pursue unhappy experiences, because she came to associate such experiences with the pleasure of feeling close to her mother.

When he saw that his daughter was becoming increasingly listless and that the nightmares she had begun to have after her mother's death were not abating, Jill's father brought her to see a psychotherapist whose practice was guided by smart love principles. At first, when her sessions ended, Jill would become hysterical. She would cling to her therapist and beg, "Don't go." The therapist said that she knew Jill was worried that the therapist would leave as she felt her mother had left, but the therapist promised Jill that she would be "right here" the next time. Gradually Jill began to believe that her therapist would be there for the next session. Over the next months Jill began to recognize that the world in general was as stable as her relationship with her therapist, with the result that Jill began to feel and to function more like her old self.

⌒

Children Will Pay Any Price to Believe in Their Parents' Love

Children are social beings, and their need to believe in their ability to cause their parents to love taking care of them is paramount. When parents are prevented from satisfying their children's developmental needs because of social, economic, political, or health problems, bad advice, or because of the parents' own unperceived conflicts about enjoying the closeness of the parent-child relationship, their children will pay any price to maintain the illusion that their parents are perfect caregivers who are perfectly devoted to them. This need even takes precedence over a child's desire for physical well-being. For example, an infant's physical growth can become stunted if he cannot derive a minimally satisfying inner happiness from his relationship with those caring for him. Such a child may have withdrawn from the real world and taken refuge in his imagination, where he can create the positive parent-child relationship he was born expecting.

If they are forced to choose between a minimally acceptable level of inner happiness and physical well-being, humans will choose minimal inner happiness. As an illustration, children and adults who suffer from anorexia nervosa and starve themselves to skin and bones (or to death) do feel hungry. Enduring the pangs of hunger contributes to their sense of inner well-being because choosing not to eat and being abnormally thin show them they can exercise perfect self-control. Some physical processes are less susceptible to emotional influence than others, but emotional desires regulate whether and how we choose to satisfy those physical needs that are subject to choice.

An everyday example of the immediacy of a child's need to protect his inner well-being at the expense of physical functioning occurs when a child puts his hands over his ears in order to shut out a parent's admonishment. The child is choosing to be deaf to his parents' words because he finds hearing these words more painful than sensory deprivation. If you observe your child reacting to you in a similar way, soften the tone and content of your responses until the child feels comfortable enough to listen.

How Children Learn to Desire Inner Unhappiness

As we have said, young children whose developmental needs are not adequately satisfied unknowingly accept whatever parenting they receive as ideal and desire more of it. They unknowingly equate an inferior state of inner well-being with inner happiness. A four-year-old in our practice who found solace in withdrawing from activities and sucking his thumb believed that this was the best pleasure to be had in social situations. Only the adults in the room could know that he was missing out on the superior enjoyment to be had with his friends.

Children who learn to crave unhappy experiences don't recognize this distortion of their fundamental optimism. A dramatic illustration of this phenomenon can be seen in severely abused children. No matter how horrible the harm they suffer with their parents, these children remember their early experiences with their parents as ideal. It is no wonder that abused children who are placed with loving foster or adoptive families often experience intense yearnings for reunion with their abusive parent(s), frequently forget the abuse, and, if they are forced to review the abusive incidents, usually blame themselves for the misery inflicted by their parents.

"MOMMY ONLY HURT ME BECAUSE I WAS BAD!"

Four-year-old Alice had been placed with a foster family after her mother repeatedly burned her with matches. The child maintained that her mother had acted properly because she had been "bad." She begged for another chance to return to her mother and promised to be so "good" that her mother would never again get in trouble for punishing her.

The horrible abuse Alice had suffered had not altered the child's inborn conviction that her mother was a perfect caregiver. Alice's caseworker arranged for Alice to enter a long-term, supportive, professional relationship so that she could gain the strength to face the reality of what her mother had done. Only with that fortification would Alice be able to relinquish the belief that she was responsible for the abuse she had received.

～

Although older children who are abused may know in their minds that they do not deserve harsh treatment, in their hearts they unknowingly equate abuse with ideal caring. For this reason, even when these children are placed in a nurturing foster home, they frequently make every effort to provoke the anger of their foster parents in a driven attempt to re-create the misery they experienced with their birth parent(s).

In explaining the process by which humans acquire inner unhappiness, we have found it helpful to use the analogy of a baby gosling that has bonded to a human "parent." It is by now well known that if a gosling is hatched apart from other geese and tended by a human, he will follow his human caregiver with the same single-minded intensity with which other goslings follow a real mother goose. The imprinted gosling steadfastly pursues the human caregiver without recognizing that the human is not an ideal parent.

This misled gosling will develop less than optimally because the human cannot provide the same quality of nurture that the mother goose can. From the day he hatched, this gosling has unknowingly developed a distorted concept of ideal parenting. Even if the mother goose is subsequently introduced to her gosling, the gosling will not recognize the goose as his mother, but will continue to follow the human. The gosling will reject the ideal parenting available from the mother goose and will continue to pursue what any human observer would recognize as the substandard care he gets from following its human "parent."

The major obstacle preventing people from healing themselves is that they are unaware that their inner well-being is less than optimal. Children whose emotional needs were incompletely satisfied have no standard of comparison to alert them to the fact that their unpleasant self-experiences do not represent an ideal inner happiness. If they encounter others fortunate enough to have developed a stable inner well-being, they cannot perceive the striking difference between the others' self-experience and their own self-experience. For example, young children who feel depressed typically assume that other children feel exactly as they do, and that their own emotional state, though painful, is normal and optimal. Parents of an unhappy child can guide her toward an awareness of her sad feelings by offering her positive experiences that demonstrate their love of caring for her, experiences that strengthen her inborn desires to experience positive pleasure. Children must know real happiness in order to perceive that their depressed feelings are inferior and undesirable.

Self-Caused Unhappiness Is Preventable

Unprovoked human unhappiness has long been an object of Western thought and has been the target of a century of psychological observations. But even with all this effort we have yet to see a satisfactory explanation for everyday unhappiness and dysfunction or a reliable road to stable inner happiness. Essentially, all of us have been told that some degree of inner unhappiness and an inability to regulate our appetites and desires consistently are woven into our human nature. The message is that some degree of unhappiness is normal, and we'll just have to live with it. Some examples are the baby who cries inconsolably, the toddler who frantically resists bedtime, the six-year-old who has a behavior problem at school, the teenager who is sullen and uncommunicative, the graduate student who writes excellent papers that are marked down because she hands them in late, and the businessman who cannot stop overeating or bring himself to exercise.

We believe we have found a viable alternative to this gloomy outlook. We feel certain that every child can grow up to possess an unshakable inner happiness and the ability to make unconflicted, positive choices. Therefore, we propose expanding the definition of abnormal emotional development to include acquired inner unhappiness and the associated incapacity for consistent self-regulation. Our years of clinical experience have shown us that typical human unhappiness is correctable as well as preventable.

The average person's state of inner well-being falls short of the human potential for stable inner happiness. Some manifestations of inner unhappiness that are commonly classified as normal include recurrent nightmares; persistent but mild depression; chronic difficulties in regulating one's personal life, work life, or love life; repeatedly choosing unsuitable friends; and unexplained changes in mood. Because we all have the capacity to enjoy stable inner happiness and to make and follow through on constructive choices, this condition should be considered "normal" and should be defined as an attainable condition. We hope that armed with this new understanding of normality parents will be better able to help their children attain their true birthright.

How to Know When Your Child's Unregulated Behavior Is Caused by Inner Unhappiness

All children engage in unregulated behavior. That is, every child will on occasion be unable or unwilling to choose behavior that is safe, sensible, constructive, or socially desirable. Unfortunately, most people don't recognize that many of the vulnerabilities and out-of-control behaviors that children engage in are both temporary and appropriate for their age. As a parent you can learn to distinguish unregulated behavior that is the result of normal immaturity from unregulated behavior that is the product of inner unhappiness. If the unregulated behavior results from normal immaturity, it will be episodic. For example, a six-year-old may occasionally be angry and rejecting, but she will quickly reestablish warm relations with her parents. Over a period of a year or two any unregulated behavior that is normal for a particular developmental phase will come under the child's control. Children who have had trouble going to bed will go contentedly, children who have been contrary will become generally cooperative and helpful, and children who have been grabbing other children's toys and refusing to share their own will start to show a genuine, unforced desire to take turns.

In contrast, when unregulated behavior stems from inner unhappiness, children will frequently appear deeply unhappy, fragile, depressed, irritable, or inattentive; they will not turn to parental love and care for soothing; and their unregulated behavior will become entrenched instead of diminishing over time. For example, while it is normal for toddlers to experience episodic shyness, children who continue to hold desperately to their parents in the presence of strangers and do not appear to be growing out of this behavior probably are suffering from chronic inner unhappiness.

Certain unregulated behaviors are seen only in children who have acquired inner unhappiness. Examples are significant depression; frequent temper tantrums; significant phobias that interfere with a child's abilities to live her life (for example, a child who is so afraid of thunder that she refuses to go outside when it is simply raining); repetitive, unprovoked, aggressive behavior (hitting, biting, verbal abuse, cruelty to animals); and habitual isolation from or hostility toward parents.

Handling Caregiving Lapses

Even the most enthusiastic and dedicated parents will have their occasional off moments pursuing personal aims when their children need parenting attention. We call these **caregiving lapses.** There will be times when fatigue or stress blinds you to the fact that your child's immature behavior is temporary and appropriate for her age, and you may well react with irritation and impatience. Or maybe you are thinking about something else when your child is talking to you. If you are generally a responsive parent, a caregiving lapse will not interfere with your child's development of an enduring inner happiness, because the lapse is an aberration. There is a difference between occasional caregiving lapses and the consistent inability of a parent to satisfy a child's emotional needs—which does cause a child to develop inner unhappiness. If you consistently respond to your child with loving attention, your occasional caregiving lapses will not derail your child's emotional development, since your relationship with your child will be such that she trusts in her ability to reengage your caregiving by alerting you to the disappointment she is experiencing. For example, a teen who was telling her mother that she had a difficult day at school because her new teacher was very critical suddenly realized that her mother was not really paying attention to her words. She said, "Mom, I need you to listen to this!" Her mother immediately refocused on her daughter's recounting of her bad day.

A FATHER BECOMES ENGROSSED IN A BASKETBALL PLAYOFF

A father we know had learned how to be sensitive to caregiving lapses. One day he was watching a basketball playoff on television. His two-and-a-half-year-old son, Alex, amused himself for a while, but then he began to ask his father to read to him. The father, engrossed in the game, kept saying, "In a minute — play with your trucks just a little longer." Finally, Alex took a wiffle-ball bat, swung it, and knocked over a full can of cola.

Alex's unusually aggressive behavior put his father back in touch with his son's needs. Instead of becoming angry, the father noted matter-of-factly that it was not a good idea to spill the drink, but he also acknowledged to Alex that he knew he had made Alex wait longer than he could comfortably tolerate. The father cleaned up the spilled cola and then read the boy a story. Both father and son felt relieved and happy about reestablishing closeness.

Some parents and experts would argue that by taking responsibility for Alex's outburst, this father rewarded antisocial behavior and encouraged his son to become demanding and obnoxious. But the father perceived that Alex's response was appropriate for his age. He realized that just as one-year-olds cry when their parents leave, two-year-olds cannot wait very long for their parents' attention without coming unglued. The father knew that although he had expected too much patience from Alex given the child's age, if he was able to respond with kindness rather than criticism, Alex would feel cared about and understood, and would actually be better able to wait the next time.

We certainly do not mean to imply that parents should apologize every time their children get out of control. This was a special circumstance in that the father had unintentionally incited Alex's behavior by failing to respond to his needs. If Alex had engaged in unprovoked destructive behavior, the father would have responded by regulating his behavior without assuming responsibility for it. For instance, the father might say, "Alex, dear, you can't eat crackers in the living room if you are going to put them on the floor and walk on them."

Parents are frequently hard-pressed to find sufficient time, rest, and emotional energy to respond to their children. *Yet children's wants and needs do not recede just because parents lack the physical, emotional, or financial resources to meet them.* With a smart love perspective beleaguered parents can work on recovering quickly from caregiving lapses that involve failing to attend to their child or mislabeling their child as overly demanding and unreasonable when the child is only expressing developmentally appropriate needs for love and attention.

SMART LOVE HELPS A SINGLE FATHER COPE WITH A BAD DAY

A single parent had been consulting us about his relationship with his young children, ages five and three. He was feeling resentful because he believed the children were old enough to be more understanding of the stress he was under as a single working parent, and he felt they should be more appreciative of his efforts on their behalf. In talking with him we focused on helping him see that his children were still too young to look at the world from his perspective, especially when things went wrong.

One day the father returned exhausted from a long day at work, picked up his two exuberant children at their day care center, and came home to his apartment, only to be confronted by a stopped-up toilet and the sight of the children's parakeet lying dead at the bottom of its cage.

Horrified by the loss of their pet, both children became hysterical. The father made every effort to calm them. He talked about how much they would all miss "Bluey," and promised to buy a new parakeet the next day. He then turned his attention to the plugged-up toilet. When the children continued to wail and to demand his undivided attention, he finally exploded, "Can't you see I've got to do this? Now go to your room and I'll get you when the toilet works." The children reacted to his exasperation by crying even harder as they retreated to their room.

In the moment of silence that followed, the father saw that in his irritation at the stuck toilet, he had lost sight of how devastated his children were by the loss of Bluey. He also reconnected with the fact that his children were too young to understand and either respond with sympathy or stay quiet in deference to the frayed emotions he was feeling upon encountering this crisis at the end of a long and exhausting day.

He rounded up the children, dried their tears, and explained that he had not meant to become angry, but that he was feeling upset himself. He said he missed Bluey, too, and that once the toilet was fixed, they would have a "memorial service" and share their memories of their pet. The father heated up a pizza and played a video for the children. Once they were comfortably settled, he finished work on the toilet. The children devoured the pizza and enjoyed the video. They cheered up even more after they all talked about Bluey together. Most important, they were immensely relieved that their father had returned to his normal affectionate and understanding self. The night ended peacefully.

Smart love guidelines can help you gain an accurate understanding of what you can expect of your child at different ages, so that when for whatever reason you are feeling overwhelmed, you will find it easier to rebound and give your child the love and attention she needs. When you're at the end of your rope and your child continues to act like a child, you will have enough insight into the situation that you can avoid feeling betrayed or unappreciated.

As we have said, caregiving lapses do not leave children with emotional scars because they are exceptions within a generally nurturing relationship. Think of these lapses as being like a few broken threads in a rich tapestry woven by parents who continuously encourage and affirm their child's abilities to elicit their unconditional loving responses. Your child's emotional development would be derailed only if the lapses were to become the norm rather than the exception.

The unconditional nature of your bond with your child is born not of self-sacrifice but of the pleasure of responding to your child's developmental need to feel she is causing you to love caring for her. Unless external circumstances or inner unhappiness interfere, you will be pleasantly surprised to find that the satisfaction of helping your child develop a lasting inner happiness and an abiding sense of competence usually supersedes other pleasures that formerly took center stage in your life. And because children whose emotional needs are adequately satisfied are happy and affectionate, you will be able to bask in the mutual warmth that anchors the parent-child relationship.

When Parents Find It Difficult to Enjoy Their Children

There are, of course, some parents who consistently find it difficult to enjoy parenting their children. They may often feel overwhelmed, plagued by self-doubts or self-criticism, angry, exhausted, or depressed. If you are such a parent, you, too, can apply the principles of smart love to become better at parenting and thereby help your child to feel happier and to be more functional. When you adopt this approach you may find that the experience of being a parent will become noticeably more rewarding. And as you feel more in touch with the joys of parenting, your child will become ever more relaxed, affectionate, and fulfilled.

Unfortunately, when the parent-child relationship is characterized by ongoing conflict, parents are often advised to respond with stern measures. The unfortunate result is that their children become more alienated and more dysfunctional, and the parents then feel more helpless and disaffected. A more constructive way of addressing problems between parents and children involves helping parents to recognize the ways in which their personal needs are interfering with their parenting aims.

Parents Who Are Emotionally Unable to Respond to Children's Needs

Parents who are emotionally unable to satisfy their children's developmental needs probably do not realize that their own personal needs episodically obscure their efforts to be consistent and responsive parents. It is not uncommon for parents whose own inner unhappiness makes them uncomfortable with and unable to enjoy the closeness of the parent-child relationship to be diverted from meeting their children's developmental needs either by burying themselves in work or by giving in to the lure of recreational pleasure (such as surfing the Internet, watching TV, and so forth).

MAIZIE BIRD TAKES A VACATION

In the whimsical children's book *Horton Hatches the Egg,* Dr. Seuss imagines that animals' parenting commitments might also falter if they had the same distractions available to them that human parents have. Maizie Bird, a flighty and lazy bird, gets tired of sitting on her egg and asks Horton the elephant to care for it while she takes a short vacation in Florida. The delights of Florida prove so seductive that Maizie never returns. Horton remains on the egg in spite of numerous tribulations, because, in contrast to Maizie, who is dazzled by personal gratifications, he is steadfast and cannot be distracted from the commitment to egg-sit.

There are a number of other ways in which parents' own emotional needs can interfere with their abilities to satisfy their children's developmental needs. For example, there are parents who unknowingly busy themselves with their children to avoid parts of their own lives about which they are conflicted (such as romantic intimacy); to explain why they feel unhappy (exemplified in statements such as "If I didn't have to spend all my time looking after you, I would have a better life"); or to blot out their depression by distracting themselves with continuous caregiving activities. Children who fill this need for their parents feel responsible for maintaining their parents' emotional well-being, and at the same time they miss out on the all-important experience of seeing themselves as being able to inspire their parents' unconditional love of caring for them.

One sure sign that personal needs are interfering with parenting aims is when you find yourself blaming your child for your own emotional discomfort, as expressed in feelings such as boredom or anger or in wishes to isolate yourself from your child. It will help at these moments to focus on how much your child needs your positive attention. When you have some quiet time to yourself, try to identify possible sources of dissatisfaction in your own life and to develop strategies for making your days more rewarding.

Parents Who Have Difficulty Tolerating Their Child's Expressions of Unhappiness

Some parents unknowingly make use of their child's positive attitude toward them to soothe their own inner unhappiness. Such parents may need to virtually abdicate their parental role in order to avoid arousing their child's anger, because setting limits seems too risky.

TRAPPED IN THE CAR

One father who had gone grocery shopping with his two-year-old daughter, Nancy, stayed in the car with her (and a quart of melting ice cream) for over two hours because she began to cry and to push him away angrily when he tried to bring her into the house. Finally, after Nancy fell asleep, her father carried her and the groceries inside.

The father consulted us because he just didn't know what to do when his daughter became upset. He felt utterly helpless. We explained that his inability to take action was rooted in his need that his daughter never experience him as frustrating any of her motives. But when he failed to regulate her behavior, Nancy got the message that her unhappiness was as overwhelming to him as it felt to her.

As we analyzed the situation, he came to see that he could have brought his daughter inside and still shown her that he recognized and cared about her sad feelings, saying something like, "I know you are really upset because you want to stay in the car, but the groceries need to go in the refrigerator." Following the principle of loving regulation (see page 8), he could have done his best to help Nancy make the transition, saying, for instance, "Let's go in and play your drums." But if she continued to protest, he would have had to come to a point where he realized that it was not in his daughter's interest to try to prevent her tears at all costs. Once he brought her inside, he could have tried everything he could think of to cheer her up, proposing, for instance, "Let's make a tower with the soup cans."

The father saw that his daughter would benefit from these guidelines, so he began to implement them. Although for a period of time Nancy still cried when she didn't want to get out of the car (or had to leave another place she was enjoying), the father discovered to his surprise that if he used loving regulation to help her make the transition, Nancy quickly recovered her equilibrium. Their relationship steadily improved, and he felt increasingly competent as a parent.

～

Some parents permit their children to make self-destructive choices in order to keep the peace. One mother whose child resisted bedtime allowed her to stay up so late at night that the child was too tired and cranky to enjoy the next day's activities. Other parents of an adolescent who regularly stayed out past curfew said nothing for fear that he would erupt in anger. As we shall see later in this chapter when we explore permissiveness, children are harmed when parents fail to set limits and regulate behavior in a positive and supportive fashion.

Parents Who Unknowingly Avoid Parenting Pleasure

Parents who themselves suffer from inner unhappiness may be so uncomfortable with the prospect of enjoying the parent-child relationship that they avoid it. Without realizing it, these parents frequently respond to their children's needs for experiencing a positive relationship by creating moments of discord, distance, and isolation.

SYSTEM OVERLOAD

A father consulted us because his relationship with his daughter was not going smoothly. In the course of the discussion, it became clear to us that the father was unknowingly uncomfortable with the fun to be had with his five-year-old. For example, without realizing it, he would create distance between himself and his daughter by answering the child's eager questions with long answers that were entirely over her head. The child would become bored and restless during the explanation, at which point the father would reproach the child for not paying attention. In this way, a moment of closeness became a time of conflict and unhappiness.

Once the father understood that he was responsible for alienating his daughter, and not vice versa, he learned to notice moments of closeness and monitor himself lest he do something to ruin the mood. Gradually, the conflict ceased. The father was immensely relieved and pleased with the good times he and his daughter began to enjoy together.

∽

In other instances parents who are made uncomfortable by the closeness of the parent-child relationship react by physically avoiding their child. These parents may lead a whirlwind life and leave their child to be raised by sitters, or they may simply leave their child physically alone. When these parents do allow themselves to experience parenting pleasure, they frequently react to the satisfaction of meeting their child's needs by feeling put upon. For example, they may blame their child for depriving them of personal satisfactions. A parent might say, "I gave up my sewing project to help you with that math problem, but it wasn't necessary because you could have done it yourself," or "I stopped reading to play cards with you, and now you're not even concentrating."

Parents who know that their child's deepest desire is to have a positive, close, loving relationship with her parents will be better able to see that their own personal needs, and not their child's, are the cause of any negative feelings they experience in the course of parenting. This increased self-awareness will help free them wholeheartedly to pursue the pleasure of caring for their child.

Parents Who Are Angry at Their Children

Although all parents become angry at their children on occasion, anger is never a constructive response from a parent. Unfortunately, parents are often told that angry feelings are indispensable to good parenting—that it benefits children to know that certain behavior is so out of bounds that it makes parents angry. Instances in which expressing anger has been deemed appropriate include times when children run into the street, play with matches, talk back, write on walls, or stay out past curfew and don't call home.

Because children of all ages draw on the relationship with their parents to sustain their inner well-being, parental anger is never growth-promoting. As we have mentioned in Chapter 1, if you repeatedly get angry at your child, he will copy you and learn to treat himself poorly. If a child is too young to stay out of the street on his own, try to stay close enough to physically redirect him; if he is inclined to play with matches, store them where he cannot reach them. If you are temporarily distracted and your child does something destructive or dangerous, stop the behavior, but try to stay positive and be more attentive in the future.

Understanding Your Anger

Even though you will feel angry with your child at times, there is all the difference in the world between believing that your anger is justified (with the result that you reinforce your child's belief that he is responsible for it) and realizing that anger does not further the goal of giving your child lasting inner happiness and an abiding sense of competence. It is not uncommon for parents to become angry when their child gives them a bad scare. But once you understand that anger makes you less effective as a parent, you will be motivated to hold your anger, thereby relieving your child of the burden of your irate feelings. For example, if you become outwardly furious with your young child who has run dangerously close to the street, feel free to give him an immediate hug and say, "I'm sorry I yelled, honey. You didn't do anything bad—it is my job to make sure you don't go near the street until you are old enough to realize that cars can really hurt you. Let's go back to the playground and swing."

Parents also tend to become angry when their child behaves in a way that is appropriate for his age, but the parent is judging the child's behavior based on what would be unacceptable in an adult. A teen may complain about having to do chores or absentmindedly leave the refrigerator door open, defrosting all the frozen goods. Parents may become angry if they conclude based on this behavior that their teen has become permanently selfish, irresponsible, and disobedient. They would find it easier to dispel or moderate their angry feelings and respond constructively to their teenager if they kept in mind that the developmental pushes and pulls of adolescence typically, though temporarily, make teens forgetful and resistant.

When Anger Becomes Abuse

A few parents become so angry at their child that they are driven to physical or emotional abuse. Sometimes abusive parents blame the child for causing their anger. They also may think that they are acting in their child's best interests. To them violence is a means of moral education—and children need to be "taught a lesson." Or perhaps they conclude that their child deserves harsh treatment because he has deliberately provoked them. Other parents lose control and then feel guilty about their violent outbursts. There are some abusive parents whose understanding is so impaired by mental illness that they do not even realize their child exists or they project other identities (such as Satan) onto him.

But abusive parents also feel love and concern for their child, even while their perspective is distorted by impulse-ridden behavior, paranoia, substance abuse, or other forms of inner disquiet. If you find you are getting out of control with your child, seek help.

Parental Kindness Does Not Always Promote Emotional Growth

It may seem difficult to understand how dedicated and caring parents could produce unhappy, even dysfunctional, children, unless you blame inborn temperament, the child's willfulness, outside influences, or the parents for having treated the children too well (spoiled them).

When parental kindness grows out of genuine love and concern and is not the product of parents playing out their own personal needs, children cannot get too much of it. When children know that they can engage and hold their parents' committed love, they derive a fundamental and lasting inner happiness. Smart love provides parents with a grounding in children's developmental needs, and parents who follow its tenets will nurture children who are happy, functional, and giving—and not children who are "spoiled," unhappy, troubled, or self-defeating.

When parents who are consistently kind have an unhappy, even dysfunctional, child, the explanation is not that they have spoiled their child by being too nice to her; instead, despite their best efforts, their caregiving has not been adequate to address their child's developmental needs. Perhaps the parents have been driven by the need to preserve their own peace of mind by preventing their child from showing anger or unhappiness.

When kindness to children is in the service of parents' personal needs, it is conditional. Children of such parents are likely to adopt a conditional type of regard for themselves. Their inner well-being may evaporate at crucial moments of sickness, success, or failure.

One father we know lavishly praised his eight-year-old son for his talent at drawing but felt uncomfortable and showed subtle, yet unmistakable, disapproval whenever his son drew faces that looked unhappy. The father's responses to his son's drawing were unknowingly steering his son away from expressing unhappiness.

BEAR GOES OUT THE WINDOW

We were helping one mother whose kindness to her children was to some extent a product of her need to soothe her own inner unhappiness. One day she was driving her three-year-old son, Sam, to nursery school on a busy expressway. It was hot, and the windows in the car were partly down. Without realizing the strength of the wind rushing by the car, Sam held his favorite bear out the window to give it some "fresh air." To his great surprise, the bear was blown away. Sam immediately burst into hysterical tears. His mother responded very sympathetically, "Oh, what a shame! Stop crying, and I will buy you a new bear and have it for you after school." Sam exerted great effort and controlled his tears.

What Sam really needed at that moment was to share his unhappy feelings with his mother. But he was prevented from doing so because she was so uncomfortable with his distress that she quickly promised to replace the lost bear on the condition that he stop crying. As had happened in the past, her generosity was motivated to some degree by her need for her son not to be sad. As a result of experiencing such interactions repeatedly, Sam silently came to believe that sad feelings were shameful and bad. Over time, if he continued to feel unlovable when he was upset, he would have experienced great difficulty with life's inevitable setbacks and frustrations.

Once she realized the effect of her behavior on her son, this mother learned not to insist that Sam stop crying when he was distressed. She saw the importance of allowing him to seek solace in their relationship, and she developed the ability to provide an available and sympathetic ear when he was shocked and sad. When a toy became lost or broken, she was able to resist placing conditions on her offer of a replacement. Most important, she was not surprised, angered, or disappointed if Sam continued to cry for a while in spite of the fact that he knew a new toy would be forthcoming.

Possessions Are Not a Substitute for Smart Love

Material things are a wholly inadequate substitute for the care-getting pleasure children really desire in their hearts. It can be difficult for parents to understand that a "spoiled" child is unhappy and behaves in ways that affront adults because she has received too little rather than too much positive attention. Or maybe she has received a lot of attention, but not the kind she truly required.

A child who receives material things instead of the parenting she really needs loses in at least three ways:

- She doesn't receive the positive, responsive parental attention she needs to develop an enduring inner happiness.
- She learns that happiness is measured by material gain.
- The child gets blamed for her unhappiness, because the parents are convinced that they have done their best to satisfy the child's every want.

Made angry by their child's unhappy, "spoiled" behavior, parents may withhold toys or other treats. This deprivation makes the child feel even more desperate and alienated because she has learned to accept material things in place of the parenting she really wants. When a child's behavior then worsens in response to deprivation, parents are further convinced that showering their child with gifts spoiled her. Material gifts neither foster nor inhibit inner happiness. There is no inherent connection between wealth and good parenting or a child's inner happiness, except insofar as parents must have adequate means to provide the time and space to raise a child.

Some Support Isn't Helpful

Children naturally need and appreciate their parents' involvement in important aspects of their lives, but sometimes parents' encouragement of their children's efforts arises from personal needs. For example, one parent may need his child to either become like him or become the person that the parent wished he had become. We know of one father who spent hours every night helping his son with math and who felt betrayed and became irate when the boy decided to major in English in college instead of following his father into engineering.

Sometimes parents are supportive of a child's efforts in part because they themselves depend on their children's accomplishments for their own sense of inner well-being. At every science fair there are parents who have initiated and dominated their child's project to increase their child's chances of winning. Such support often backfires, with the child refusing either to participate or to work up to the standard the parent has set.

As we have described, one crucial developmental task is that the child learn to base his secondary happiness on the pleasure of making good choices and pursuing those choices effectively, rather than on his success at gratifying any particular wish. When parents' personal needs cause them to become overly invested in helping their child succeed at a given activity, they give their child the message that success rather than a good effort is what matters, thereby interfering with the process in which the child's all-powerful self is supplanted by a competent self. Children who remain subject to their all-powerful self will be outcome-oriented and therefore will be vulnerable to life's inevitable disappointments. But children who grow up to base their secondary happiness on the satisfaction of making a sustained effort will not experience an interruption in inner well-being when events do not turn out as they desire.

Permissiveness Is Not Smart Love

Permissiveness can be defined as a style of parenting that fails to impose necessary regulations on children's behavior. Parents who are permissive believe they are acting in their children's best interests. Permissiveness is rooted in parents' inability to tolerate their child's anger or unhappiness, which prevents them from stepping in and governing the child's behavior when appropriate and thus protecting their child from the consequences of their immature behavior. The problem is not that permissive parents spoil a child by being too generous or too nice. As we have explained, granting children's wishes whenever possible is growth promoting. Permissiveness harms children because it teaches them that their all-powerful selves are right to believe that they are too strong to be interfered with. It prevents children from outgrowing the belief that their well-being is contingent on always getting what they want when they want it—an impossible goal—and it interferes with the development of a competent self (see page 4).

PARENTS WHO FOUND IT DIFFICULT TO BE IN CHARGE

Tom's parents consulted us because four-year-old Tom was having problems with self-control. At preschool his teachers and peers were constantly angry at him for his aggressive behavior. After talking to his parents it became clear to us that when Tom desired to do or to have something that was not good for him, his parents were uncomfortable about opposing his wishes. As a result, at home Tom watched TV programs that frightened him, rode his bike recklessly inside the apartment, and hit and pushed his parents when he was upset.

In spite of their heartfelt intentions to make their son happy and their belief that they were facilitating this goal by not interfering with Tom's need for "self-expression," his parents' failure to manage Tom's out-of-control behavior was interfering with his ability to develop a stable, healthy capacity for self-regulation. The confusion he felt when outsiders did not respond to his needs as his parents did only intensified his aggression.

With counseling these parents began to see the importance of keeping Tom's behavior within bounds that were both constructive and also appropriate for his age. They learned how to use loving regulation to limit his TV watching to programs that were fun and educational, to restrict his bike riding to the park, and to gently but firmly keep him from hitting or pushing them. At first Tom was outraged when his wishes were thwarted. But we had helped his parents to anticipate this initial fury, and to be ready to stand their ground while remaining calm and positive. Eventually, Tom accepted the new guidelines at home. His newfound ability to accept guidance from adults carried over to school, and his classroom behavior began to be more like that of his peers. As a result, he began to enjoy school and, much to his delight, began to receive invitations for play dates.

∾

Environment Counts, Too

Our assertion that you can help your child attain lasting inner happiness and the ability to regulate his desires does not ignore the existence either of unalterable, unpleasant large-scale realities, such as drought, famine, war, and social inequality, or significant personal losses, through accident, disease, or death. It is certainly true that terrible social and economic conditions can prevent parents otherwise capable of giving optimal care from doing so. In times of war, children are separated from their parents, and the parents of children born into poverty have to work long hours and thus are robbed of the ability to stay home with their young children or to provide quality substitute care.

Social enlightenment about children's emotional needs and the development of social supports to help parents to meet those needs are crucial to promoting widespread human well-being. Social reforms that would be meaningful for children and parents (such as subsidies that would allow parents to remain at home with young children or laws that would prevent parents who choose part-time work when their children are small from being penalized by their employer) have been thwarted from many directions, including erroneous but popular theories that imply that reform is futile because the important causes of human unhappiness are inborn; well-publicized failures of utopian solutions, such as communism; the widespread assumption that short-term economic gain is preferable to long-term human happiness; and the lack of sufficient understanding about how children become stable, happy, and accomplished or chronically unhappy and dysfunctional.

Even though we devote little space in these pages to addressing the complex and arduous efforts to find solutions for pressing social problems that interfere with parents' abilities to parent successfully, we certainly believe these problems deserve serious and sustained attention. We hope that the understanding of childhood we present in these pages can contribute to the building of meaningful and comprehensive social and economic supports for children and their parents.

Children who acquire inner unhappiness and who grow up in pockets of poverty and violence will be especially prone to develop symptoms of alienation, aggression, and lack of concern for their own or other's welfare. Environment affects children's emotional development in two ways: environmental factors can determine whether parents who would otherwise be capable of meeting their children's emotional needs will have the opportunity to do so; and environmental factors can affect the balance between a child's inner equilibrium being maintained primarily by positive pleasure or primarily by destructive pleasure or unpleasant experiences. A community that offers a broad spectrum of athletic and cultural opportunities to its youngsters helps children learn to seek positive pleasure.

Every child who has acquired inner unhappiness bases her inner equilibrium on a combination of positive pleasure, destructive pleasure, and unpleasant experiences. Environmental factors can dramatically affect this balance. When children who suffer from inner unhappiness grow up in a neighborhood where there are few positive opportunities owing to a lack of resources, and where there is a gang culture that values violence and accepts prison sentences as an inevitable part of life, these children are more likely to use destructive experiences as a way of maintaining their inner equilibrium.

We badly need social reforms that will ensure that all parents who are able to meet their children's emotional needs have the opportunity to do so, and also that children unfortunate enough to acquire inner unhappiness have a chance to build the most satisfying lives of which they are capable. Children who acquire inner unhappiness but who are well fed and well clothed and whose every talent is encouraged and cultivated will have a vastly more enjoyable life than children who have inner unhappiness and whose surroundings are dangerous and depriving, who are also in danger of being killed every time they step outside their house, and who constantly lose close friends and family members to drugs and violence.

FOR SOME CHILDREN, DETENTION CAN BE GROWTH-PROMOTING

The director of a pretrial juvenile detention facility observed that when youths were taken from the streets and incarcerated, they would make giant scholastic leaps, showing a year or two of progress in just a few months. She attributed these dramatic gains to the fact that "[t]he first thing we give a boy or a girl is the gift of feeling safe. No bullets ripping by their door, no need for drop-down drills. A child in terror cannot learn; terror freezes the brain."[3]

Many capable parents are prevented from parenting effectively by events that are beyond their control, such as serious illness, social upheaval, or economic deprivation that forces them to work outside the home when their children are very young. Lawmakers should consider the needs of our children and parents when drafting potential social initiatives. For instance, when the government pushes single parents of young children who depend on public assistance out of the home and into the workplace, often children are harmed and their parents are embittered, thereby creating worse, not better, citizens.

∼

In this chapter we have described how children can unknowingly develop a chronic inner unhappiness when:

- personal, social, political, or economic circumstances interfere with their parents' abilities to make parenting goals their top priority;
- parents do not realize that young children will interpret their every experience, whether negative or positive, as the intended effect of perfect parenting;
- parents want to respond positively to their children but are unable to prevent themselves from being angry, intrusive, disapproving, or negligent; or
- parents are permissive. That is, their positive responses to their children are shaped by their need to soothe their own inner unhappiness, rather than by an ability to enjoy helping their children become truly happy and competent. These parents cannot provide their children with the loving regulation the children need because the parents cannot tolerate their children's anger or tears and, therefore, cannot bring themselves to govern their children's out-of-control behavior.

Parents Are Not to Blame

Because parents have so often been blamed for children's problems, when we assert that children develop inner unhappiness when their parents are unable to respond to their developmental needs, parents might assume that we blame them, and especially the mothers, for children's problems. But this is emphatically not what we mean. We know that parents do their best to make their children happy, and they want to understand how and why their children become unhappy. Moreover, they are eager to learn how to guide unhappy children back on the road to a happy and productive life.

The fact that some parents find it difficult to respond to their children's developmental needs in no way implies that they lack good intentions, are not trying to do their best, or are not loving and kind to their children. They may be stymied by external constraints or physical illness; they may have been given poor child-rearing advice and have an inaccurate understanding of their children's true developmental needs; they may themselves suffer from inner unhappiness, which interferes with their ability to parent effectively.

Cause and moral responsibility are not equivalent. To equate the two is in effect to say that the person who was unaware that she was coming down with a cold and who unintentionally spread the virus to an elevator full of people was morally responsible for their subsequent illness. In other words, parents do not intentionally cause their children to develop inner unhappiness, and they do not bear the moral responsibility for this unwanted outcome.

Parents who are themselves burdened with inner unhappiness may have difficulty separating their own personal needs from their children's developmental needs. This explains why children of the best-intentioned parents can develop inner unhappiness. To illustrate, suppose a young child expresses an emphatic and irritable "no" in response to her mother's interference with her wishes to stay in the park and play. The mother may have trouble deciding how to respond to her child's behavior. If she lets her child remain, is this because she is facilitating her child's developmental need to exercise choice whenever possible, or is she being influenced by her personal need not to have her child feel unhappy or angry with her?

Suppose this mother insists that the child leave the park. Was she right in judging that her child needs a nap more than the child needs to gratify her desire to stay and play? Or did the mother insist that the child leave because the child's rebelliousness challenges the mother's personal need to feel in control of the child's behavior? A good rule of thumb for parents faced with this dilemma is, if the child is not showing signs of being so cranky or tired that she obviously needs to leave, there is no harm done by remaining a few more minutes.

All parents retain the inborn desire (even though it may be in latent form) to love their children well and without reservation. *In all of our clinical work we have never encountered a parent who wasn't trying his or her very best to make the right decisions for his or her child.*

It is only superficially comforting to believe that children are unhappy because of their inborn temperament, or the evil or baseness of human nature. If we adopt this belief we are conceding that nothing can be done about such immutable causes. It is ultimately much more hopeful and helpful to recognize that children develop chronic inner unhappiness out of love for their parents, and, in turn, that parents can learn to apply the principles of smart love to help unhappy children change.

Chapter Three

Recognizing and Reversing
Children's Inner Unhappiness

Parents can best help unhappy
and difficult children when they understand how inner unhappiness
affects their children's behavior and experiences. The two most
important consequences of inner unhappiness are (1) that the child's
well-being remains entirely vulnerable to the ups and downs of everyday life—for instance, a lost backpack, a grouchy teacher, or a rude
classmate can send a child into a tailspin; and (2) that the child's well-
being is also at the mercy of unperceived needs for self-caused unhappiness—for example, an infant may bang her head repeatedly against
her crib railing, or a child may pick at her cuticles until they bleed.

Inner Unhappiness Makes Children Especially Vulnerable to Life's Ups and Downs

When children's needs are responded to generously and positively,
children acquire the inner resources to function flexibly and effectively in the real world; whereas when children's needs are not adequately met they develop inner unhappiness, thereby becoming
vulnerable to disappointments and impaired in their abilities to cope
with everyday life. No matter how successful people become later in
life, if they developed inner unhappiness as a child, their well-being
remains tied to external events and can be disrupted by the disappointments of everyday life, because their well-being continues to
depend on their ability to get what they want when they want it. The
most popular child will fail to get a party invitation she covets, the
most successful businessman will encounter financial reversals, the

most charismatic politician will fail to get a bill passed, the most competent farmer will lose crops due to bad weather, and the most powerful athlete will lose a game. When this happens, in addition to the frustration of not getting a sought-for desire, the individual who lacks stable inner happiness will experience an interruption in her good feelings about herself. Setbacks are unavoidable. What can be avoided are the accompanying feelings of unworthiness. If your child seems especially vulnerable to everyday loss, you can increase her resilience by using the smart love guidelines outlined later in the chapter.

Because the inner well-being of unhappy and difficult children remains tied to their success or failure at getting what they want when they want it, when these children are confronted with a loss, they may dissolve in tears, develop a reactive indifference, or lash out in fury. For example, while receiving a sought-for award may lead them to feel on top of the world, the failure to gain the award may cause them to feel worthless. Inner unhappiness can make even apparently inconsequential losses feel devastating. This inability to separate inner happiness from the influence of external events endows everyday disappointments—from a lost toy to a last-minute change of plans to a critical remark—with the power to throw these children's lives into disequilibrium. When parents recognize this special vulnerability and consistently lend a sympathetic ear to their child's distress, the child who has developed inner unhappiness gains an alternate source of well-being that will make it possible for her to feel calmer and more worthwhile when things don't go as she wishes.

The inner well-being of children who have acquired inner unhappiness remains tied to external symbols. A child's unshakable primary happiness derives from her certainty that her parents are unconditionally committed to satisfying her developmental needs. This reservoir of inner well-being makes it possible for the child to finish adolescence in possession of the reliable ability to make positive choices and pursue them competently and with enjoyment. Sadly, children who have not developed true inner happiness must rely on experiences with no intrinsic connection to self-worth to supply themselves with inner well-being. They may knowingly or unknowingly attach their sense of inner security to social symbols (such as being accepted by a particular circle of friends), or to material symbols (such as possessing a coveted toy), or to status symbols (such as pricey clothes or an advanced degree). Much human aggression, from wars to simple altercations, occurs because people with inner unhappiness are knowingly or unknowingly convinced that their life or honor rests on the preservation of various external symbols, including religious, cultural, national, regional, or familial symbols. People who launch themselves into these aggressive confrontations feel that they are defending or avenging their very essence. Although these symbols have intense personal meaning, objectively they may be as impersonal as a collectible baseball card or a corner office.

The child who has acquired inner unhappiness unknowingly maintains the illusion that she can control everything that happens to her. The child who lacks inner happiness unknowingly clings to her all-powerful self's claim to control events because she has not developed alternative sources of well-being to tide her over when things go wrong. The persistence of the child's illusion that she has or could have the power to bring about any and all desired outcomes explains irrational, self-destructive behavior (for example, the child who jumps out of trees in the belief that she will land unhurt, and the teen who knows smoking causes cancer but doesn't believe that smoking will adversely affect her health).

The child who has acquired inner unhappiness often needs to dominate others. Children whose inner happiness rests on getting what they want when they want it frequently have trouble with relationships because they never cease to experience others' wishes as potential threats to their own inner well-being. They may destroy rewarding friendships through fierce competitiveness, by experiencing others' successes as pointing to their own inadequacy, or by endless squabbles over minor but entrenched differences of opinion, as with the child who always has to be the one to decide which game she and her friends will play.

Children with inner unhappiness may react to everyday disappointments in a number of ways, including experiencing a nagging sense of insecurity, shame, forgetfulness and unintentional inattentiveness, or unprovoked irritation with someone else. Their reactions can be as severe as suicide or homicide (for example, the teenagers who killed themselves because their parents would not let them date each other).

Whether their reactions are mild or severe, children whose inner well-being remains vulnerable to everyday disappointments, even those as minor as losing a pen or going to a movie only to find it is sold out, lack the deep satisfaction of knowing how they will feel the next day or even the next hour or minute.

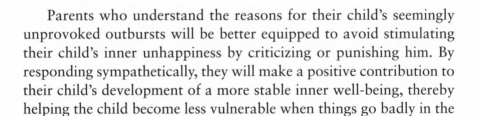

REVERSAL OF FORTUNE

A ten-year-old we know was ecstatic when he was able to buy the Boardwalk property in a *Monopoly* game, but he dissolved in tears and swept the game pieces onto the floor when his holdings were wiped out. Children fortunate enough to have a reliable inner happiness are disappointed to experience a sudden reversal of fortune, but because their inner well-being remains stable, they would not be driven to trash the game to restore a sense of equilibrium.

Parents who understand the reasons for their child's seemingly unprovoked outbursts will be better equipped to avoid stimulating their child's inner unhappiness by criticizing or punishing him. By responding sympathetically, they will make a positive contribution to their child's development of a more stable inner well-being, thereby helping the child become less vulnerable when things go badly in the future.

Symptoms of Inner Unhappiness

The symptoms of inner unhappiness resolve themselves into persistent patterns of poorly regulated behaviors that are not caused by a child's developmental immaturity. Many of the symptoms that are typical or considered benign in a given society go largely unnoticed, but those that are atypical or seem dysfunctional are viewed as abnormal. Caregivers and professionals often respond to the symptoms as though the symptoms themselves were the primary problem, but symptoms only serve as indications of the presence of inner unhappiness.

As we have discussed earlier, in a given culture a certain level of unhappiness is accepted as a normal by-product of being human. In

Western culture, some expressions of inner unhappiness that are commonly misperceived as being normal, or are seen as being within a normative range, are

- expressions of low self-esteem—"I never can get it right";
- regularly feeling slightly "down";
- difficulties studying or working effectively, controlling weight, consistently acting in one's best interests; and
- persistent feelings of unrest and discontent.

Other common symptoms of inner unhappiness may go unrecognized by the person who suffers with them because the person misperceives them as benign. Some of these symptoms are even valued by the culture—for instance, Western culture values overwork, a driven materialism, and perfectionism.

Some children who have inner unhappiness insist that they are happy and feel "fine," even though to their parents and teachers they may appear dejected. Moreover, the presence of inner unhappiness does not prevent children from appearing to be cheerful and "sunny." But their need to create unhappiness for themselves will find other means of expression. For example, they may pick friends who constantly disappoint them or may keep themselves off balance emotionally by forgetting important tasks.

In general, children who acquire the need to be unhappy often create problems for themselves without knowing it. This phenomenon is easily observed in those who unknowingly court disaster and who are utterly astonished and feel victimized when disaster strikes, such as the out-of-control adolescent skier who seriously injured someone else and blamed the victim for crossing his path, or the child who broke his leg trying to walk down a banister and blamed his sister for daring him.

Children with inner unhappiness frequently sabotage relationships because they prevent themselves from accepting kindness, friendship, or love at face value. No matter how well they are treated by someone else, they wait for the real (angry, mean, unpleasant) other person to emerge. When a little boy was told by his parents that they loved him, he reacted as though he were being tricked and exclaimed, "No you don't!" His parents, who had been consulting us about their son's depression, did not take his outburst personally; instead they responded sympathetically, "It must be painful to think we don't love you. We will keep trying to help you see that we really do!"

Certainly children with an unshakable primary happiness sometimes feel unhappy, for instance, when they have stomach flu. But this experience of unhappiness does not taint their ongoing sense of inner well-being, and, most important, they do not cause their own unhappiness. Whereas, as we have seen, children whose emotional needs are not adequately satisfied unknowingly develop needs to re-create the inner unhappiness they originally experienced in the relationship with their parents.

When children are exposed to traumatic experiences, such as emotional, sexual, or physical abuse, their need to cause themselves to suffer may be expressed in severely dysfunctional behavior. Severe symptomatic behavior includes childhood psychosis, chronic school phobias, antisocial behavior, and eating disorders. When children with severely dysfunctional behavior do not respond to smart love parenting guidelines, they may require psychological treatment.

Suicide (and attempted suicide) is the most extreme manifestation of inner unhappiness. By far the majority of people who commit suicide do so in spite of the fact that they possess adequate nourishment and good health. They kill themselves because they have the delusional conviction that death offers their only hope for inner peace. For any number of reasons, such people cannot find a way to satisfy their acquired but unrecognized needs for inner unhappiness except by committing suicide.

Fortunately, most people with acquired needs for unhappiness can satisfy their needs for unhappiness without resorting to suicidal self-hatred. Usually, a period of depression or self-castigation will sufficiently gratify an individual's reactive need for painful experiences, after which time he will be able to maintain an inner equilibrium without the need to kill himself.

THE BOY WHO WASN'T CHOSEN

When a child we knew to be troubled with inner unhappiness was not chosen for a coveted part in the class play, he first reacted with a storm of anger at himself for having been so "stupid" as to try out. Despite his parents' efforts to cheer him up, for several days he found it difficult to get out of bed in the morning. In time, his self-castigation was sufficient to gratify his unperceived need to suffer in response to a severe disappointment. Eventually, with some gentle assistance from a teacher, in combination with his parents' ongoing support, he attempted to find a silver lining in the disappointment. He ultimately signed on as stage manager.

Sometimes severe symptoms, such as phobias, nervous tics, disabling depression, schizophrenia, or homicidal rage, make their appearance for the first time in children (or adults) who previously appeared quite normal. These symptoms may disappear as quickly as they came, or they may become chronic. Although it seems that the serious symptoms appeared out of thin air, the individual actually had acquired an inner happiness that was maintained mainly by constructive pleasure until an event occurred to shift the balance toward needs to suffer.

The person with inner unhappiness maintains her inner equilibrium through a combination of positive pleasure, destructive pleasure, and unpleasant experiences. This balance can change based on her experiences. When serious symptoms suddenly manifest themselves, it is because some life experience has strengthened the person's reliance on unpleasant experiences (phobic behavior) or destructive pleasure (substance abuse) to provide a sense of inner well-being.

A YOUNG GYMNAST STARVES HERSELF TO DEATH

Some time ago, a young, immensely talented and dedicated gymnast died of anorexia nervosa. According to news reports, she developed the eating disorder after overhearing the judge of one of her events remark that she would receive better scores if she lost a few pounds. As a consequence of the judge's comment, the girl starved herself to death. Her unperceived need to suffer apparently overpowered her constructive desires to be a healthy and accomplished gymnast. Her tragic death illustrates the degree to which other important adults besides parents can have negative as well as positive effects on the way children with inner unhappiness satisfy their need for an acceptable inner well-being.

The Desire for Unhappiness

Acquired, though unperceived, needs for unhappiness account for a lot of perplexing human behavior. An example is the child who believes that she is happy while she is engaging in self-defeating or self-destructive behavior.

Children usually have no idea that they are driven by wishes for inner unhappiness—for example, the boy who unknowingly provoked other children to hit him and then felt outraged and victimized. Sometimes children may be aware of self-defeating or self-destructive impulses, but they may feel powerless to resist them—such as a child who has a school report due but cannot bring herself to do the research.

Others may believe that the unhappiness they knowingly cause themselves is acceptable. They may experience suffering as atonement for a misstep—for example, the child who slapped herself in the head when she made a mistake; or they may find a way to hurt themselves as a way of soothing themselves—for example, the teenager who cut herself when she felt anxious. Some children who have acquired inner unhappiness seek out unpleasant experiences under the misapprehension that the resulting discomfort will make them feel better. When they do pursue pleasure, it is frequently for the purpose of relieving inner unhappiness rather than for its own sake. Examples are the overweight child who responds to every low moment by eating candy, and the teenager who craves compliments about her appearance to counteract her own feelings of ugliness. But pleasure that is in the service of easing inner unhappiness can provide only fleeting relief. Sometimes the pleasure being used to soothe unhappiness is actually destructive, as is the high produced by heroin or cocaine.

Inner Unhappiness Can Cause Children to React Aversively to Pleasure

Children whose emotional needs have not been adequately satisfied develop conflicting desires. On the one hand, they retain their inborn desire to gain inner happiness through positive pleasure; on the other hand, because as babies they were convinced that the unhappiness they experienced when their developmental needs were not accurately responded to was the ideal happiness intended by their perfect parents, these children unknowingly acquired needs to seek unpleasant experiences. The result of these conflicting desires is a lack of inner peace. When the child gratifies her unperceived need for unpleasant experiences, her pleasure-seeking wishes are frustrated. When she achieves even a moment of success, the pleasure she feels frustrates her unperceived need for unpleasant experiences and stimulates her to make herself unhappy.

Children's unperceived needs to make themselves unhappy cause them to react negatively to positive experiences. This **aversion to pleasure** is the reason that the behavior of children who have acquired inner unhappiness may temporarily worsen in response to genuine caring. Unfortunately, parents and teachers often draw the conclusion that only stern measures will be effective in such cases. These negative responses to accomplishments and pleasurable experiences often occur in school, so teachers and coaches who read these pages will find frequent opportunities to use the smart love guidelines in this book to help children who are making themselves unhappy.

A STUDENT GOES TO FRANCE IN SPITE OF HERSELF

A mother consulted us because she was concerned that her high-school-aged daughter, Cynthia, frequently seemed to make self-defeating choices. Cynthia was an excellent French student and was also knowledgeable about current affairs. She was a shoo-in to be chosen as the delegate from her school to an international conference in France. Yet Cynthia reacted aversively to the pleasure represented by this exciting possibility. She convinced herself that preparing for the conference would be too much work, and she announced that she had decided she would not be applying. But after she made that decision she was overcome with regrets. All the following week, she dwelt on the fun she would be missing. She was consumed with anger at herself for "blowing" this unique opportunity.

Fortunately for Cynthia, her mother and her French teacher understood that without realizing it Cynthia was being buffeted by competing drives for constructive pleasure and for unhappiness. As a result, they did not become angry or disapproving when this prize student didn't apply for the delegate slot. Nor did they feel Cynthia needed to be taught a lesson by having to stay home. Both her mother and her teacher were determined to support Cynthia's desire to choose the better path for herself.

The teacher said that she could see that Cynthia wanted to reverse her decision. Cynthia nodded but said she felt she couldn't change her mind. Her withdrawal from consideration for the delegate's slot was common knowledge at school, and she was afraid she would look foolish. The teacher emphasized that people often make imperfect choices, and that the important thing was to realize that you don't have to live with a bad choice but can try to undo it. She added that it was still not too late to apply for the slot, and that she would wholeheartedly support Cynthia's candidacy.

The teacher emphasized that Cynthia might be teased by her classmates for vacillating, but given the nature of the opportunity, it would still be worth putting her name on the candidates list. With her teacher's and her mother's encouragement, Cynthia gathered the strength to make public her change of heart. She was chosen as the school's delegate and had a memorable experience in France. Even more important, with the help of two caring adults, her desires for constructive pleasure were strengthened.

When children are at the mercy of conflicting needs for both pleasant and unpleasant experiences, they often follow a happy moment (making a brilliant catch in a baseball game) by unknowingly satisfying their needs for unhappiness (dropping the next easy fly ball). For these children, even the most genuinely satisfying achievement or experience is tinged with disappointment, which explains why they frequently react to gifts by finding something wrong with them, or respond to achievements by conjuring up displeasure. An adolescent who heard she had been selected for the debate team found herself unable to stop castigating herself for accidentally ripping her favorite pair of jeans. One six-year-old who struggled mightily to learn to read and finally succeeded responded to his teacher's congratulations by saying, "But it doesn't matter because all the other kids are already on the next level."

These aversive reactions to success and pleasure are actually quite common, but more often than not they go unnoticed or when noticed are misunderstood. A teenager who was elated to hear that she had been accepted by the college of her choice tarnished her happiness by "accidentally" slamming her fingers in the car door on her way home to tell her parents. One child who won an award for a science project to which she had devoted many hours was unable to enjoy it because she secretly felt she did not deserve it. The pain associated with feeling unworthy actually made her feel virtuous for not being "stuck up."

When children react aversively to pleasure, their parents often conclude that their concerted efforts to help their children are not working or may even have been counterproductive. But it is inevitable that a child with inner unhappiness will have at best a mixed reaction to pleasure. If the child reacts negatively to what should be a pleasurable experience, this is actually a sign that a swing toward happiness has stimulated a reaction toward unhappiness. If parents can avoid becoming angry or discouraged in response to their child's aversive reactions to pleasure, they can turn these reactions into growth-promoting experiences. Parents who can maintain a positive and loving attitude in the process of helping their child become aware of her conflicting responses to pleasure can help their child make sense of her upsetting feelings. Eventually the child's aversive reactions may begin to diminish.

A BOY REACTS TO THE PLEASURE OF A PONY RIDE

Craig, a four-year-old who was plagued by frequent, violent temper tantrums, passionately wished to be a cowboy when he grew up. He was utterly thrilled when his parents took him to a county fair for a pony ride. When the ride was over, Craig loudly and insistently demanded cotton candy. His parents responded that they were about to have lunch, but that he could have cotton candy for dessert. Although Craig knew and normally could accept the family rule that he could not eat candy just before a meal, this time he became hysterical and flung himself to the ground kicking and screaming, "You never give me anything I want!"

In the past Craig's parents would have reacted to this seeming ingratitude with remarks such as, "How can you say that when we brought you to the fair and gave you the pony ride you wanted?" or "What's the use of doing anything for you when you can't remember it for five minutes?" With our support they were trying some smart love guidelines. Instead of reacting with exasperation or anger to Craig's tantrum, they understood that he was reacting negatively to the pleasure of the pony ride. They simply said, "Come on, let's have lunch, and then you can have cotton candy. You know, even cowboys eat lunch before they eat candy." Craig looked up tearfully and asked, "They do?" His parents nodded. He picked himself up and accepted the hand his mother offered him. At lunch, his father said, "You know, maybe you were so upset about not getting the cotton candy right then because, you just got the pony ride you wanted and you were feeling so happy that a part of you couldn't take it." Craig listened but made no response.

A few days later, Craig's parents took him to the toy store, where he was allowed to choose one toy. When he requested and was denied a second toy, he again flung himself to the ground screaming. His mother sat down next to him and quietly and affectionately remarked, "You know what? I think this is just like what happened after the pony ride, when you were so upset about the cotton candy. It's feeling hard to enjoy the toy you chose." Craig slowly picked himself up off the floor. Soon he was playing happily with the new toy.

Over the next few months Craig ceased to react to pleasant experiences by immediately asking for something he couldn't have and then throwing himself to the floor in a tantrum when his request was denied. For some time, he would become irritable after he got something he especially liked, but eventually he gained the ability to enjoy special activities and presents without spoiling his own good feelings.

⌒

The child with inner unhappiness may seek out opportunities to undermine potential success. For instance, parents may want to be aware that the child who constantly procrastinates about doing schoolwork may be doing so out of the need to create unpleasant experiences for herself.

A TEEN RECOGNIZES HER MOTIVE TO UNDO HER HARD WORK

We were working with the parents of Carol, a high-school sophomore, to help Carol become aware that she frequently got in her own way when things were going well. After an arduous competition, she was selected as a reporter on the school newspaper. When she told her parents the good news, they congratulated her heartily. Then, very gently, they reminded her that although she felt only happiness at being selected, based on past experience some part of her might be uncomfortable with feeling so much success and might try to interfere with that pleasure by causing her to make a mistake. Carol nodded thoughtfully. The next day, she told her parents at dinner, "I caught myself submitting a story without double-checking my facts. When I checked them, I realized that I had misspelled the name of the teacher I was interviewing. Thanks for reminding me to be careful!"

As you can see from these examples, if parents know that their child has a track record of reacting aversively to pleasure, they can anticipate these responses, handle them with equanimity and sensitivity, and see them as opportunities to strengthen their child's ability to choose constructive pleasure. In this way, parents can help their child develop an awareness of her need for unhappiness, and a functional determination to keep this compulsion from interfering with her life.

Rage Is Always a Product of Inner Unhappiness

There is an important distinction between rage and anger. Anger refers to appropriately aggressive emotions and/or behaviors that occur in response to unprovoked, painful events. Certainly, it's healthy to feel angry if you've been mugged. This emotion is felt by everyone—it is not a sign of inner unhappiness. Children who repeatedly treat themselves and others with unprovoked aggression are expressing inner unhappiness in the form of rage. Rage can be either consciously felt or known only by its effects. People are often unaware of their own rage. For example, an adolescent we know felt nothing but admiration for his girlfriend when she outscored him on an important math test. But that day he forgot to meet her after school and left her waiting on a corner even though he had previously been reliable.

The distinction between felt rage and anger is illustrated by the contrasting reactions of two six-year-olds to unprovoked attacks by schoolmates. The child who reacted with rage continued to fight long after the boy who had attacked him gave up. He stopped pounding on the aggressor only when a teacher stepped in and separated them. Even then, the boy remained consumed with fury. He screamed at his teacher for interfering, and he spent the rest of the morning resentful and upset. He returned home in a foul mood but never mentioned the incident.

The child who responded with anger first defended himself by pushing the other child away, and then he told the other child that he wasn't going to play with him if he was going to act like that. He proceeded to find other children to play with, and he made certain to tell his parents about the incident when he got home.

Every Child Is Born with the Potential for Inner Happiness

Personality can be defined as patterned ways of evaluating and responding to life experiences. After decades of clinical experience and familiarizing ourselves with the relevant research, we have concluded that the most important aspect of personality—the stability or instability of a person's inner happiness—is entirely determined by the nurture a child receives.

A child whose parents have attended to his developmental needs adequately has the inner freedom to develop a personality that is flexible and adaptable. He will develop a true self-awareness because, since there is no hidden agenda running his life, he is able to make appropriate choices in the areas of values, relationships, interests, and work without running into internal opposition. His choices will be neither self-destructive nor injurious to others, because he will never acquire the desire to make himself or others unhappy.

True self-awareness is possible only when an individual's developmental needs have been met and he has completed adolescence. In contrast, there are three types of incomplete self-awareness: habituated, developmental, and abnormal.

- A *habituated* lack of self-awareness occurs when we perform everyday activities without consciously attending to them. Just as we can drive from home to work without being fully aware of our actions, so we can go through the motions of other repetitive activities without fully engaging our awareness of what we are doing.

- A *developmental* lack of self-awareness is due solely to intellectual and perceptual immaturity. For example, young children are convinced that they have the power to control events and get what they want.

- An *abnormal* lack of self-awareness is the recurrent inability to remember what is necessary to keep yourself happy and healthy.

This self-destructive behavior is rooted in acquired needs for inner unhappiness. Examples are the ten-year-old who crossed the street without noticing if the light was red or green; the teen who forgot the due date of an important paper; the woman who did not pay attention to the signs of an infection radiating up her arm from a cut; and the husband who ignored the deteriorating state of his marriage.

Children who exhibit an abnormal lack of awareness are at constant risk of hurting themselves. Parents may need to give these children numerous friendly reminders, such as, "Remember, that's a big street. Please be careful crossing!" or "Let's check your equipment before you go to the hockey game to make sure you have your face guard." If children of any age have frequent accidents despite parents' attempts to help them take care, they may require the assistance of a mental health professional.

The most important characteristic of the personality of the child whose developmental needs have been met will be an inner happiness that is separate from, and impervious to, life's ups and downs. Obviously, each person will develop different talents and preferences in relation to work and play, and these will contribute to the exciting variety of human activities and achievements he or she chooses to engage in. However, these abilities and choices are neither sources of sustained inner happiness nor explanations for an individual's most important choices. Children develop an abiding inner happiness and are able to reach their full potential as the result of parents' available, informed love, not because of their genetic make-up. We emphasize that "full potential" is not synonymous with material success. Material success is not an intrinsically important goal, and, in addition, adverse circumstances can interfere with the attainment of material success even when an individual is working to full potential.

The widespread but unproven belief that personality is largely inborn has had a harmful effect on the way our society thinks about children. For example, parents are often told that their irritable and unhappy baby was "born that way" and that they should accept the baby's unhappiness the way they accept her eye color. No matter what behavior patterns healthy newborns exhibit, these can be modified by parents' responses.[4]

How to Help Your Child Choose and Become
the Person She Wants to Be

All children grow up identifying with those who are close to them or whom they admire. **Identification** is the perceived or unperceived attempt to become like an important other. Some children may desire to play musical instruments like their fathers or aunts; others may be more interested in painting like their mothers or uncles. The identifications of children whose needs have been accurately and generously responded to are always positive (produce pleasure) and voluntary (not the product of children's inner unhappiness or parental pressure). With the help of your smart love, your child will grow up actively choosing to treat herself with the same informed, abundant love she received from you. She will also freely choose to emulate those interests and talents of important others that promise to provide her with the most enjoyment.

When children's emotional needs are not satisfied, their identifications have an involuntary and frequently unpleasurable quality. Many children grow up feeling that they must follow in a parent's footsteps, and then they lack the satisfaction of having chosen their life's work. Growing up to be an architect because Mom is an architect is rarely recognized as problematic, but since involuntary identification with a parent's accomplishments has an unreflective quality, it actually can add to a child's inner unhappiness by increasing feelings of helplessness.

If parents are self-destructive or antisocial, or if they treat their children harshly or neglectfully, children will identify with these negative characteristics. A couple of examples are the child who locks his puppy in the bathroom for a time-out and the child who emulates his father's reckless driving by rollerblading carelessly.

Children sometimes copy the antisocial actions of peers, for example, by taunting children who are "different" or throwing rocks through windows. This behavior always builds on the children's preexisting negative identifications with their parents. If children's developmental needs have been positively responded to, they will not be tempted to imitate others' antisocial or self-destructive behavior.

Sometimes children identify with their parents' fantasies about them; for example, a child may want to become the artist, intellectual, or failure her parents always envisioned her to be. Children who fight off their "destiny" feel selfish and guilty. Parents would probably be less likely to make global statements about their child's personality if they realized that their child's love for them will impel her to try to live up—or down—to this image. One parent told her friend in front of her six-year-old, "David is so disorganized. I don't think he could find his head if it weren't attached to his shoulders!" Another parent continually remarked in front of his ten-year-old that she was so athletic she would probably save them college tuition by getting an athletic scholarship. While these descriptions and predictions often seem humorous, affectionate, or inconsequential to adults, they have an enormous impact on children, who may feel pressure to actualize their parents' views, or may experience shame or guilt if they have contradictory beliefs or desires.

Children who suffer from inner unhappiness will differ in the degree to which their identifications feel chosen, even though none of their identifications will actually result from a genuinely free choice.

- *A child's involuntary identification with a parent (or parent's point of view) is* active *when the child is convinced she is freely choosing a course of action.* One girl believed she had made a careful decision to go to the college her mother attended, even though she had never investigated any other colleges. When the mother realized that her daughter was not pursuing other options, she suggested that the teen might look into other colleges so as to make the most informed decision possible. The mother offered to assist her daughter to collect information about other schools. In this way, she helped her daughter to avoid the trap of acting unreflectively on her identification with her mother's choice of a college.

- *A child's involuntary identification with a parent (or parent's point of view) is* reactive *when the child's choices are dictated by the need to distance herself from her parents.* One teen was determined to grow up to be entirely unlike his father. After considering many different colleges, he turned down the college he liked best for the sole reason that his father had gone there.

- *A child's involuntary identification with a parent (or parent's point of view) is* passive *when the child simply lives out her "fate."* One boy helplessly experienced himself becoming the spendthrift, shiftless adult his father had always predicted he would become.

As you can see, a child with inner unhappiness may be in the grips of an involuntary identification even when she seems most decisive or when she seems unable to make any choice at all. Parents who understand this will be less likely to take at face value their child's decisiveness and will be better able to help their child if she is paralyzed with indecision. They will know that their child needs support to consider other possibilities and to experiment with different choices.

A BOOKWORM BROADENS HIS HORIZONS

A couple came to us out of concern for their eight-year-old, Ned, who was being teased mercilessly by other children for being a "nerd." We soon determined that Ned was fulfilling the family consensus that he was an excellent student but a poor athlete. His parents reported that they were concerned because Ned was constantly finding ways to get excused from gym class, and he did nothing active at home.

We suggested that the parents find a noncompetitive, low-key physical activity Ned could engage in with the family. The parents invited their son to go walking with them and the family dog. Ned resisted at first, but when he finally agreed to go, he enjoyed the fresh air, the companionship, and the chance to be alone with his parents and to talk with them about his science projects. Soon the early evening walks became a family institution, and on weekends the family branched out to state parks, where they did some vigorous hiking. Although Ned never developed the desire to be a star athlete, for the first time he was able to take pleasure in physical activity.

∽

Stopping the Roller Coaster of Inner Unhappiness

If your child is unhappy and difficult, you need not resign yourself to his discomfort and problems. Inner unhappiness need not be a life sentence. You can use smart love principles to strengthen your child's desires for constructive pleasure and to reduce the strength of your child's needs for causing himself unhappiness.

Because children develop inner unhappiness out of love for their parents, parents can build on that love to make their children happier. It is our experience that all parents can use the principles of smart love to make significant and constructive changes in their parenting. For example, by responding to problem behavior with loving regulation rather than with disciplinary measures, you can help a child with inner unhappiness develop a stable preference for constructive pleasure. You can use smart love guidelines at any time to guide your child at any age back to a satisfying, successful, and enjoyable life.

How to Help Your Child Choose Constructive Pleasure

Parents and other important adults can dramatically improve an unhappy child's quality of life because the child will respond well to the caring of parents and important others and to positive life experiences of all kinds. Individuals whose emotional needs have not been met maintain their inner well-being through a combination of *constructive pleasure* (for example, smooth-running friendships, academic success), *unpleasant experiences* (such as picking fights), and *destructive pleasure* (for example, overeating or unsafe promiscuous sex). This balance does not remain constant; it can be shifted by life experiences of all sorts.

Anyone who has a meaningful relationship with an unhappy and difficult child can use smart love guidelines to strengthen the child's wishes for inner well-being gained through the pursuit of constructive pleasure, and to wean him from the need for an inner well-being based on unpleasant experiences or destructive pleasure. A child's preferences for experiencing constructive pleasure will be strengthened or weakened by any event that is important to him. Examples are school successes or failures, falling in or out of love, praise or criticism from a parent, or the championship win or loss of a favorite sports team. The change can be either transitory or enduring.

Children burdened with inner unhappiness typically expect adults to misunderstand them and to criticize them. These children may unknowingly try to provoke hurtful interactions because of their needs to maintain their inner equilibrium through negative experiences. When adults understand this dynamic and respond to a child's mistakes and "transgressions" with understanding and compassion, the effect on the child can be profound.

COMPASSION TRANSFORMS A THIEF

Victor Hugo recognized the power of a caring relationship to alter the course of a life when he wrote in *Les Misérables* of the positive and lasting transformation that occurred for the thief, Jean Valjean. After being apprehended for stealing silverware from the vicarage, he was released when the bishop compassionately told the authorities that the silver had been a gift. This generous act permanently strengthened Jean Valjean's desire for constructive pleasure. He distanced himself from his long-standing feelings of bitterness and resentment, abandoned antisocial behavior, and dedicated the rest of his life to helping others.

Many adults remember key interactions with significant others that permanently changed their lives for the better. Teachers, coaches, bosses, clergymen, and other important adults can have such an effect; that is why it is helpful if they, too, understand the principles of smart love.

A COACH MAKES A DIFFERENCE

John, a boy we know, transferred to a new school and joined the baseball team. In his first game, he fumbled an easy ground ball and gave up the winning run. He felt utterly furious with himself and went to the dugout anticipating that his coach would give him the severe tongue-lashing he felt he deserved. John was overcome when his coach affectionately clapped him on the back and said, "It happens to everyone. Next time just try to keep your eye on the ball and you'll be fine. You're a first-rate shortstop." John was startled to find that his anger at himself was not shared by his coach. From that moment on, John's fury with himself whenever he made a mistake began to seem out of proportion. Instead of feeling despicable and worthless, he was able to keep in mind that others make errors, too, that he had tried his best, and that he could learn from his mistakes and improve.

Notice When Your Child Is Most Vulnerable

You can also help your child to reduce his needs for causing himself unhappiness if you notice under which circumstances he tends to fall back on destructive pleasure or to create unpleasant experiences. For example, a father told us that his daughter always went on food binges while she was studying for finals. When he offered her the more constructive pleasure of sitting with her and helping her review, she was much better able to regulate her eating.

MAYHEM AT DINNERTIME

A mother who was seeing us for parenting advice noticed that her six-year-old son was teasing and hitting her four-year-old son around dinner time. When we asked her to recall the details of what had happened, she realized that the fighting occurred when she turned her attention to cooking. She began to plan ways in which her sons could help her with the dinner preparation (mixing, stirring, setting the table). At times when the boys didn't feel like participating, she started them on projects they liked, such as finger-painting, just before she began cooking. She was very gratified to find that the hour before dinner suddenly turned calm and pleasant.

Use Loving Regulation to Minimize Your Child's Exposure to Upsetting Books, Movies, and Television Shows

In keeping with the principle of maximizing the unhappy child's desires for constructive pleasure, parents should try to minimize their child's exposure to experiences that will whet her appetite for destructive pleasure or unpleasant experiences. The child whose developmental needs are adequately satisfied grows up seeking only constructive pleasure. She does not find excessively violent or pointlessly depressing books, movies, and television shows appealing, nor does she have an inclination to identify with their values. In contrast, children who suffer from inner unhappiness will be more inclined to find such material enticing. They will function less well and will be more upset because of their exposure to sad or aggressive books, movies, and TV programs.

MY BROTHER THE BAD GUY

When a six-year-old we were seeing watched a violent television program, he would pretend that his three-year-old brother was a "bad guy" and would terrorize him by pretending quite realistically to shoot him and stab him. While in the absence of TV the child would occasionally vent his unhappiness on his brother, these aggressive acts were relatively infrequent and of short duration. When the boy watched violent TV programs, however, his imaginative play was appropriated by the aggressive scenarios. His hostile behavior toward his brother became so out-of-control that he was unable to make peace until an adult intervened.

Many children with inner unhappiness are inclined to watch an excessive amount of TV. Helping these children limit their television watching can be a real challenge for parents. When children use television as a source of well-being, it is not sufficient simply to ask them to restrict themselves to an hour of benign TV per day. Parents need to suggest alternatives that will appeal to their child's interests. One father of a five-year-old could usually engage his son to help fix things around the house; a ten-year-old really enjoyed going to the park with his mother to draw landscapes; a three-year-old liked being read to; and a teenager enjoyed playing card games.

Children with Inner Unhappiness Need Constant, Gentle Guidance

Children who have inner unhappiness require more focused attention in later years than children who were fortunate enough to have had their emotional needs met from birth. Unhappy children need constant, gentle, unobtrusive guidance toward sustaining their inner well-being through constructive pleasure rather than destructive pleasure or unpleasant experiences.

When children pursue activities that are dangerous, self-defeating, or likely to lead to poor outcomes, parents can use smart love guidelines to help their children make better choices. Parents can take comfort in knowing that their children retain their inborn desires for constructive pleasure, even though this positive force may not be obvious.

Parents can make a valuable contribution to the well-being of a child who suffers from inner unhappiness by recognizing instances when their own personal agendas prevent them from being as helpful to their child as they would like to be. They can then enlist the assistance of caring others. One mother whose three-year-old became very anxious in new situations was aware that she herself was a nervous wreck each time she had to go to the dentist. When the time came for her son to have his first dental appointment, she knew that if she were to take him, her fright at being in the dentist's office might increase her son's anxiety. She asked her sister, who was unruffled by dental procedures, to accompany her son.

Loving Regulation for the Child with Inner Unhappiness

Parents often say, "We are concerned that if we don't come down hard on problem behavior, our child will just ignore us and the behavior will continue. Our child will not learn that there are real-world consequences for misbehaving." But, as we have emphasized, the smart love principle of loving regulation allows parents to manage their children's unwanted behavior without depriving their child of the pleasure of a positive relationship.

Loving regulation stops out-of-control behavior without adding to the child's unhappiness. When you use loving regulation, you guide your child toward more constructive behavior as diplomatically as possible and without imposing sanctions or giving lectures. Your gentleness and your willingness to listen to your child's unhappy feelings will strengthen her wishes to treat herself well. Over time loving regulation will decrease the child's need to engage in problem behavior.

Children are better able to get beyond problem behavior when they are sustained by feelings of closeness with their parents. For this reason, loving regulation is always preferable to measures that rely on some form of coercion, since coercion actually strengthens the child's need to make herself unhappy by stimulating the child to copy her parents' harshness toward her.

THE HARM IN IMPOSING NEGATIVE CONSEQUENCES ON A CHILD WHO "STOLE"

Parents who believed strongly in the benefits of stern discipline and negative consequences reacted strongly when their six-year-old, George, came home from a play date with a toy that didn't belong to him. The parents asked, "Did you take that toy?" George said that he hadn't. The father replied that he didn't believe George, and that he intended to call the friend and ask whether the toy had been taken without permission. George burst into hysterical tears and admitted what he had done.

His parents first lectured George about stealing. "How would you feel if people stole from you?" they asked. "Stealing is against the law, and when you get older you will go to jail if you steal." They also restricted him from play dates for a week. Finally, the parents insisted that George call his friend and tell him what he had done, and they stood near the phone to make sure he carried out their instructions. George cried throughout this ordeal, and he seemed very depressed the next day.

When George was allowed to play at his friend's house a few weeks later, he again took a toy, but this time he hid it in his backpack and then in his room. His parents never discovered that he had taken it. As George grew older, he continued to take things that didn't belong to him whenever he was feeling particularly low. But he concealed this activity so successfully that his parents never knew about it until the day the police came to their door saying that their son had been arrested for shoplifting. At that point the boy was referred to us for help.

〜

USING LOVING REGULATION WHEN CHILDREN "STEAL"

When six-year-old Ethan took a toy from a friend's house without permission, his parents, who were working with us, gently asked where he had gotten the new toy. At first, Ethan insisted that his friend had given it to him, but when his parents repeated their question in an affectionate manner, he admitted his mistake. His parents simply responded, "You know we can't take things that don't belong to us." His mother said that she would go with her son to school in the morning and make sure that the classmate got the toy back. Ethan started to cry and said that he didn't want his friend to know he had taken the toy. His father said that he thought his friend would be relieved to have the toy back, and he doubted that he would be really angry. He gave Ethan a hug and said he knew he felt bad about what he had done. Ethan looked downcast and nodded. A few minutes later the boy asked his father to play catch with him, and his father said he would be glad to. The next day Ethan apologized to his friend and subsequently lost interest in taking other people's things.

Ethan's parents followed loving regulation in making it clear that Ethan could not take things without permission; in showing him a constructive, viable way to fix the problem he had created; and, most important, in making clear to Ethan that their admiration and love for him were undiminished by his impulsive act.

Two Steps Forward and One Step Back

When the problem behavior of a child with inner unhappiness does not appear to respond to parents' loving regulation, parents sometimes mistakenly conclude that being nice to children who "misbehave" doesn't work. But because such children have unknowingly developed needs for unpleasant experiences, they will often take one step backward for every two steps they go forward. Try to focus on the two steps your child takes forward toward happiness, and try not to be thrown by the one step backward toward unhappiness.

Children with inner unhappiness will react aversively to pleasure, including the pleasure they experience when their parents respond with loving regulation. Parents who don't see this pattern may become discouraged by their child's negativity and fall back on harsher responses. The child's behavior will then worsen, and she may cease to progress altogether.

WHEN PARENTS DON'T RECOGNIZE AVERSIVE REACTIONS TO PLEASURE

The parents of eight-year-old Connie consulted us because the girl was regularly hurting her younger brother. We advised them to arrange her day so that she had many opportunities to play and to take initiative, while at the same time they kept either Connie or her brother in plain view. Connie reacted aversively to the newly established tranquillity by landing a few blows during the infrequent times her parents' backs were turned.

Unfortunately, her parents concluded that these instances of backsliding indicated that loving regulation was not working. They began sending Connie to her room for a time-out each time she hit her brother. Connie reacted to the time-outs by blaming her younger brother for being a "little brat." It was his fault that she was being sent to her room. She grew increasingly enraged with him and took every opportunity to make his life miserable. Soon the relationship between the siblings was worse than ever.

On our advice, Connie's parents stopped the time-outs and returned to loving regulation. They accepted that Connie's unperceived needs for self-caused unhappiness would lead her to react to peaceful times with her brother by provoking or hitting him, so they tried never to leave the children alone together. Moreover, they did not overreact on those infrequent occasions when Connie went back to acting aggressively.

Relations between the siblings gradually improved. Three months later, when the girl's father had to leave the room and, as usual, asked that one child accompany him so that the siblings would not be left alone together, his daughter said earnestly, "That's OK, Dad, we'll be all right. We're playing, and I don't feel like hitting him today." Her father heard the conviction in his daughter's voice and replied, "That's great! But if you start to feel differently, let's agree you will call me." The girl assented, and the siblings played peacefully while their father was occupied in the next room.

Parents have a tendency to grow impatient when their child's behavior improves very slowly in response to loving regulation. To them the troublesome behavior appears to be within the child's control; if she wanted to, the child would stop biting, refusing to eat, or disobeying teachers. They believe that the child can take control of her behavior; she is just being obstinate in clinging to antisocial or self-defeating ways.

It is important to remember that children never make a genuinely free choice to behave in ways that are self-harming or socially unacceptable. As one five-year-old we were seeing said plaintively, "When my brain tells me to get in trouble, I have to do it." Because "misbehavior" is the product of an underlying, though unperceived, need to bring on unhappiness, children cannot simply decide to abandon the compulsion, any more than afflicted adults can easily stop overeating or having a short fuse.

When parents respond with anger, disapproval, deprivations, and other punishments to symptoms such as thumb-sucking, stealing, or truancy, children feel misunderstood, and consequently their unhappiness will tend to increase, and their need for their symptoms will strengthen. When parents punish a child for each instance of wayward behavior by restricting her from an activity she enjoys, the child becomes further alienated from her parents. For example, depriving a truant child of telephone privileges may or may not get her to go back to school on a regular basis, but it will never accomplish her parents' true goal: to increase the child's appetite for the enjoyable process of improving her mind. Children miss school for a reason, and parents who practice loving regulation will focus on trying to understand the underlying cause.

HELPING AN EIGHTH GRADER WHO DIDN'T WANT TO GO TO SCHOOL

Carrie, an eighth grader, began to resist going to school. When pressed, she was unable to give a reason for her truancy. Her parents followed a friend's advice to ground her one night for each day she missed, but Carrie silently accepted the restriction, and her attitude remained as negative as before. The friend suggested withholding her allowance, but the parents intuitively felt that harsher measures would be counterproductive.

When these parents consulted us, we suggested that they stop punishing Carrie for her truant behavior and focus instead on showing her that they really wanted to understand her negative feelings. They tried asking Carrie if she was feeling worried or upset about some aspect of her school experience. Carrie denied that anything was wrong. Her parents told her that school was impor-tant and she had no choice about going, but if something was bothering her, they really wanted to hear about it. She continued to insist that everything was fine, that she was just "bored." Her parents saw an opening and asked which classes "bored" her the most. She said mainly Spanish—she could never seem to get her accent right, and the other children laughed at her when she was called on. Her parents responded that being ridiculed might make it difficult to go to class or even to school. They offered to ask a Spanish-speaking friend to spend some time with her at night working on her accent. Carrie agreed, and over the next few weeks, as her accent improved, her attendance at school improved as well.

We emphasize that Carrie became willing to share her concerns with her parents when they approached the problem of her truancy without showing disapproval or imposing sanctions. Their change of tack made credible their expressed desire to help her remove whatever obstacle was preventing her from wanting to be at school.

The smart love principle is *while parents should try to strengthen their child's desires for constructive pleasure, they should not force her to do the right thing.* Genuine, lasting change will occur only if the child with inner unhappiness learns to choose constructive pleasure from a desire to feel happier, and not because she is coerced by disapproval or the threat of punishments. For this reason, smart love is incompatible with "tough love," which we discuss in detail in Chapter 8.

Don't Reward Children with Inner Unhappiness— Encourage Them Instead

Just as parents should avoid responding negatively to their child's problematic behavior, they should not use rewards to induce a child to behave more constructively. Rewards are harmful because they override children's power to choose by manipulating them into accomplishing specific goals. Rewards actually function coercively. They rob children of the benefit of recognizing for themselves that they are capable of making good choices and pursuing them well. The child who is tempted by a reward learns to focus on the reward and ceases to evaluate the quality of the choices available to her. To illustrate, rewarding children for getting A's in chemistry will not help them to develop a love of science; in fact, there is evidence that rewards may degrade whatever interest children have in a school subject. In addition, rewards have a hidden punitive component: the child is attracted by the promise of a reward and feels hurt and punished if she doesn't get it.

As an alternative, offering children **encouragement** when they show that they want to choose constructive pleasure is helpful. Unlike rewards, encouragement is not contingent on any particular outcome—the child gets the encouragement whether or not she attains or even tries for a given goal.

ENCOURAGING A THIRD GRADER WHO HATED MATH

We suggested to the parents of Joe, a third-grade boy who was having difficulty with math, that they ask him whether he would like help with his math homework. He said that he didn't think so. His parents replied, "OK, but if you change your mind, we would be happy to see what we can do." A few weeks passed, during which we kept counseling the parents to be patient. At dinner one night, Joe said, "I really hate math!" When his parents asked why, Joe replied, "I just don't understand how to multiply and divide fractions, and I don't even want to learn about it!" Joe's parents again suggested that some assistance might make the process more enjoyable. Joe said, "I don't think I would like math even if I were a genius, but if you want to try, it's OK with me."

Joe's parents took turns sitting with him as he worked through problems and helping him when he got stuck. The first night, he got very frustrated after the third problem and said, "I can't do anymore—you do it!" The father said, acceptingly, "OK, I'll work on the rest of the problems for you, but you watch and make sure I'm doing it correctly. I'll do my thinking out loud." Joe paid close attention. The next night, he worked all but one problem with his mother's help before he asked her to finish for him. The third night, he was able to complete the entire assignment with their help. Over the next few months, Joe's math grades improved from D's to B's. Most important, he willingly sat down to do his math after dinner and stayed with the homework assignment until he completed it. Joe felt comfortable asking his parents for help when necessary. Because his parents didn't offer rewards for good grades, but, instead, encouraged Joe's desire to enjoy the pleasure of being competent at math, the boy felt that he was in charge of and responsible for his math progress, and he experienced his parents as furthering his own wish to improve.

Principles for Helping the Child Who Has Developed Inner Unhappiness

- Keep in mind that deep down, your unhappy and difficult child wants to feel happy and fulfilled.
- Be accessible and supportive.
- Create opportunities for your child to experience constructive pleasure and positive identifications.
- Understand that your child will react aversively to pleasurable experiences, including the pleasure of making constructive choices.
- Limit negative influences.
- Use loving regulation.

- Don't punish.
- Don't reward.

Parents Hold the Key to Human Happiness

With smart love principles you can give your child the kind of happiness that will allow him to attain his highest potential. The greatest improvement in the quality of human life will come not from brilliant discoveries about the nature of matter or technological innovations, but from parents whose love and insight give their children lasting inner happiness and thereby leave a legacy of competent, caring individuals. Talent at parenting is not a function of intelligence, education, or wealth, but of sensitivity to children's developmental needs and sustained effort to satisfy them. When the children of such parents grow to adulthood, they will not be attracted to antisocial behavior, greed, narcissistic self-involvement, or self-destruction. Because they have acquired their own unshakable inner happiness and sense of competence, they will make others happy and make the world a more secure and welcoming place.

Chapter Four

❧

The First Year:
Smart Loving Your Baby

Contrary to conventional wisdom, newborns do not enter the world undifferentiated blobs aware only of themselves. Rather, every baby enters the world an optimist with regard to human relationships. Infants are born adoring you, wanting to be just like you, and convinced that they are so lovable that you will always want to respond to their needs for affection and care. Babies are convinced that you cause their every experience, and that every experience represents ideal parenting. Infants interpret every feeding, feeling, visual pattern, or touch as your loving response to their wishes to be cared for. Every time you respond positively to your infant's needs, she discovers that reality matches the ideal world she was born expecting. She will be well-launched on her journey toward a happy and meaningful life and will have no need for painful experiences.

The days and weeks after birth are your opportunity to show your baby that the optimism she was born with is well-founded. This is the start of an exciting process of getting to know your child and, thereby, becoming an expert at making her happy. Every baby believes she is causing your unconditional loving responses, but babies differ in the type of caring they find most soothing. Some babies like looking at the world over your shoulder; others are happy and interested being cradled in your arms. As you learn how to comfort and please your baby, you will feel a growing sense of competence and confidence, and she will become convinced that she can communicate her needs and cause the caring responses she most desires.

Your Infant's Point of View: The Meaning of Her Cries

With the help of smart love, you can ensure that your infant will never lose his inborn optimism. Instead, he will discover that the joy he feels in your presence is the most effective balm for discomfort and frustration. By the time they are a few weeks old, unless they are experiencing insistent physical pain, infants whose developmental needs are adequately satisfied will not be inclined to cry frequently or intensely. If they do cry, their tears will remind them that help is on the way.

Parents who are not aware of the importance of responding immediately, gently, and positively to their infant's discomfort may unintentionally teach their baby to cry hard the moment he feels unhappy (for example, when he feels hungry, overstimulated, or tired). When a baby's crying is regularly ignored, his subsequent unhappiness reminds him that help does not come when he is upset, and the baby learns to respond to discomfort by crying more intensely and more disconsolately.

If a baby's tears don't predictably evoke a caring response, eventually he will become withdrawn. The child becomes convinced that his misery is what his parents desire for him, and, therefore, that the unhappiness is desirable. You cannot prevent your baby from experiencing some kinds of unhappiness, such as indigestion, colds, or the pain of teething. But you can help your infant avoid the more costly emotional misery he will feel if you follow popular advice to "let him cry." Babies who are left to cry feel powerless and incompetent. Whether or not you can determine the exact reason for your baby's misery, by consistently responding to your crying child, you show him that everyday difficulties do not have to diminish his inner happiness, because he can always elicit your loving assistance.

You may have been told that babies who are picked up and soothed every time they cry will either become too tender emotionally to handle frustration, or learn that crying gets attention. But many parents find it heart-wrenching to allow their baby to cry miserably "for his own good," and they are enormously relieved to hear that deliberate unresponsiveness is actually harmful, not helpful, to children.

Babies cry because they experience two separate kinds of unhappiness. First, they really are hungry, tired, frightened, in pain, or overstimulated. Second, they assume that their parents are aware of and desire their misery. When you soothe your baby, you show him that you want him to feel happy rather than unhappy. Children who have been responded to generously will, when they are older, surprise everyone with their ability to tolerate the ups and downs of daily living without losing self-esteem and self-confidence. This strength will arise from their ability to emulate the manner in which their parents responded lovingly to their tears. Infants grow into resilient children and adults because they have experienced an abundance of caring and not a history of deprivation.

The smart love guideline is *always try to comfort a crying child*. Because of his immaturity, your infant can express unhappiness only by fussing or crying. Try to respond to the crying infant as if he is articulately asking for your loving help, rather than as though he were trying to manipulate you by making imperious and irritating demands. When you do your best to keep your infant happy and comfortable, he learns to treat himself equally well. By responding consistently and in a caring way, you protect him from acquiring needs for unhappiness and you secure his emotional health. The inner happiness you make possible for your child will also improve the quality of his physical, social, and intellectual development. Therefore, try to ignore all advice that tells you to be rigid about schedules or to worry about spoiling your child with too much attention.

In Western society there is a long-standing belief that children are inherently antisocial and need to be civilized. Actually, infants are born social. They come into the world seeking the pleasure of relationships. You may feel uncertain and anxious when you find yourself spending long hours at home alone with your firstborn. Perhaps it will help to remember that your baby enters the world adoring you and possessing abundant goodwill toward you. All parents experience moments when their newborn seems inexplicably inconsolable. The knowledge that your baby cries only from discomfort, and never with the intent to anger or manipulate you, may help you to persevere in the attempt to uncover the source of your baby's unhappiness or, failing that, to continue the effort to make your baby as comfortable as possible.

THE "INCONSOLABLE" BABY

New parents consulted us about their six-week-old baby, because three or four times a day, particularly in the afternoon and evening, she would become hysterical and cry inconsolably. Her parents would offer food, burp her, check her diaper, rock her, and sing to her, but nothing seemed to work. They brought her to their pediatrician, who could find nothing wrong. The baby was eating, sleeping, and growing appropriately, but still she cried. Her parents bought books that told them that their daughter was born irritable and that there was nothing to be done. They found themselves alternating between feeling miserable at their helplessness and feeling furious with their infant for seeming so intractably unresponsive.

We told these parents how wonderful it was that, in the face of their daughter's continued wails, they persisted in their efforts to soothe her, especially since they were so often advised to "let her cry." By continuing with their attempts to ease their baby's unhappiness, they were showing her that even when she felt most uncomfortable, she need never feel insecure about her ability to cause her parents to respond lovingly to her needs.

After we observed them with their baby for a two-hour period, we saw that these parents, enchanted with their firstborn, were overstimulating her. From the moment she opened her eyes from a nap, they were constantly talking to her, holding her up in the air, adjusting her clothes, and generally doing things "to" her. Like many first-time parents, this mother and father were so thrilled with their baby and found playing with her so enjoyable that they didn't give the baby a chance to feel in control of her world.

We suggested that if their daughter woke up content, they let her enjoy being awake for a few minutes before they picked her up, that they not jiggle her up and down while holding her, and that as long as she was enjoying a particular position (such as viewing the world from a shoulder or lying in her bassinet) they not move her. All of these suggestions were designed to help these parents to give their baby a greater sense of control over her world, without diminishing her inborn belief in their ongoing commitment and availability.

The parents called us two weeks later to report that to their surprise and delight their daughter had virtually ceased her periods of hysterical and inconsolable crying. They said she was now content almost all the time, and that the experience of parenting had become as enjoyable as they had always hoped it would be. When we saw this family for a follow-up visit a few months later, the baby was smiling, socially engaged, and self-confident, and her parents were

proud of their ever-increasing expertise at understanding and responding appropriately to her needs.

Your Crying Infant Is Not Manipulating You

We cannot overemphasize that your crying infant is not trying to manipulate you, and that responding lovingly will *build* rather than corrupt his character. *Manipulation is a word that never applies to babies.* Crying is the child's way of expressing misery at feeling both overwhelmed and also incapable of eliciting your loving assistance. Crying is not a calculated act. Anger or withdrawal on your part convinces the child that he is unattractive to you (and, therefore, to himself) when he is unhappy. The child whose tears evoke parents' anger or seeming indifference grows into the adult who compounds everyday sadness and disappointment by feeling unlovable when he is unhappy. Remember that you are the source of your young child's greatest happiness. If you freely supply your loving attention, your child gains a storehouse of well-being that will last a lifetime and see him through every disappointment and frustration.

Parents can usually find ways of soothing their infant when daily care causes distress. For example, bathing a newborn can be upsetting for the child. Many infants do not like the feeling of being lowered naked into water. The smart love principle is *try to keep your baby as happy as possible*. There is no reason to give your baby a true bath until he is old enough to enjoy it. Premoisturized cleansing tissues or a well-wrung washcloth applied to face and bottom will provide acceptable hygiene without upsetting your baby unnecessarily.

Your Infant's Point of View: The Meaning of Being Fed

The experience of being fed will build your baby's trust and confidence and increase her desire for the pleasure of your company. Feeding your baby can also give you unalloyed pleasure. Whether breast- or bottle-fed, the infant soon learns to suck effectively and to be nourished by the joy of being in your presence as well as by the food she receives. She will increasingly use this time to gaze at your face, to coo, to touch, and to smile.

Try to give and get the full enjoyment from feeding your baby. Ideally, feeding should not be a time for refereeing the disputes of older children, making lists, calling customers, or entertaining guests. Nor should you worry about whether your baby is being fed too often. Feeding your baby when she cries will not be harmful in the event that her distress is not caused by hunger. If you think that your crying baby is hungry but find that she remains upset when she is offered milk, no harm is done. Try to look for another explanation for her tears. Perhaps she is coming down with a cold or needs to burp, to sleep, or to change position. If you refuse food to a crying baby who is hungry, her inability to satisfy her need to be fed will dent her inborn optimistic belief in herself as a valuable and effective person.

Ignore all advice to let your hungry baby cry until the next feeding time. Your baby's cries of hunger express two separate sources of unhappiness: (1) the discomfort of the hunger pangs, and (2) the painful conviction that you want her to feel miserable. By responding to your infant's cries, her hunger pains will be eased, and, just as important, she will see that she is so lovable that she can inspire you to make her happy.

Babies need both food and to believe that their adored parents want them to feel satisfied. Because they are born believing that their parents are perfect caregivers, when infants are left to cry hungrily, they mislabel the misery they feel as a desirable state intended by their parents. Over time, these infants will develop ongoing needs to re-create this discomfort in their lives. *The ultimate source of all self-generated adult misery is that, believing our parents were perfect caregivers, we emulate the way our parents cared for us.*

Weaning

The timetable for weaning babies varies widely across cultures, and for good reason. In some cultures, mother's milk is by far the most abundant, nourishing, and germ-free source of nutrition, and children who are breast-fed longer will be healthier and hardier. In cultures where nutritious, safe foods are widely available and working mothers may need to leave the infant in the care of others for considerable periods of time every day, there are good reasons to wean children early.

In general, babies who are under one year of age adapt better to changes than children who are between one and two-and-a-half years old. For this reason, when the child is eleven months it is often a good time to begin gradually weaning the breast-fed child and to help the bottle-fed child make the transition to drinking from a cup. After they turn one, children may demand the breast or bottle by name, and they may not be easily distracted by or attracted to the new cup you give them.

Whatever age you choose for weaning, do it gradually and in a way that fits your child's daily rhythm. For example, some children wake up happy and adventurous, and the first meal of the day is a good time to offer them a cup rather than the breast or bottle. These children may be overtired by nightfall and may need to nurse in order to get to sleep peacefully. Other children are sleepy and want to be held in the morning, and they may be outraged if you offer them a cup when they want the breast or bottle. But they may be willing to try out a cup at lunch or at night.

Sometimes parents are advised, "Just take away the breast [or bottle] and give her a cup. She will cry, but she'll get over it, and the process won't take forever." The problem with this advice is that the priority is the child's compliance, rather than her feelings. If you force your child to use a cup, she learns that growing up is traumatic and that you want to make her feel sad and upset. If you let her make the choice to drink from the cup when she is ready, you will preserve her closeness to you and increase her feelings of competence and enjoyment.

Solid Foods

It can be difficult for parents to keep in mind that their real goal in offering their child solid foods is to show her that solids can be enjoyable, not to get any particular food into her stomach. Every baby likes some foods and food groups better than others, and there is every reason to respect and build on those preferences. Your baby will be getting vitamins in any event, and she will not be harmed if you don't push foods she doesn't like. If you make mealtimes enjoyable and unpressured, she will develop a positive attitude toward solids, and you will help your child develop into a good eater with varied tastes.

Once your pediatrician says your baby can begin eating finger foods, you have an opportunity to reintroduce foods that may have been rejected in the jar. For example, the fun of picking up peas and popping them in her mouth may attract the child who wanted nothing to do with peas that were puréed and spoon-fed.

How to Help Your Baby Put Herself to Sleep Happy

Sadly, parents are often advised to let babies cry themselves to sleep at bedtime. There exists a popular but entirely unrealistic and harmful notion that infants should not bother their parents at night. Even more detrimental is the notion that if infants are always comforted when they are having difficulty sleeping, they will take advantage of this responsiveness and become manipulative little creatures who will subsequently rob parents of their sleep and evening free time on a regular basis.

When infants are left to cry themselves to sleep, they can only conclude that they are not lovable enough to engage their parents' desires to comfort them. The same is true of older children who have trouble sleeping but whose parents don't respond to them. When a child's tears do not elicit parental concern, he may infer that when he can't sleep and he is unhappy, he is bad and unlovable. If he actually stops crying, it may be because he has abandoned hope that help will come. When sleep experts recommend that parents let their child cry until he develops the ability to go to sleep on his own, they overlook the detrimental impact that being left alone and unhappy will have on a child's emotional development.

Try to put your infant to bed sleepy but not asleep in order to help him learn to drift off himself. If your infant cries, make every effort to comfort him until he can fall asleep peacefully. Although in the first year you may have to return numerous times to your baby's side to rock him, provide a drink, or rub his back, your baby will learn both that you are reliably responsive to his expressed needs and also that he can put himself to sleep in a pleasurable and contented manner (and not in despair at his inability to raise a positive response from you). A baby who is comforted in this way will become a child who is an accomplished and reliable sleeper. You will reap many peaceful nights as the result of your efforts in your baby's first year.

Sleep-deprived parents of a crying baby often feel very tempted to let their infant cry himself to sleep so that they, themselves, will be able to get some rest. We ourselves know from experience how exhausted parents of infants can become. But we also know that the extra mile you can go for your baby now will pay enormous dividends later. Because your infant has no way to know that you are tired and need peace and quiet, when he is left to cry himself to sleep, he believes that you are actively deciding to leave him to feel helpless and miserable. As with hunger, so with sleep—he will conclude that his unhappy state is what you intend for him, and, therefore, he will develop ongoing needs to emulate your caregiving and make himself unhappy.

When you are aware both of the negative impact that being left to cry will have on your infant, and also that your baby's need for your nighttime heroics is temporary, even though you are tired, you will have more reason to make the effort to go to your baby and try to help him get to sleep comfortably.

Developmental Milestone: Your Baby Smiles at You

One of the great milestones in your child's development also marks a high point in parenting pleasure. When she is about three months old, your baby's eyes will fix on your face and she will light up in a smile of utter joy. This is the culmination of a process that starts when your infant is a few weeks old and begins to smile somewhat indiscriminately whenever she feels she has caused your loving attention and, thereby, made herself particularly happy. As the first three months pass, your baby increasingly identifies special faces as the source of her greatest pleasure. The ecstatic grin that your baby saves especially for you indicates that she is delighted both with you and with herself for causing you to love her.

Developmental Milestone: Stranger Anxiety

Sometime around the age of eight months, your child will exhibit a temporary developmental vulnerability known as stranger anxiety.

Although it appears to be unhappiness, stranger anxiety is actually a developmental achievement that results from your infant's newfound capacity to recognize and to prefer your face over all others. Previously your infant may have been outgoing, relating well and happily to strangers, but now unfamiliar faces may make her lower lip begin to tremble, and she may actually burst into tears until your beloved face reappears. If you mistakenly see your child's reactions in adult terms, you may feel embarrassed, make excuses ("he's teething," "he's tired"), or stiffen your hold so that your infant senses your disapproval. Or worse, you may assume that your child has become too dependent on you, so you decide to become less available just at a time when your child needs you to be especially responsive.

Indeed, you have reason to feel immensely pleased and proud when your child reacts with unhappiness to a new face. Because of your attentive love, your infant realizes that his relationship with you is the source of his highest pleasure. Your infant looks for you, reserves his brightest and widest smiles for you, and wriggles with delight in your presence. When a face other than the faces that make him feel joyful appears unexpectedly, he feels the absence of his accustomed pleasure in his relationship with you. And because his immaturity prevents him from knowing that you remain nearby, he fears that he has lost your face forever. His cries express the pain of losing his relationship with you.

Once you know that your infant's discomfort signals a vulnerability that is both temporary and also appropriate for his age, you will see the importance of responding to his expressions of stranger anxiety by immediately showing him your reassuring face. This response sustains your infant's inborn belief that he is causing you to make him happy and to ease any unhappiness that comes his way. Your reassuring response furthers his inclination to turn to his relationship with you for love and comfort. As a result he will be far less likely to fall back on less growth-promoting ways to soothe himself, such as clinging to a blanket, withdrawing, or crying angrily.

Over the next month or two, your infant's understanding will mature to the point that he will be aware of and able to take comfort from your presence even when confronted by a strange face (although on an off day, he can still be thrown by encountering a strange face when he expects a familiar one). This process of maturing allows him to grow out of stranger anxiety, but, paradoxically, because your infant at the same time becomes more attuned to your presence or absence, he also becomes more vulnerable to a different type of developmental discomfort—separation anxiety.

Developmental Milestone: Separation Anxiety

Stranger anxiety and separation anxiety are often confused, but they are quite different developmental vulnerabilities and occur at different times. As we have said, stranger anxiety starts at about eight months of age. It occurs when your infant is shocked to discover the presence of a face that brings less pleasure than the familiar parental face she was expecting. Separation anxiety appears near the end of the first year, and it involves your infant reacting to your departure as though it signals the end of all earthly security and contentment. Separation anxiety can occur when you merely leave the room, or when you place your child in the care of other adults with whom she is familiar. This vulnerability is caused by your child's increasing recognition of the importance of the unique pleasure she feels in your presence. Previously, when you absented yourself temporarily, such as when you went to the bathroom or briefly disappeared into another room, your infant hardly seemed to notice. Now, because of her intellectual maturation, she may notice an absence of even a few seconds and begin to cry.

If you view your child's actions in adult terms, you may conclude that she is spoiled or terribly insecure because she can't bear your being out of her sight. Or you may feel overwhelmed at being desperately needed, or you may decide that your child has become overly clingy and has somehow gone astray on the road to independence. Parents who envision their child as being permanently timid or dependent may try to jolly, coerce, or shame her into behaving like older children. What is really needed, though, is to recognize that your child is exhibiting temporary, healthy vulnerabilities that are appropriate for her age.

You will strengthen, not weaken, your child's inner resources if you avoid triggering or ignoring your child's sensitivity to separation anxiety. When your child is most vulnerable, if you need to go into another room you might tell your child, "I am going to the kitchen to get a drink. Would you like to come?" In a few months, you will be able to go into another room without triggering unhappiness in your child.

ONE MOTHER'S SOLUTION

A mother we know preferred showers to baths, but her eleven-month-old regularly burst into tears when the mother closed the opaque shower door. The mother temporarily switched to baths in order to be more visible and accessible. Her child happily played with toys on the bath mat next to the tub while the mother bathed. The toddler's self-confident activity was much more rewarding to the mother than persevering in taking showers that were accompanied by hysterical crying.

When your child is acutely vulnerable to separation anxiety, try to avoid changing babysitters or taking on added responsibilities outside the home. An important smart love principle to keep in mind is that *you will advance your child's development if you give her your loving attention whenever she requests it and you are able to offer it.* You can be secure in the knowledge that your responsiveness will produce a happy, optimistic, confident, productive, and caring human being.

Don't Measure Your Child's Behavior by Adult Standards

As we mentioned earlier, there is a popular misconception that children are miniature adults with an adult's capacity for self-governance. It is surprising that although children are clearly less physically, socially, intellectually, and emotionally mature than adults, they are frequently held to adult levels of morality and social accountability. Parents who would never dream that young children could possess the maturity to cross streets or plug in appliances by themselves often assume that young children possess an adult capacity for altruism and self-regulation. Caregivers frequently hold children morally responsible for inconsistent, impulsive, clinging, or overly aggressive actions.

This behavior actually stems from developmental immaturity.

Parents are often told that immediately responding to the cries of children who are three months and older will encourage them to become unduly demanding. A best-selling parenting book gives the following advice to a mother whose seven-month-old baby starts to "act up" when she comes home from work:

> Like most babies his age, your baby's already learning how to be manipulative. And like most good mommies, you're falling right into his trap. Even at this tender stage your baby is shrewd enough to see that playing the abandoned and neglected victim is the best way to guarantee that he'll get an extra dose of love and attention when you arrive home. He plays on your insecurities, instills the guilt, and gets what he wants.[5]

This baby isn't manipulating his mother; he is trying to communicate how unhappy he has been and how interminably long he has been waiting for her. The authors' assertions about the infant's wily motives, moreover, are disproved by scientific evidence that completely contradicts the notion that infants can fake unhappiness. We would discourage this baby's parents from feeling manipulated and hardening their hearts; on the contrary, we would encourage them to respond with extra warmth and attention.

Returning to Work

Perhaps the most emotionally charged issue for new parents is whether and when both parents of young children should return to the workplace. Some parents may find our discussion of this subject disquieting, but we feel we should provide guidance for parents who need or want to work and who also want to help their children develop a lasting inner happiness and the resulting ability to reach their full potential.

The reality is that children thrive better if they have at least one parent available to them for the majority of the day until age three. Children will not necessarily become alienated or otherwise dysfunctional if both parents work full-time in the first three years, but they will benefit enormously when one parent is able to limit work to part-time hours.

Children Need Quantities of Time as Well as Quality Time

In spite of its popularity, quality time—the notion that parents can compensate for being gone a significant part of the young child's day by offering the child periods of intensely focused attention—does not result in a high quality of life for young children. If you look at the world as young children do, five minutes can seem like forever. Before age three, children know their parents' intentions only from their immediate behavior. Consequently, when both parents depart for work and are gone for nine or more hours at a time, children under three can't be certain that their parents love them and want to be with them. When children miss their parents, they experience unhappiness, and they assume that their parents intend for them to feel this way, and that unhappy feelings are therefore desirable. Children who are left for long hours in substitute care on a regular basis before the age of three can modify their ideal of inner happiness to include experiences of anxiety and an unhappiness born of lack of control over the source of their well-being. Even though they may become successful in other ways, these children can develop active needs to experience inner discomfort under the misapprehension that this unpleasantness is equivalent to inner happiness.

Parents' availability and loving responsiveness together constitute a yardstick by which very young children measure their self-worth. Only their parents can sustain the inner happiness of very young children and ensure that children do not develop needs for unhappiness.

Certainly, we are aware of the harsh reality that often there is no choice regarding the parents' need to work. Far too many parents must return to full-time work shortly after the birth of their baby. That many parents want desperately to stay home with their young children but are forced to leave them represents a profoundly destructive flaw in the way our society and culture are ordered. We need reforms that will allow children under three to have one parent with them for the majority of the day. Other societies, such as France and the Scandinavian countries, have made this happen by providing substantial subsidies and parental leave with job security. Although such a program would be expensive, we all know how much it costs to pick up the pieces of broken minds. Our society will never change its policies toward parental leave until there is a comprehensive understanding of essential human nature and child development, in combination with the determined efforts of parents and other advocates for children who find the current situation intolerable.

Although many parents do not have a choice about working, sometimes both parents of children under three years of age choose to work full-time outside the home, and some even absent themselves with a heavy social schedule or a full menu of hobbies. These parents might spend more time with their child if they understood the true consequences of their choice.

Balancing Your Child's Needs with Your Need to Work

We speak out on behalf of children with full recognition that our views may be unnerving to some parents. Those people who have spent years cultivating their careers fear that if they take significant time off to be with their children, their careers may be retarded or derailed altogether. Certainly many parents are intrigued with and challenged by their work and are reluctant to reduce the time they devote to their work. But it is misleading to give parents the impression that they can have it all—that both parents can work *full-time and* raise a baby who can be counted on to grow into a confident adult with stable inner happiness and no motive to experience unhappiness.

We certainly do not think that it is a woman's duty to be shackled to her home and children. What we suggest is that either one of the parents of a child under three years of age make the temporary commitment to work no more than part-time so as to give that child the gifts of enduring inner happiness and an abiding sense of competence. This choice may temporarily cramp the parents' standard of living, but over the course of a lifetime, three years is a relatively short period. The first three years really do fly by, and they are filled with tender, humorous, loving moments. It would be a shame to miss out on these memories.

Some Guidelines for Working Parents of Children Under Three

• Do not believe experts who tell you that your baby will be just as happy if you work full-time. Nothing is better for your baby than *quantity* time with you.

- Try to avoid having both parents work full-time as long as there are children under the age of three at home.

- For those who are able, have children before you start your career or after it is sufficiently established so that you can take significant leave time; for example, maybe you have tenure, have made partner, can hire people to replace you, or have accumulated enough seniority to take time off with or without pay.

- Try to choose a career or a workplace that strongly supports family life and allows flexible hours or working at home. If you can arrange to work during the hours when your baby takes her longest daily nap, you will exponentially increase the care-getting pleasure you are able to give her.

- Do what you can to organize other parents (1) to increase your employer's awareness of the importance of parental leave and to emphasize the positive impact generous policies would have on your loyalty and productivity, and (2) to increase public awareness of the need for the kinds of society-wide flexible leave policies that many other societies have implemented. *The future is our children.*

- If you feel you must continue to work full-time for financial reasons, ask yourself if you really need the money or if you are trying to maintain a lifestyle you could afford to cut back on for a few years. Children would much rather have you spend more time with them than have fancy clothes, a big yard, a new car, expensive toys, or costly vacations.

- If both parents are working full-time, try to stagger your working hours so that each of you will have larger blocks of time to spend with your child.

- If you go to work and you can afford to do so, offer your child an in-home substitute caregiver. The stability of having the same caring person in her life when you are not there will be very reassuring to your child. It is very important to design the arrangement in a way that will best meet your child's needs. Screen applicants thoroughly. If the caregiver will also be doing housework, make it clear that the child's needs come before the laundry, the cooking, or the cleaning. Try to find someone who will commit to staying at least three years.

Once you have hired someone, watch carefully for worrisome changes in your child, such as sudden periods of irritability, difficulties in eating or sleeping, regressive forms of soothing such as head banging or hair pulling, or a marked decrease in smiling. If these danger signals occur, and there is no obvious reason, change caregivers. If these signs persist, try to get time off from work for a while.

• If you must work full-time and cannot afford high-quality in-home care, try to find a day care setting with low staff turnover and a high ratio of staff to children. Examine the staff's qualifications and get references from other parents. Also try to visit at odd hours. After your child is enrolled, take seriously any significant changes in your child's mood or behavior (see earlier). If the changes in behavior continue but there is no good explanation, make a change in day care arrangements.

• If both parents must work full-time while your child is under the age of three, use the smart love principles and guidelines that follow to make the most of the time you spend with your children.

How Working Parents Can Make the Most of Their Time with Their Children

Working parents of young children can feel very disheartened when their child shrieks and clings to them desperately when they leave for work. When they come home, their child may seem indifferent to them, burst into tears upon seeing them, or generally be cranky and upset during the relatively short time they have together before bed-time. Parents who can accept that the angry, withdrawn, or crying child is asking for their loving assistance will find that they can respond to their upset child confidently and effectively rather than guiltily and ineffectually.

Young children who become upset, indifferent, or angry when you leave for work or return home are really trying to communicate how badly they feel and how much they want to be comforted. *They are not manipulating you.* When you are able to respond sympathetically and gently to your child's anger, withdrawal, or tears, she will experience the well-being that stems from knowing she is able to cause you to respond lovingly to her needs. This is the reason that working parents should not try to jolly, shame, tease, or distract their child when she expresses unhappiness when her parents leave home or return from work. Parents who become angry at, hurt by, or unwilling to listen to their young child's irritable or melancholy reactions to their work schedules inadvertently confirm the child's belief that her parents have chosen to make her unhappy.

In contrast, parents who can accept their child's upset feelings about their work schedules demonstrate to their child that they care and want to help. These parents will know the satisfaction that comes from offering their child the support she needs.

SMART LOVE IMPROVES A FATHER'S HOMECOMING

A working father found himself feeling increasingly alienated from his one-and-a-half-year-old son, Greg. When this father returned home from a long work day and an exhausting commute eager to play with his son, he was disheartened when his son averted his gaze and appeared indifferent to his arrival. The father, feeling wounded, would say, "Well, if you don't want to play, I'll go read the paper." Even though the little boy would eventually come over to the father's chair to show him something, the father never entirely recovered from his son's initial unresponsiveness.

Disturbed by the anger he was feeling, the father consulted us. We suggested that he try to respond to Greg's unenthusiastic greeting as though the child were requesting the father's understanding and affection, rather than as though he were rejecting his father. On our advice, when the father returned home he would sit down next to his son and comment gently on whatever activity Greg was engaging in ("That's a pretty picture, a tall tower," and so forth). If Greg did not answer, the father would continue, "You know I missed you, honey." At this point, Greg would usually give his father a big hug. Within two weeks of showing Greg that he realized his withdrawal was both a measure of how much he had missed his father and also a silent plea for the balm of his father's love and attention, this father was delighted to see that his son began to look excited and happy upon his arrival home.

The father's new perspective on his son's behavior allowed him to minimize the harmful effects of his long absences at work, and also to maximize the enjoyment and affection he and Greg were able to have during their time together.

SMART LOVE IMPROVES A MOTHER'S LEAVE-TAKING

A working mother arrived at her job each morning feeling utterly traumatized by the experience of leaving her two-and-a-half-year-old son, Max, at day care. He would begin to shriek hysterically the moment the car pulled up in front of the door, and the mother had to drag him out of his car seat. Max kicked and screamed while she carried him in and then clung to her like superglue, crying desperately. The day care staff pried his fingers from her clothes, assuring her that he always stopped crying within a few minutes of her departure.

The mother left with a mental image of her son's hysterical, tear-streaked face that haunted her for the rest of the day. Her friends told her that her son's tears were his attempt to upset her as revenge for being left at the day care center. They insisted that any attempt on her part to "coddle" Max would simply teach him that he could manipulate her by crying. This mother's intuition told her there must be another way. She decided to consult us because she was (correctly) convinced that her son's daily misery was both genuine and also detrimental to his emotional development.

One source of Max's upset was his feeling of powerlessness at being unable to have the one thing he wanted more than anything in the world—his mother's continued presence. His mother needed her job, and part-time work was not an option. So we asked her if she could rearrange her mornings to respond to her son's need to believe that he was lovable enough to engage her ongoing love and attention.

Max's mother took a day off from work and spent it with her son at the day care center. That visit reassured her that the center was well run, and it gave her son a chance to experience being at day care in the glow of his mother's presence. While at first Max was anxious, fearing that she would leave, he soon took her hand and showed her around. He proudly painted a picture and gave it to her, and he had her read his favorite book to him and a friend.

The mother then decided to get Max up earlier so that she could spend an hour with him at the day care center on her way to work. The relief and self-confidence Max felt when his mother met his need to have her stay for a while cushioned his transition to day care. By the time the hour was up, he was busy playing, and by the end of the first week, he actually gave her a kiss good-bye and went back to his play. The mother was deeply relieved at her son's new equilibrium, and her own work day was, accordingly, much happier and more productive. Within a few weeks she found that she could shorten her time at the day care center to fifteen minutes without upsetting Max when she left. In addition, because she had given her son the gift of feeling that she would make every effort to respond to his needs, he was much happier generally, and their time together at home was closer and more enjoyable.

Developmental Milestone: Your Baby "Talks" to You

Babies are born familiar with, and attracted to, the human voice. By paying attention to your baby's sounds, you can begin to have a dialogue with him within the first months. You will notice little sounds of contentment, especially during feeding. If you imitate these vocalizations, your baby will produce them with increasing frequency, until you and your baby are having a genuine conversation, in which each partner "talks" and listens in turn. Your baby will be transfixed by his capacity to engage you in this exciting and gratifying dialogue, and you will experience a special and satisfying aspect of parenting. In addition, as your baby discovers that "talking" is fun, he will be inspired to do more of it.

As your baby learns that things have names, your dialogue will expand as you introduce him to the world. Some parents are eager to teach their children everything from the alphabet to the names of all the states. The smart love guideline is to *subordinate specific teaching objectives to the more important aim of enhancing your child's inner happiness and sense of competence.* You will most effectively help your child to reach his full intellectual potential if you tailor your teaching goals to increase his enthusiasm and self-confidence. Try to satisfy his wishes to explore his environment, rather than teach any particular content, like numbers and colors. Name the things in which your baby exhibits most interest. For example, follow the eight-month-old's gaze and discuss what he is looking at ("Isn't that a nice dog? Would you like to pat him? Wasn't that fun. Shall we pat him again?"). If you manage to tailor your responses to your baby's interests, you will find that sometime after your child is ten months old he will begin trying to say words (*dog, pat, again*) with gusto.

Encouraging your child's curiosity is beneficial, but try to avoid testing your child to see how much he has absorbed. Once a baby begins pointing at things, parents often try to reassure themselves about the child's progress by asking him, "Which is the car?" "Which is the blue one?" These questions make the child feel put on the spot or, worse, as though he has displeased his beloved parents if he doesn't know the answer or doesn't want to give it.

Try to ask only questions you are certain your child can answer and will enjoy answering ("Where is your blanket?" "Do you want some milk?"). In addition, if an answer is not forthcoming, immediately supply it so that your child will feel no sense of inadequacy ("Oh, there's the blanket. Do you want to hold it?").

This is not to say that you should not play games, like peekaboo or "counting fingers" with your infant. Games appropriate for babies differ from tests in that they are either purely for fun or are enjoyable ways to learn. Games can provide moments of real, constructive pleasure.

Because your baby was born seeking positive pleasure in his relationship with you, if you introduce your child to the world in a way that fits his interests and developmental stage, your child will react to your caring leadership by enthusiastically absorbing words and concepts. If you are able to make learning fun and unpressured, your child will seize on the information you offer with the same eagerness with which he reaches for food or snuggles up for hugs. In this way, you will inspire him to become a confident and voracious learner.

Your Infant's Point of View: Trying Is Learning

If an eight-month-old has been calmly but unsuccessfully attempting to put a round block into a square hole, your own concerns about success and failure may cause you to step in and guide your baby's hand to the correct opening. But if your infant is comfortable with deferred accomplishment, offering assistance may give her the message that unfruitful effort dissatisfies you, and soon the experience of trying and not immediately succeeding may become dissatisfying for her. Allow your baby to keep trying as long as she is content. When you can remain relaxed and comfortable as your baby tries repeatedly to put a block through the wrong hole of a block sorter, your child will learn that her parents remain just as positive and involved when she is trying as they do when she succeeds.

The smart love principle is *do not interfere with children who are content with their own effort,* even if the effort is unsuccessful and frustrating by adult standards. This principle may sound simple to implement, but you would be surprised at how anxious adults can become over a child's goal-oriented struggles and how tempted they will be to short-circuit a learning process by providing help. Even interventions as subtle as moving a rattle within the reach of an infant who is engaged in zestful but failing attempts to get it into grasping range can interfere with the child's growing self-confidence.

On the other hand, when a child signals that she needs help, offer it immediately and don't make her wait with words like, "Try again," or "I know you can do it." Parents sometimes fear that by following the principles of smart love they will make their child unfit for the real world by eliminating all frustration. With the help of smart love you will prepare your child for the real world by nourishing and expanding her inborn happiness and confidence. If you are responsive to your child's requests for assistance, you will show your child that she can try to do things herself as long as she enjoys the effort, but that she can always fall back on her relationship with you. In other words, your child learns that you will neither interfere with her wish for competence nor leave her to feel unhappy and helpless if the fun has worn off. With this level of trust your child will have an abiding confidence in her effectiveness, a long attention span, and a high tolerance for frustration. She will also feel optimistic and comfortable about asking for help when she needs it. In other words, she will be an eager and successful learner.

Developmental Milestone: The Mobile Baby

Sometime in the first year, the wonderful security you felt when you put your baby down will vanish as you realize that he is now on the move. First he rolls over, then he slithers, crawls, and, sometimes by a year, he walks. Your approach to the mobile baby should reflect the same strategies you used when he was a newborn—try to keep him happy and confident, soothe his tears when they are unavoidable, and avoid conflict.

Try to baby-proof your child's environment so that he is free to explore. For those moments when you cannot follow him, you can fill a playpen with his favorite toys so that it is a haven and a source of pleasure. Some parents will tell us, "I just couldn't bring myself to move everything out of the living room—it looks institutional without the knickknacks, photos, and flowers, and the baby has to learn sometime there are things he cannot touch." When the baby approaches a breakable or dangerous object, these parents then say a commanding "no!"

Parents who take this approach may keep both their possessions and their baby safe, but at the same time they may also sap their baby's confidence and dent his optimism. Since the baby is not mature enough to make his own determination about which objects are breakable or dangerous, parents' loud admonitions appear completely arbitrary and may cloud the child's initiative with apprehension and self-doubt. You must find ways to protect your young child from his own adventurousness, but it is better not to do so with an emphatic "no!" Babies and toddlers who are on the receiving end of a "no!" are too young to understand or learn anything except that their beloved parents are angry at or disappointed in them for reasons that seem unfathomable. It is far better to make the environment safe for your baby or to gently redirect your baby when he is going after something he can't have.

Physically guiding and refocusing your baby takes much more physical energy than a verbal prohibition uttered from a seat across the room, but you will be repaid for this extra expenditure of effort; your child will gain a happy and loving approach to life.

Tips for Living with Your Mobile Baby

The smart love guideline is *protect your baby's confidence and curiosity by not holding him responsible for avoiding hazards and delicate objects.*

- Try to avoid saying "no!"
- Baby-proof your home so he is free to explore.
- If he is determined to eat sand, keep him away from the beach or out of the sandbox until sand begins to look less delicious.
- If he thinks his older sister's computer is a banging toy, keep the door to her room closed.
- Make sure you are always near enough to your baby to protect him from danger by scooping him up and hugging him.

If you follow these guidelines, by the time your child is old enough to understand your explanation that something is dangerous, fragile, or unhealthy, he will want to avoid it out of self-interest, not out of fright at your harsh tone. Most important, your use of the smart love guidelines will help your baby grow to be a toddler and a two-year-old who is terrific rather than "terrible."

Smart Loving the Infant Who Suffers from Inner Unhappiness

At times the first weeks or months of life do not provide infants with the happiness they were born expecting. In spite of parents' best intentions, they may be unable to satisfy their infant's emotional needs. Or an infant may experience significant discomfort for other reasons, such as physical illness. Such infants can unknowingly develop needs for unpleasant experiences. Once infants acquire an inner unhappiness, they can be very difficult to soothe. For example, they may arch their backs and scream louder and louder when picked up or held. If you are the parent of an unhappy infant, the challenge is to attract her to the pleasure available in your relationship and not to become angry or discouraged when she reacts negatively to the loving attention you offer her.

HELPING AN INFANT WITH INNER UNHAPPINESS CAUSED BY A SERIOUS ILLNESS

A couple came to us because they were very concerned about their baby, Bobby. He had been born with multiple defects in his intestinal tract. His parents remained with him in the hospital throughout the painful surgeries that were required to correct his bowels. Even though his parents were ready and able to respond to his emotional needs, Bobby's view of the world, befitting his age, led him to conclude that the nearly constant physical pain he experienced was caused and intended by his parents. As a result, he unknowingly developed needs to re-create this discomfort. Fortunately, his parents remained with him around the clock and held and comforted him whenever possible, so Bobby also preserved his inborn wishes for positive relationship experiences.

When Bobby was released from the hospital at the age of three months with his intestinal tract repaired, he had great difficulty sleeping, and he was a poor eater because he had learned that eating caused him pain. Worst of all, he was fretful and unhappy. He would allow his parents to hold him for short periods, but after a while he would become rigid and cry. He rarely smiled, and he seemed most content when left alone in his crib.

When his parents consulted us, we suggested that the next few weeks and months were of critical importance to Bobby. We advised them that if he was not to slip into intractable emotional isolation, they had to reacquaint Bobby with the desire for an inner happiness based on the pleasure of the parent-child relationship. The parents started to make every effort to offer Bobby abundant experiences of care-getting pleasure without overstimulating him or becoming discouraged when he reacted negatively to the pleasure of being cared for. Learning how to help Bobby enjoy his relationship with his parents was a process that required great thoughtfulness and perseverance. For example, his parents discovered that if they simply picked him up when he awoke in the morning, he became very upset and cried miserably. On the other hand, they found that if they came into the room talking softly, rubbed his arms and legs for a few minutes, let him look at a terry-cloth rabbit, and only then picked him up gently, he remained calm and positively engaged.

His parents also noticed that Bobby reacted to the pleasure of smiling and being smiled at by becoming irritable and upset. So they stroked him, talked to him softly, and smiled at him, but when he began to get restless, they put him in his infant seat and sat next to him while he looked around for a while. Then they would start talking to him endearingly again.

Although Bobby had occasional miserable moments and even miserable days, his parents were very gratified to discover that over the next ten months their responsive, informed love had a profound impact on their son. By the time he was a year old, he was a good eater and sleeper, laughed and smiled easily, and exuded confidence and security.

Infants Who Can't Sleep

Infants' inner unhappiness is often expressed as an inability to go to sleep or to stay asleep. We have already discussed why no infant should be left to cry herself to sleep. This is especially important for infants who have developed needs for unhappiness. If these infants are left to cry they eventually fall asleep, but their sleep is born of hopelessness and helplessness, not of contented pleasure. Parents who follow the popular advice to let infants cry themselves to sleep only intensify their child's unhappiness. The meaningful question is not "What will make my baby sleep better?" but "What will make my baby happier?"

Whatever the reason for your baby's wakefulness, you want to help her get to sleep by offering her the pleasure available in your relationship, not by depriving her of that comfort. Try putting her down when you think she is sleepy, singing to her, rubbing her back, finding her favorite blanket, or discover other effective ways to soothe her, and then leave the room. If your baby cries, return and help her until she feels comforted, and then leave again. Over time, as your baby learns that her cries will be responded to, she will become contented and sleep.

The smart love approach to infants with sleep problems is more demanding and time-consuming than the popular prescription to let infants cry, but it has the advantage of helping to make infants better sleepers by making them happy. Just as parents rarely balk when they are told they have to get up in the middle of the night to give children medicine or take their temperatures, we have found that when parents understand the healing they impart by responding to their infants' cries, they will usually accept the interruptions to their sleep as reasonable and necessary.

Infants Who Rarely Smile

Perhaps the most accurate barometer of how a baby is feeling about herself, you, and the world is her smile. If your baby is three to nine months old and does not smile easily, rethink her daily experience. Certainly, no baby will feel like smiling every time she is smiled at, but most babies who are in a familiar setting, with familiar people and toys, and who are not ill or overtired will smile readily. If your baby seems "serious" most of the time, ask yourself:

- Is the baby healthy? Have your pediatrician give her a checkup.
- Is the baby being overstimulated by too much tickling, bouncing, and so forth?
- Is the baby being left to play alone for long periods without seeing a smiling, loving adult face or being gently held?

• Is the baby being responded to immediately when she cries?
• If the baby has a babysitter or is in day care, do you know how she is spending much of her day?

Babies are very resilient. If you identify and remedy those aspects of your child's daily life that are dampening her natural zest, most likely you will soon find that she is dazzling you with her smile once again.

Chapter Five

～∾～

Ages One to Three: Smart Loving Your Toddler or Preschooler

The changes that occur between your child's first and third birthdays are both thrilling and challenging for you and your child. The most important developmental achievement is the establishment of stable primary happiness. Your child acquires stable primary happiness when he realizes that your love of caring for him is undiminished even when you are temporarily unable to respond to him.

During these years your child will make lightning progress in learning to negotiate the world by walking and talking. As all parents know, children at this age possess an unswerving determination and are convinced they are so powerful that they can do and have anything. They haven't the slightest notion that they could be seriously hurt. The words "I want" and "no" predominate in their growing vocabularies. Even though this phase is commonly known as the "terrible twos," we believe it can be a time of "terrific twos" for parents and children. Using the principles of smart love, you can help iron out the rough spots and guide your young child to become happier and more resilient.

Developmental Milestone: Your Child's Primary Happiness Becomes Unshakable

Between the ages of one and three, children are moving toward the most important milestone in all development—the establishment of enduring primary happiness. Primary happiness is the conviction that every infant brings into the world that she is causing her parents to pay loving attention to her developmental needs. Until about the age of three, your child's primary happiness is unstable because it is largely dependent on your responses to her intense need for focused parenting, and you will not always be able to respond immediately.

If you have met your child's developmental needs with consistent, loving attention, by the time she turns three her primary happiness will have evolved into an indelible certainty that she can be effective in eliciting your unconditional love of responding to her. Her happiness will no longer depend on her moment-to-moment ability to get your attention.

We are introducing this developmental milestone for establishing primary happiness for the first time in these pages. Parents should look for a special vulnerability just before their child achieves this developmental goal. Your child will temporarily have an intense need for your focused attention.

Your Child's Point of View: Wanting and Needing Extra Attention

Starting sometime around your child's first birthday, in keeping with the vulnerability to separation anxiety we described in the last chapter, your child's involvement with you will begin to deepen significantly. Increasingly, he makes clear that he cannot get enough of you. He wants to show you every speck of dust he lifts carefully from the floor, have you comment admiringly on each repetition of a hundred similar physical feats, and have you read to him every book on his bookshelf. *This passionate wish for direct involvement with you is actually a sign of his maturity.* Your child now recognizes the superiority of the happiness he feels when you are caring for him (talking to him, reading a story, responding to his requests). Activities that do not require your direct involvement, such as when your child is painting while you talk on the phone, may be pleasing, but your child now identifies these as qualitatively less satisfying. His newfound recognition of the superior pleasure of your focused caring frequently leads him to insist that you switch from personal to parenting activities ("Paint with me, Dad" or "Watch me jump, Mom").

When you respond promptly and affectionately to your child's wishes for your focused attention, your child will see that he has the power to make himself truly happy. Once your child recognizes the difference between the pleasure of your focused involvement and any creative substitutions you may offer (for example, he wants you to play cars with him and is unwilling to be distracted from this goal by being given blocks with which to build a tower while you do housework), he is understandably eager to engage you. Your child's increasing preference for more satisfying (focused) caring over less satisfying (less focused) attention is a crucial accomplishment.

If you are not aware that your child's seemingly insatiable appetite for your focused attention is both appropriate for his age and temporary, you may worry that you have created a clingy and dependent child who will never be able to play or learn by himself. But his preference for your focused involvement need not alarm you; nor should you feel put upon, manipulated, or worried that he is developing an unhealthy type of dependency. There is a popular but mistaken notion that by consistently responding to your child you will create a monster with an insatiable desire for adult attention. Parents are often told that the main developmental task of children from the age of one to three is to become independent of their parents, and that the child should be weaned from parental attention rather than offered it freely. As a means of fostering independence, parents are frequently advised to encourage children to play alone and to tell children that they cannot expect their parents always to do what they want.

We reiterate that your child's wish for your total involvement is healthy. Your consistent responsiveness will produce a satisfied, fulfilled child. Because the child is now able to discriminate between the closeness that accompanies your positive involvement and the less satisfying pleasure he experiences during times when your attention is elsewhere, your child naturally prefers the superior pleasure and wants as much of it as he can get. Once you understand the significance of this developmental leap, you can feel enormously gratified by your child's newfound desires for deeper involvement with you. It is very important that you put aside personal activities whenever possible and respond to your child's fervent requests for focused attention.

When you respond to your child's request that you interrupt a personal pursuit—reading a novel, talking on the phone, straightening up the house—and offer him your loving attention, you show your child that you share his preference for the pleasure of your relationship. The child's certain knowledge that he is effective at acquiring his heart's desire—your love of caring for him—is synonymous with the attainment of an unshakable inner well-being.

When you make clear to your child that, whenever possible, you will choose to defer personal desires so as to respond to his developmental need for your undivided attention, you strengthen your child's growing ability to distinguish between causing you to respond to him and causing your unconditional wish to respond. At those times when you cannot interrupt an activity (you must keep the evening meal from burning on the stove), try to convey both your genuine pleasure at your child's desire for your involvement and also your determination to respond as quickly as possible: "I would love to read to you— I can't think of anything more fun. Just let me get this cooking finished and I'll be right with you." Although your commitment to meet your child's developmental needs has always been there, with his maturing intelligence your child can now perceive that he retains the power to cause you to want to care for him even when temporarily he cannot cause you to respond to a particular request.

"TALK TO ME, MOM!"

A mother we know was cleaning the stove while two-and-a-half-year-old Peggy was eating breakfast. Peggy smiled at her mother and said in a happy voice, "Sit down and talk to me, Mom." Her mother smiled back and said, "I will in a minute, but I have to finish cleaning. I'll give you some crayons, though." Peggy replied enthusiastically, "No, Mom, come talk to me now. It will be lots of fun!"

The mother realized that her daughter was unwilling to go on coloring by herself in her mother's presence. The mother recognized that her daughter's newfound ability to prefer focused attention from her parents over other pleasures made the child especially vulnerable to disappointments in their relationship. She reminded herself that a positive response would help her daughter to reach that crucial developmental milestone when unshakable primary happiness is established once and for all. So it was clear that cleaning the stove at that instant was not a priority. Although she felt a little frustrated at leaving the job unfinished, she was careful not to blame her child, who, after all, just wanted to enjoy her company. She sat down next to her little girl and said, "You're right—let's talk!"

You Can't Spoil Your Child with the Right Kind of Attention

You may have been warned that the constant gratification of your child's desires for your attention will make him unfit for the real world. The reality is that your child's intense desires for focused parenting will be temporary if you are consistently able to respond positively to him. Gratifying your child's wishes, especially his desires to engage your focused attention, will not spoil your child. It will not make him hopelessly self-centered or unable to postpone gratification. In fact, your child's all-encompassing need for your focused attention will decrease when he becomes certain of your unconditional wish to respond to his needs and provide the attention he wants.

In contrast, if you ration your attention out of concern that too much is harmful, your child will never feel fully certain of his ability to elicit the caregetting pleasure he wants and needs. When children find that they cannot count on their parents to respond to their needs, they initially react by intensifying their demands for parental involvement. If these demands are not responded to, children may even turn away from the ungratifying relationship and disavow their wishes for closeness.

If you try to gratify your child's needs and wishes whenever possible, you will help your child to acquire a lifelong sense of competence and inner well-being. This unshakable inner happiness, in turn, will allow your child to become good, to do good, and to do well. For this reason, on a temporary basis, try to give your child's wishes priority, provided these desires are safe and do not conflict with your essential personal aims (stopping for gas, putting away frozen foods).

By fulfilling your child's developmental needs and wishes you will not spoil your child. You will be giving him the tools to become a happy, competent, and socially engaged adult. Your smart love assures your child that he is causing you to love caring for him, and this certainty, in turn, provides him with a well-being rich enough to share with others.

When You Cannot Put Aside Your Personal Needs

Clearly, there are occasions when you will be unable to put aside your personal needs and desires. A pot may be about to boil over, or the boss has called with a question that must be answered immediately. At these times, try to convey to your child both your desire to give him your undivided attention as soon as possible, and also your understanding of and pleasure at your child's wishes for closeness and involvement. For instance, you could say, "I would love to read you a story—that's a great idea. I just have to finish this one thing and I'll be right with you." As a result of his maturing intelligence and the reservoir of trust accumulated through your history of positive involvement, your child will increasingly recognize that in your heart you would prefer to respond to him even at moments when you must continue to pursue another activity.

You will also find that because your small child is so in love with you, he will be thrilled to participate in almost any activity. Many daily chores can be transformed into cooperative and enjoyable moments in your relationship. If you have to mop the floor, there is no reason a toddler cannot be given a small mop and allowed to help. A trip to the store can be fun if it is not rushed and you let your child assist in the choice of foods. "Come and work with me" is very appealing to children of all ages; "Do it yourself" may seem like you are withholding your love, and may lead to conflict and resistance.

Spacing Siblings

Because children under the age of three still need a lot of your focused attention if they are to develop an unshakable primary happiness, we believe it is better to wait at least until your child turns three to introduce a competitor for your love and attention. Try not to act on the wish for more children until the parenting attention one child needs will not interfere with the parenting attention that is appropriate for the other.

Certainly, babies are often born before older siblings turn three. Moreover, with the growth of fertility technology, multiple births are increasingly common. If you have two or more children under three years of age, try to use family, friends, or financial resources to amass time to spend alone with each child. In this way, each child will have chances to experience uninterrupted care-getting pleasure. Even if you cannot get others to help you, you can often find some time to spend alone with one child when the other is sleeping or playing with a friend. If you can manage any time, even as little as half an hour a day, alone with each child doing something the child especially enjoys, you will significantly enhance that child's primary happiness. Each child will have a chance to bask in the warmth of your special relationship, which will make him less resentful of his sibling. The time you devote to each child will increase the likelihood that the siblings will experience each other as friends and allies rather than as enemies and competitors.

Developmental Milestone: The Appearance of Secondary Happiness

We have just described how your child will develop an enduring primary happiness when she realizes that she has the unfailing ability to cause you to love caring for her. What developmental steps to self-governance remain for the three-year-old who has developed lasting primary happiness? Clearly, she is not ready to enter the world on her own. Not until the end of her adolescence will she acquire a stable form of secondary happiness. As we described earlier, primary happiness is generated within the parent-child relationship; secondary happiness results directly from the pleasure generated by engaging in everyday activities, such as building with blocks, running, or looking at pictures in a book.

We group the activities that produce secondary happiness into three categories. Intellectual desires are wishes for pleasure related to learning, knowing, understanding, creating, negating, differentiating, navigating, and so forth. Social desires focus on the pleasure associated with relating to others. Physiological desires are wishes for physical pleasure and include the satisfaction of essential physical needs, such as eating and breathing, as well as the gratification of nonessential physical aims, such as swinging or bike riding. Because these categories are descriptive, there is some overlap. For example, the adolescent who decides to play on a basketball team may be motivated by both the desire to develop a new circle of friends and the pleasure of playing ball. The planning of game strategies may also be intellectually satisfying. Artistic pursuits, too, gratify a combination of intellectual and social desires, and some arts, such as dance, are physically satisfying as well.

Like primary happiness, secondary happiness entails a distinct developmental transformation. As we have seen, primary happiness is unstable at first because it falters at moments when your child is unable to elicit your focused attention. Secondary happiness, too, is initially unreliable, because when your child is small, her secondary happiness depends entirely on her ability to attain whatever satisfactions her heart desires. Satisfaction is tied to the gratification of specific wishes—young children want what they want now (for example, to have the teddy bear another child is playing with or to take the ball from the dog's mouth).

By the end of adolescence, your child's secondary happiness can become as stable as her primary happiness, because it will rest on the certain pleasure of making constructive choices and pursuing them well. At the end of adolescence, the secondary happiness of children whose developmental needs have been met will be completely separate from their success or failure at gratifying any particular wish. Just as smart love guidelines will help you help your child to develop an unshakable primary happiness, they can also guide you to help your child develop permanent secondary happiness.

The First Phase: "I Want What I Want When I Want It"

Anyone who has watched a two-year-old spy another child with a new, desirable toy and march up and grab it is aware that in the beginning the quest for secondary happiness has an intense and imperative immediacy. Initially, your child's secondary happiness depends entirely on her ability to have exactly what she wants. Two-year-olds who are prevented from taking another child's toy, or whose toy is wrested from them, may well cry and persist single-mindedly in the attempt to get the desired object until they are successful or are successfully diverted to a new goal. If you realize that this intense version of "I want what I want when I want it" is normal and temporary, you will be better able to respond to your toddler's determined acquisitiveness with good humor and sensitivity.

Your Child's Point of View: "I'm Unstoppable"

Your toddler's all-powerful self is inherently unstable because it rests on the immature and illusional belief that she has the ability to gratify her each and every desire. Each gratified wish, in turn, confirms the all-powerful self's fantasy of omnipotence. Your child takes the exalted claims of the all-powerful self for granted. She believes she can overcome any interference with her wish to get what she wants when she wants it. Of course, children know that certain desires go ungratified (for instance, you might not buy your child a coveted box of candy). But in an unreflective corner of the child's psyche, her all-powerful self continues to derive satisfaction from the conviction that it *could* have prevailed and, indeed, will prevail in the future.

How to Respond to the Child Whose Favorite Word Is *No*

The all-powerful self is the source of the child's passionate attachment to the word *no* in what is popularly termed the "no stage." Toddlers' no's are not signs of the emergence of an antisocial menace that needs to be curbed. The ever-present "no" expresses their belief in their power to control their environment. This illusion of power has a special urgency because at this age toddlers are especially vulnerable to the loss of secondary happiness that occurs whenever they don't get what they want when they want it.

Let's say you go to a lot of trouble to make your two-year-old's favorite lunch. But when you put it on the kitchen table and say, "Lunch is ready!" she says, "NO EATING." You may be tempted to say, "I just made your favorite food! Come and eat right now!" or, "If you don't eat your lunch right now, you can't have anything to eat until dinner," but it is much better to avoid a confrontation. She may be saying "no" to something she really wants as a way of showing she is in control. If you respond with acceptance, you give your child the space to change course. You might say, "OK, but I think your teddy bear really likes this food. Would you like to feed him?" If the child says another "no," try sitting down and eating yourself. If your child is hungry and you don't make a big deal of her refusal, she will likely wander over and eat when she's ready. If she continues to play and avoid the food, put it in the refrigerator and wait awhile until she says, "I'm hungry." At that point, she will feel she is in control of her eating, and she will be more likely to appreciate the good food you have made.

In general, it is better to approach children who have temporarily adopted *no* as their favorite word by going underneath their radar. Instead of saying, "Lunch is ready," try giving a choice. For example, ask, "Do you want milk or orange juice with your lunch?" Or "Do you want the Winnie-the-Pooh plate or the Little Mermaid plate?"

One parent asked us what to do when her child demanded a peanut butter and jelly sandwich instead of the lunch the mother had just prepared. She said to us, "Doesn't she need to learn that I am not a short-order cook, and also to eat what's put in front of her?" We suggested that she try asking her daughter what she would like for lunch before she prepared something. This worked, because once her little girl felt she had more input into the menu, her all-powerful self was less driven to categorically reject the food on her plate.

We suggest that you try to accommodate your young child when she decides she wants something different from the food she requested and you made. If you go along with the revised menu, your child will both enjoy her food and also thrive in the warmth of your relationship. The other alternative—trying to force her to eat—only sets the stage for eating battles and problems and casts you unnecessarily as an adversary rather than an ally.

Two other arenas in which parents commonly find themselves at war with their toddler or preschooler are in making the child follow a health and safety rule and in getting the child to leave an activity she is enjoying. Try to make a plan you think has the best chance of resulting in a smooth transition. If it fails and your child becomes upset, don't prolong a battle you know she has to lose. At the same time, try to allow her to save face and feel in control whenever possible.

CAR SEAT WARS

One father reported that car seats were an everyday battle with eighteen-month-old Peter. The father confessed that he was terribly upset by the events of the previous day. Although he had tried every distraction he could think of and then offered a bribe, when he tried to shoehorn his son into his car seat, Peter kicked and thrashed so hard the father finally slapped him, even though he didn't believe in hitting children. Peter stopped fighting, but he cried as though his heart would break for the entire trip.

We suggested that the father tell his son that, although he wanted to say yes whenever possible, he couldn't give in when Peter's health or safety was at stake. We advised that the father never move the car an inch unless Peter had his seat belt on, and that he insist that everyone else in the car wear their seat belts as well. We recommended that the father keep any discussion friendly but short, and strap his son in before the child became completely hysterical and the father lost his temper. Even though the father still had to force Peter into the car seat, he found it easier to remain gentle and understanding, with the result that Peter went into his car seat with an undiminished primary happiness.

"NO GOING"

A mother who had been seeing us for parent counseling was in the park with her two-and-a-half-year-old, Avery. In spite of her best efforts to be diplomatic in raising the topic of leaving the park, when she told her son it was time to leave, Avery uttered an emphatic "no" and took off in a dead run in the opposite direction, forcing the mother to chase after him. The other parents watched in amusement and waited for her to discipline the boy for being "disobedient." Even though the mother was not in the mood for a sudden sprint, she realized that there was no need to reprove her child and every reason to remain positive and warm. She knew that Avery was not deliberately flaunting his disrespect for her authority; he was driven by his all-powerful self to demonstrate that he could do what he wanted when he wanted. Because of her consultation with us, the mother knew that Avery was running away to shield himself from the emotional pain he felt when things didn't go as he wished.

For this reason, when the mother caught her son, she tried to avoid confronting him with the fact that he could not have his way, and she managed not to get angry at him for behavior that was really normal and appropriate for his age. She said, "You are such a fast runner! Let's race back to your stroller—I bet you will win." Avery enthusiastically took her up on the challenge. When they reached the stroller, the mother thought of something Avery would like to do on the way home, in order to help him feel he was choosing to leave. She said, "Your squirt gun is in the stroller. Would you like to water the grass as we go?" Avery happily climbed in and began squirting the passing landscape.

∿

In contrast to the need to hold hands when crossing the street or the need to wear seat belts, there is usually no urgency about leaving the park. Allow enough time for the process of departing so that after you say it's time to go you can let your child play for a few minutes until her belief that she is too powerful to be made to leave is no longer uppermost in her mind.

Parents sometimes say, "I was brought up to believe children should be respectful of adults. When my son says 'no' to a direct order, I feel I have to make him obey for his own good." Unfortunately, when the toddler's all-powerful self is determined to prove that it is too strong to be interfered with, parents frequently overreact by holding their child to adult standards of conduct. They may feel enraged at what appears to be scornful disobedience and willful disrespect. Parents are then more inclined to respond with strong, harmful measures, such as using a raised and disapproving voice, sending the child to her room, telling her she can't engage in her favorite activity, criticizing her severely, or even slapping or spanking her. Keep in mind that the child between the ages of one and three is in a temporary phase in which she is driven to try to prove her immunity from interference. Because feeling all-powerful is an important source of well-being for the young child, if you can be understanding and diplomatic at moments when you must interfere with your child's wishes, you will help her to outgrow this illusion on her own timetable. On the other hand, trying to force a young child to face the limitations of her powers is sure to backfire. Some children react by becoming depressed; others cling even more desperately to their illusions of invincibility.

Smart Love Perspective: The Value of the All-Powerful Self

Although the all-powerful self needs governance, it is not a negative force. Because the all-powerful self is impervious to self-doubt, it plays the valuable developmental role of helping your child to persist in new activities in the face of the failures that are inevitable when one is learning. It is not unusual to see a toddler try ten times to get a piece of meat on her fork before she actually succeeds. As adults, we would feel discouraged by this failure rate. The toddler's all-powerful self gives her the confidence and optimism she needs to renew her efforts.

Loving Regulation for Your Toddler or Preschooler

Parents often say, "We understand that our toddler needs our love and understanding, but what happens when he hits his friends, won't go to bed, or tries to run into the street?"

In the temporary period when young children derive secondary happiness only from getting what they want, they seem unable to wait a moment for anything. Their requests may be followed by an insistent "I want it *now!*" If you fall into the trap of holding your child's behavior to adult standards, you may mistakenly conclude that if you don't force your child to be polite and patient, he will become a demanding, narcissistic grownup.

When you recognize that every young child's secondary happiness starts out with outcome dependence (getting the new toy he wants, staying at the playground, having the cookie he sees in the bakery window), and that this emotional vulnerability to frustration is a temporary developmental phase, you can react to your child's intensity with good humor or at least with forbearance. With ongoing parental kindness and affection and the benefit of loving regulation, you can help your child sustain his secondary happiness when he can't have what he wants. This reservoir of feeling cared for makes it possible for children to develop into adults who can encounter life's unpleasant surprises with an unshakable inner happiness and renewed effort.

If you see your nineteen-month-old child begin to eat crayons, say mildly, "Crayons aren't for chewing," and remove them in a friendly and affectionate manner. Then substitute something edible or safely chewable. Lecturing the child about the dangers of eating crayons, frightening him with a loud "no!" or imposing other disciplinary measures will teach him to treat himself and others harshly. Children who are never yelled at or punished will stop wanting to eat crayons as they grow older.

If your child grabs for the stove knob, try not to yell a startling "no!" but move the child away and give a friendly suggestion of an alternative. For example, you might say, "These knobs are not good to play with—they can be hot and give you an *owie*. Let's turn the knobs on your play stove." Yelling at your child will make him afraid of you and show him that you explode unpredictably—and yelling will not teach him about the properties and dangers of hot objects.

If the child persists, you can just say, "I think we need to go play in another part of the apartment for now." If the child cries, you can carry him out of the kitchen and affectionately help him begin a new activity. The smart love guideline is not to send the screaming child to his room, but to *accompany him and help him to feel better*. In this way, you help your child to distinguish between the disappointment he feels when he doesn't get what he wants and the abiding good feelings available to him as a result of your commitment to make him happy.

Giving your child a time-out in his room teaches him that everyday disappointments are doubly upsetting. First, he doesn't get his wish to cook. Second, the forced isolation from you is painful in itself and also causes him to imitate you and feel as negative about himself as he believes you feel about him. Because repeated time-outs undermine children's inner well-being, they make children more dependent on external gratifications and, therefore, less able to tolerate frustration.

THE CHILD WHO WAS TOO ILL TO SLED

A father who was seeing us for parent counseling turned to the principle of loving regulation when his ill three-year-old, Mike, became upset because he couldn't go sledding as promised. The father said, "I know you have been looking forward to going sledding, and there is new snow, but you have a fever, and it would make you much sicker to go outside. How about if you sit in my lap, and I will read you a story?" When Mike continued to cry, his father adhered to the principle that nothing would be gained by upsetting the child further with responses such as, "If you don't stop this screaming, you can't go sledding tomorrow," "You have to spend five minutes in your room until you calm

down," "You can't have a treat," or "You have to learn that you can't always do everything you want," and the like.

Instead, the father continued to hold his sobbing son. After a while, Mike stopped crying, at which point he accepted his father's suggestion that he might like to help feed the goldfish.

When a toddler's all-powerful self is determined to prove that it is too strong to be interfered with, parents frequently overreact by holding toddlers to adult standards of conduct. Take the example of the child who hauls back his arm and is about to throw a ball directly at your face. You can try a diversion ("Instead of throwing the ball at me, how about rolling it for the dog?"). But if it becomes clear that the child is going to throw the ball at you, you might say firmly, "Don't throw that ball, it can hurt me. If you throw it, I will have to put it away." A toddler who is completely under the spell of his all-powerful self may ignore this warning and heave the ball right at you with a laugh. If you misperceive children as small editions of adults, you may feel enraged at what appears to be scornful disobedience and willful disrespect. You may be more inclined to respond with strong measures, such as speaking in a raised and disapproving voice, sending the child to his room, telling him he can't engage in his favorite activity, criticizing him severely, or even slapping or spanking him.

Children going through this temporary phase certainly need regulation, but anger and disapproval will harm, not help. Disciplinary responses to children's expressions of aggression actually hinder children from developing the capacity to regulate themselves in an unconflicted and effective manner. By alienating children from parents, disciplinary measures force children to turn to growth-inhibiting sources of inner well-being, such as thumb-sucking, renewed defiance, or withdrawal. Worse yet, because children adore their parents and want to grow up to be just like them, when children are treated severely they adopt this same harshness toward themselves and others.

By following the principle of loving regulation, parents can spare children the emotional trauma caused by repeated isolation or alienation from parents. In the example just described, you need only say to your child, "You remember I told you that if you throw the ball at people's faces, I will have to take it away until you can play with it safely," and then remove the ball from the scene. If your child protests, you could say, "I know you feel bad now. We can try a little later to see if you can play with that ball without throwing it at my face. Meanwhile, would you like to hit a balloon back and forth?" Once you regulate your child's behavior, try to make your child happy.

You need neither withdraw from your child nor lecture him on the need for obedience and respect for others. You can regulate way-ward behavior without making your child feel ashamed, bad, and as though whenever he feels angry or upset, those he adores cannot tolerate having him around. *The lack of control that is associated with your child's illusion that his all-powerful self will always prevail is not an emerging personality trait; it is appropriate behavior given the child's developmental phase.* Loving regulation controls unwanted behavior, but unlike discipline it will not alienate your child or teach him to dislike himself.

BEAR GETS A BATH IN THE TOILET BOWL

If you take an important phone call only to discover that while you were talking your toddler was giving her teddy bear a bath in the toilet, you need not lecture your child about the dangers of toilet germs, frighten her with loud no's, or isolate her with time-outs. Using loving regulation, you can simply remove her from the scene with a mild comment like, "Toilets are not good for baths. Let's take Bear to the sink and wash him with special [disinfectant] soap."

Many parents do not realize that it is both unnecessary and harmful to lecture, reprimand, or punish their toddler for playing in the toilet. Try to maintain a positive attitude as you gently redirect your young child. This loving regulation will successfully disengage her from the toilet bowl without causing her to feel she is bad. This interest is only temporary, because your child will certainly outgrow the wish to play in the toilet as she matures. Until that time, she needs friendly supervision to keep her away from it.

Children become good citizens because they want the good feelings of being like those they admire, not because they have been subjected to negative consequences. If you treat your child with love, understanding, and respect, he will grow up to treat others that way, even if these positive traits are rarely apparent until after he turns three.

If your three-year-old is hitting a smaller sibling, try to prevent physical mayhem by sitting between them or picking up the older child until the aggression stops. You need to tell your older child that you cannot let him hit his younger sibling, but there is no reason to be disapproving with him. For example, you need not lecture him about following the golden rule or not preying on those who are younger and weaker.

Most people who break the law know right from wrong, so lecturing your child about how to behave will not guarantee that he will grow up respecting the rights of others. Moreover, since your child will imitate you, lectures may actually interfere with his socialization by making him feel criticized and alienated and causing him to want to make his siblings and peers feel equally small.

With the help of loving regulation you can simply defuse your child's aggressive behavior without expressing disapproval, and in so doing you will give your child a model of relating that he will strive to emulate. As soon as he outgrows his inclination to go after what he wants regardless of who or what is in his path, your child will want to be just like you—supportive, gentle, loving, and loyal.

Statements to Avoid

Parents often ask us how to distinguish between discipline and loving regulation. One rule of thumb is that disciplinary statements take this form: "If you don't do X, you can't do/have Y" where Y is arbitrary. An example is the father who asked his son three times to put his snow boots on and then said, "If you don't put your boots on right now, you can't have an ice cream cone when we are out."

Parents using loving regulation will impose only those consequences necessary to protect the child who fails to respond to a directive. They will add no other consequences. To illustrate, a three-year-old insisted on wearing sneakers instead of boots on a snowy day.

His father simply said, "OK, but then you won't be able to stomp around in the snow. If you want to walk in the snow drifts, you need to wear boots so your feet will stay dry and warm." The little boy considered this for a moment and then agreed to put his boots on.

If his son had continued to insist on wearing sneakers, the father would have brought the boy's boots along in case the boy discovered that playing in the snow was more important to him than wearing sneakers. The father's objective was to make sure that his son didn't go out in the snow inappropriately dressed; it was not to teach the boy that he would be sorry if he didn't make the right choice.

Permissiveness Is Not Loving Regulation

Permissive parenting differs from parenting with loving regulation in that permisive parents do not control children's harmful impulses. Permissive parents often go along with children's wishes that should not be granted because they find it difficult to tolerate their children's anger or unhappiness. Some examples are parents who allow protesting or crying children to continue an activity when the children really need to eat, parents who give their children more candy than is good for them because their children become upset when limits are imposed, and parents whose children are frequently exhausted because the parents can't bear the children's angry reactions when they are told it is time to stop playing and take a nap.

Permissive parents may believe that they are giving their children exactly what they need and want, but permissiveness interferes with children's development of stable inner happiness and prevents them from reaching their full potential, because when children are not helped to regulate themselves, their all-powerful selves have full sway. Children whose behavior goes unregulated continue to believe that they have the power to realize each and every desire. Their secondary happiness stays yoked to the gratification of specific desires and, therefore, remains at the mercy of the ups and downs of daily life. These children also learn that the unhappiness they feel when they are disappointed is overwhelming to their parents and cannot be managed either by their parents or by themselves.

How to Make Your Toddler's or Preschooler's Day Run Smoothly and Happily

Understanding your child's special point of view will help you to avoid treading unnecessarily on your toddler's developmental sensitivities. When your toddler's all-powerful self drives her to disobey every prohibition and test every boundary, you can baby-proof your child's environment so that she will experience as few disappointments and as little conflict with you as possible. You may also want to avoid taking the child of this age to places with tempting displays that can't be touched. Since toddlers are periodically driven to prove that they need tolerate no restrictions, they will always find a way to push the envelope. Better they do their testing at a playground where they might throw some sand out of the sandbox than in a bookstore, where they may try to demonstrate their immunity to interference by removing the jackets from all the expensive hardcover books.

ANTIQUING CAN WAIT

Parents whose favorite hobby was antiquing began to find that entering an antique store with their eighteen-month-old was no fun at all. Lynn was irresistibly drawn to touch the fragile objects. When her parents tried to carry her, she screamed to get down. The child experienced the prohibition against touching the displays of delicate objects as a direct and irresistible challenge. Her parents resorted to firm "no's" and even a slap or two on the hand, but the result was a sobbing, clinging child. Then the parents could not enjoy looking around because Lynn was miserable. They also noticed that their daughter had nightmares after a day spent antiquing. They came to us asking how they could get Lynn to "behave" in stores.

We explained that Lynn was old enough to break things but too young to make her own determination that certain things were breakable and couldn't be touched. Therefore, she could only see her parents' interference with her wish to touch as arbitrary and unfair. When her parents' responses escalated to include a scary tone or physical punishment, Lynn felt that for reasons she couldn't fathom, she was a bad girl. As a result she cried and felt devastated. Worse, because she adored her parents and believed they took perfect care of her, she began trying to treat herself exactly as she felt they had treated her.

The unpleasant feelings that resulted from the nightmares felt just like the emotions evoked by her parents' responses.

When Lynn's parents understood the effects of their unrealistic expectations on their daughter, they were willing to get a babysitter when they wanted to visit antique stores. On family outings, they went to the children's sections of museums and the city playgrounds, where Lynn could gratify her need to touch everything in sight. The family expeditions became happy times again, and Lynn's nightmares stopped as abruptly as they had begun.

When children are confident that they can elicit their parents' unconditional loving responses and, in addition, are given a wide latitude to satisfy their desires, they will come to accept a few nonnegotiable health and safety rules, including using car seats, taking medicine, and holding hands crossing streets with good grace. In addition, they will acquire the emotional space to realize that blindly obeying their all-powerful selves can cause them unhappiness. The more you make it possible for your child to experience the genuine pleasure of making constructive choices and pursuing them well, the less she will be attracted to the unrealistic pleasure represented by the false claims of her all-powerful self to know everything and to be able to do anything. As a result, your child will become increasingly capable of tolerating failures and disappointments without feeling a loss of face.

NO TIME FOR PAINTING

The parents of two-year-old Penny consulted us because they were finding it difficult to cope with her refusal to listen when she was told she couldn't have something she wanted. The more her parents lectured her, the more determined Penny became. After speaking with us her parents realized that Penny was not being willfully disobedient; she ignored her parents' attempts to interfere with her wishes only because disappointments made her feel desperate and vulnerable.

A few weeks later, Penny was told that there was no time to paint before dinner. She cried briefly in frustration, and her all-powerful self tried to maintain the illusion that she could paint if she wanted to, with the result that she carried a paintbrush around and pretended to paint with it. But Penny's parents were careful not to expose her need to pretend that she could have her way. When she waved her brush in the air and announced, "Look, me painting," they simply said, "We see!" and did not argue with her.

Sometime after her third birthday, when she was again told there wasn't time to get out her paints before dinner, Penny accepted the reality that painting was out for the moment. She cheerfully got out her crayons and began coloring.

Your toddler or preschooler needs more of your time and focused attention than people usually think. It is popular wisdom that toddlers and two-year-olds, who are beginning to look more like children and less like babies, should be increasingly independent. Accordingly, parents are instructed not to "baby" their children by doing for their children things that their children are capable of doing for themselves, like getting socks from a drawer or putting on mittens. But the smart love guideline is that *your child will better accept your occasional need to interfere with her wishes if you honor her requests whenever possible.* When you can't grant a particular wish, showing your child that you will help her find an alternative (you don't have time to get her socks, but big sister can; she can't bang on the glass table with a hard plastic flute, but she can use a foam rubber baton) emphasizes that you do want her to make her own choices and to have fun.

When your child is in this phase, you can try to arrange her day so that she has the broadest possible scope to gratify her blossoming sense of personal choice. Try to anticipate and prepare for your child's need to feel in control. For instance:

- Allow extra time for an errand that would normally take a few minutes so you won't have to hurry your child or pull her away from what interests her.

- Recognize that transitions will be difficult. Give your child some advance notice and then help point her in the direction of other gratifications. Say, "Let's go home and see our doggy," "Let's get into the stroller and have some raisins," rather than, "Remember, I told you two more minutes. Time's up and we have to leave now."

- Avoid asking questions unless you really mean to give a choice. "Do you want milk or orange juice?" is fine, but don't ask the child, "Do you want to go out?" when you have planned an errand on which the child has no choice but to accompany you.

- Try not to give your child a false sense of freedom. One mother was disturbed because her twenty-month-old constantly ran away from her on busy sidewalks, but the real problem was that the mother was putting the child down on the pavement at times when she wasn't willing or able to follow her. This mother could have avoided a conflict if she had kept the child occupied in her stroller until they reached an area that was more appropriate for toddler explorations.

- Avoid protracted discussions about things that must occur. If a child needs to take medicine and protests, don't cajole, bargain, or describe all the dreadful things that will happen without the medicine. Merely show the child that you recognize it is very difficult not to have a choice ("I know you don't want it now, but you need to have it") and get it over with.

How to Help Your Child When He Can't Have What He Wants

In trying to instill in your child the ability to regulate himself, especially the ability to delay gratification, you may have been advised to remind him that he cannot have everything he wants when he wants it. Parents are often told to say, "Everyone has to wait," or "You cannot have it until you stop screaming/whining/crying." But strict or disapproving responses to your child's wishes only make matters worse. In addition to the frustration that caused his tears, your child will experience the added hurt that his beloved parents don't understand that he feels miserable because what he wants seems desperately important.

Children whose parents are most responsive and least withholding feel loved and lovable, and as a result they are better able to tolerate frustration. As two-year-olds, these children will generally be terrific rather than terrible. They will certainly make clear their unhappiness when their wishes are frustrated, but they will also respond to the inevitable disappointments with resilience and a strong desire to get help from their parents, rather than by turning to more isolated kinds of soothing, such as overeating or becoming glued to the television set.

When parents repeatedly admonish a child or make him comply with strict rules in order to acquire what he wants, his experiences of wanting things may begin to take on a traumatic hue. As a result, he may become more impulse driven and more easily irritated, or he may assert himself reactively by turning away from what he really wants in order to preserve a sense of being in control.

A typical example is when parents employ popular but unnecessarily negative and, therefore, counterproductive disciplinary measures in response to their two-year-old's tears at having to leave the playground. They may say, "If you're going to scream like that when we leave, we can't come here anymore," or "If you don't stop screaming, we won't stop at a restaurant on the way home," or "If you don't stop screaming, you are going to have a time-out on that bench over there!" The child who is spoken to in this way frequently responds by saying he doesn't want to go to the playground or the restaurant anyway. Depriving and isolating a child may well quiet him, but these measures always increase the child's unhappiness by teaching him that his parents disapprove of him when he is upset. Since children want to be just like their parents, they may copy the parents' behavior and learn to dislike themselves whenever they feel unhappy. Fortunately, the child who melts down when his wishes must be thwarted can become resilient if his parents learn to respond to his raw emotions according to the smart love guidelines.

SMART LOVE HELPS A CHILD LEAVE WITHOUT TEARS

The parents of two-year-old Jake came to us because Jake would throw fits whenever it was time to leave a place where he had been having fun. The parents would react by losing their tempers. Then both they and Jake would feel even worse.

With the help of the smart love principles Jake's parents changed their approach. The results of this change became evident one day when Jake had been playing for an hour and a half at a children's museum. After providing their son with advance notice ("We know you're not finished playing with the water table, but we need to go soon"), the parents said, "It's time to go and get lunch now." Jake burst into loud crying. His parents responded with the calm insistence that it was time to leave. When he continued to scream in spite of his parents' attempts to help him see the positive side of the transition ("When we get to the restaurant, you can squeeze the ketchup onto the hamburger yourself"), his parents gently but firmly picked him up and carried him out of the museum. They made no attempt to reason with him until he calmed down about five minutes later. At that point, his mother said sympathetically, "It was really hard to stop playing and leave when you were having such a good time." Jake nodded vehemently and then relaxed and became his usual sunny self.

Through loving regulation these parents could be effective in responding to their son because they controlled their son's recalcitrant behavior, but they did not add to his unhappiness by disapproving of him, lecturing him, or imposing disciplinary measures.

A month later, when Jake was told it was time to stop another activity that he was enjoying and go home, he looked at his parents and with great feeling said, "I sad." The parents' loving regulation had provided their son with the support necessary to become more in charge of his feelings of not wanting to leave. As a result, he had become able to share his feelings with his parents. His father responded, "I know, it is hard to stop doing something you enjoy." Jake then went along with his parents in a cooperative mood and without tears.

When Jake was two and a half, he had to be the first to leave a birthday party at which he was having a wonderful time. He left without conflict, but on the way home he confided, "I really didn't want to leave." His parents were pleased to see that their son had developed the capacity to leave a place where he wanted to stay without feeling devastated, depressed, or angry. Even though his parents had caused him to leave the party early, Jake was able to sustain a loving closeness with them that allowed him to maintain his inner well-being even when he couldn't have what he wanted.

~

How to Help the Child Who Has a Bad Dream

It is popular wisdom that nightmares are as inevitable as colds. Yet we have found that children whose developmental needs are adequately satisfied will not create terrifying dreams for themselves. They won't wake up in the night reporting hair-raising encounters with monsters, witches, dragons, or other angry beings, because, having never acquired needs to cause themselves unhappiness, they will not have any desire to frighten themselves. At worst, these children may have occasional unpleasant dreams because they have had an unpleasant experience during the day, such as a bad fright, or they may react to some physical discomfort that occurs during sleep by having an upsetting dream. The smart love guideline for helping the child who has had a bad dream is *respond with solicitude to the discomfort that stimulated the bad dream.*

ANTS IN BED

A two-and-a-half-year-old we know awoke one night crying. She said she'd had a dream about ants climbing all over her. It was clear to her mother that April, who had a history of dry skin, was itching badly.

Mother: You were having a dream. I think you were thinking about ants in your sleep because you were itching.

April: I don't like ants!

Mother: I know. Let me put some lotion on you so you won't be itching.

April: I don't want any more ants in my bed.

Mother: You probably won't dream about ants anymore now that your skin feels better.

April: *(pause)* I want to dream about you.

Mother: That would feel a lot nicer, wouldn't it?

April: Yes.

Mother: Night night.

April: Night night. *(She went back to sleep.)*

Although April had an unpleasant dream, it was stimulated by physical discomfort. It did not terrify her, and she trusted that her mother would help her feel better. She had no more bad dreams once her parents began putting lotion on her skin before bedtime.

～

TEDDY BEAR FALLS

A mother we know recounted to us an unpleasant dream of her three-year-old, Sandy. The boy, who hardly ever hurt himself, had fallen down in the playground during a game of tag and had had to go to his pediatrician to have gravel removed from his skinned knee. That night Sandy called his mother to his room and said he had dreamt that his teddy bear fell out of bed and broke its leg. His mother hugged him and said that he was probably having that bad dream because he was still upset about hurting his knee. Sandy nodded emphatically and asked for a new Band-Aid for himself and one for his bear. After the Band-Aids were applied to both patients, Sandy slept undisturbed.

∾

A child's occasional bad dream can usually be traced to a discomfort that occurs during sleep or to an upsetting event the child experienced in the daytime. But frequent nightmares reflect a child's ongoing need to make herself unhappy, and they are a call for help. Later in this chapter, we offer suggestions for responding to the child who is having frequent nightmares.

How to Help the Child Who Resists Bedtime

When sleep problems occur, loving regulation is the most effective way to make bedtime peaceful and happy again. Using the smart love principles you can make sure your child gets the rest he needs, and you can make bedtime a cozy period during which you and your child can enjoy each other's company.

You are living with a small creature who is in love with you, himself, and the world around him. Why would he want to leave all that and go to sleep? The toddler or preschooler who wants to stay up at least until you go to bed is not being manipulative or willful, and he is not trying to torture you. You will find it easier to maintain your equilibrium if you see your child's resistance to bedtime as understandable and appropriate to his age.

All advice to bribe, punish, or ignore children who are unhappy and resistant at bedtime is ultimately unhelpful. Children who are yelled at, threatened, locked in their rooms, or ignored, may well give up and go to sleep, but they will also conclude that their beloved parents want them to feel miserable, and they will learn to treat themselves harshly. For example, in the future when they find themselves in a difficult situation, they may have great difficulty asking for help. Children who are bribed conclude that they are so powerful you have to pay them in one way or another to do what you know to be in their interest. With the loving regulation approach, you can see that your child goes to bed at a reasonable time, and at the same time you send the message that you love him, care about his feelings, and are in charge of him.

If a three-year-old who is being put to bed postpones sleeping by demanding one glass of water after another, you will probably tell him after the fourth or fifth drink that he has had enough. But try not to become irritated or angry. Although it is natural for you to wish fervently that your child would go to sleep and leave you some space to rest or do chores, try not to see his demands for water as being manipulative or hostile. They represent his immature but creative attempt to prolong the enjoyable experience of being awake. If you can respond with kindness, you will build your child's confidence that you continue to love and care for him even when you have to refuse his wishes.

You can appreciate your child's inventiveness and still decline to gratify his demands. If the child cries when you refuse to get yet another glass of water, comfort him until he stops crying. If he cries again when you leave, make the effort to return to his room *as often as necessary* to tell him briefly but sympathetically that he has had enough water and it is time for sleeping. For example, you might say, "We know it's hard to go to bed when there are so many fun things to do. But you really need to sleep. Go to sleep now, and you can have more water first thing in the morning."

Since the goal is regulation rather than discipline, by comforting your child when he cries you demonstrate that even though the water will not be forthcoming, you care whether he is unhappy and you are available to help him feel better. Your loving responsiveness will spare your child from falling asleep in a state of despair at his powerlessness to cause you to respond to him when he feels miserable, and it will teach him to put himself to sleep surrounded by the emotional warmth of your relationship.

Parents often ask us whether or not they should take the wakeful infant or small child into their bed. We believe this is ultimately a cultural issue. There is nothing inherently wrong with taking your baby or small child into your bed. In some cultures there are great advantages to doing this (for example, the child will be less likely to be eaten by a marauding animal; or if warmth is hard to maintain, the body heat of parents and siblings will keep the baby comfortable). In cultures in which entire families share the same bedroom, taking a child into the parental bed will not create difficulties for him as he grows older. In Western culture, however, there are certain disadvantages: Nighttime is one of the few times parents have to be alone together, individuals in this culture generally need to develop the ability to sleep alone, and the transition to sleeping in his own bed may be painful and difficult as a child grows older and feels increasingly entitled to sleep with his parents. We suggest that in this society it is usually better for parents to help children sleep in their own beds, because children ultimately will sleep in their own room or share a room with a sibling, and it is probably better to help them learn to put themselves to sleep in their own beds as infants. If you decide that it is better for your child to sleep in his own bed, but he keeps climbing into yours, try to remain positive, and walk the child back to his room as many times as needed to help him get back to sleep.

We want to emphasize that while smart love principles have universal applicability, we are well aware that our examples are drawn from the perspective of Western culture at the approach of the twenty-first century. The examples we provide here are specific to our own culture and time; they do not reflect the belief that one culture's style of parenting is any better than another's for raising children who are truly happy.

We do believe that in any culture when babies' tears are consistently either ignored or responded to with disapproval or punishment, the children unknowingly develop needs to experience unhappiness. Cultures that prescribe styles of caregiving that cause children to experience long periods of conscious unhappiness will still produce adults who are socially successful, consciously satisfied, and accepted by their society as normal. But these cultures will produce fewer adults who possess an unshakable inner well-being.

Developmental Milestone: Choosing to Use the Toilet

Most conflicts over "toilet training" occur because parents are afraid to allow children to choose to use the toilet on their own timetables.

Parents are often told that for her own good the child should be toilet trained by a certain age. As more time passes and the child remains in diapers, some parents begin to feel increasingly helpless and concerned. But there is no more reason to try to hurry your child into using the toilet than to worry about her walking, talking, riding a bike, or reading. It might be easier for parents to relax if they considered the unlikelihood that their child would some day play Little League, go to high school, or be married wearing diapers. By taking the long view, parents might find it easier to give their child the time she needs to make the inevitable choice to use the toilet.

We prefer the term *toilet choosing* because it highlights the true nature of the transition from wearing diapers to using the toilet; it is an opportunity for the child to gain greater autonomy and secondary happiness. When you offer your young child the option of choosing the toilet with the same relaxed attitude that you offer her opportunities to play with crayons, blocks, or dolls, then at the point that she chooses the toilet she will feel only pride, prowess, and closeness to you. What route you decide to take—potty chair, training pants, or child-sized toilet seat—is not as important as your relaxed attitude.

All advice to parents that focuses on getting children out of diapers by a certain age or at a certain time is misguided and likely to cause exactly the kind of conflicts that all parents want to avoid. Don't bargain or cajole. Don't demand that your child must be toilet trained. The fundamental goal is to protect and enhance your child's sense of competence, which is why you should give her the freedom to decide to use the toilet.

"NO MORE POTTY"

An eighteen-month-old amazed his parents by copying his older cousin and making use of the potty chair that had been standing unnoticed in his room. After announcing proudly to friends and relatives that their little boy was well on the way to being "trained," the parents discovered that their child began to show a complete lack of interest in ever using the potty again. Utterly frustrated, they consulted us.

We told them that while it was understandable that they felt disappointed at the prospect of the many diaper changes in their future, it was important to accept their son's conclusion that having tried the potty, he wanted to stick with diapers for the time being. We asked the parents to wait until their son showed renewed interest, and then they might encourage him in a low-key manner.

❦

It may be frustrating when your child "backslides," but trying to force or bribe her to choose the toilet may trigger a major contest of wills—and you will certainly lose, because no one can effectively control the functioning of another's bowels and bladder. Moreover, if choosing the toilet becomes something your child does for you or for a reward, your child will miss out on the real goal of toilet choosing—the sense of pride and enhanced competence derived from learning to regulate important bodily functions.

Perhaps you want to enroll your two-year-old in an activity, such as swimming or gymnastics, but you are told that only "toilet trained" children will be accepted. You know your child would really enjoy the activity, so even though you may have been feeling very relaxed about your child's toilet choosing, you wonder if you should try to speed up the process for your child's own good. So long as you keep in mind that using the toilet is a choice your child needs to make for herself, there is no reason not to explain to her that if she wants to take swimming or go to play school or day camp, the rule is that she must use the toilet when she is there. Your child may decide that she wants the activity enough to follow the rule. We know one little boy who used the toilet during day camp and went back to wearing diapers at home. Fortunately, his parents were accepting of that arrangement. Alternatively, your child may conclude that the activity is not worth giving up diapers. You need to respect that choice as well.

If your child elects to stay in diapers and forgo the activity, you can probably find something enjoyable for her to do that doesn't require toilet skills. Since you want to avoid pressuring your child into using the toilet, there is every reason to try to find a satisfying alternative to the activity that is not available to her.

If you need to send your child to preschool and she is not willing to use the toilet, try to find a school that accepts children in diapers. If your child's preschool allows it, you may also want to explore using disposable training pants if your child has just started to use the toilet. If need be, you can always switch your child to a different school once she has chosen to use the toilet on a regular basis.

"I CAN'T BELIEVE HE'S STILL IN DIAPERS!"

A father went to visit friends whose three-year-old was using the potty. Ron, his own three-year-old, was not. In an attempt to be helpful, the friends tried to shame young Ron ("I didn't realize you were still a baby!") and to succeed where the father was "failing" ("Come on, Ron, let's show Dad that you really can use the toilet and get rid of those babyish diapers"). Ron responded to this pressure by crying and insisting on being taken home. He also refused to go back to his friend's house, although he had always enjoyed playing there.

The father consulted us because he wanted to know how to protect his son from the hurtful comments of well-intentioned adults. We advised him that whenever other adults criticize a child within parents' hearing, it is crucial to defend the child. We suggested that the father say something like, "Ron will use the toilet when he feels ready! There are a lot of children his age still wearing diapers, so diapers are not just for babies. They are also for big boys who haven't decided they want to use the toilet yet!"

Parents who are eager for their child to get out of diapers often ask whether it would be appropriate to motivate their child with a reward, such as a toy or a trip to the local amusement park. It is best to avoid such rewards because they only show your child how important her using the toilet is to you. Rewards will put pressure on your child, and she will feel bad and inadequate if she doesn't feel ready to give up her diapers. Further, if your child actually uses the toilet to get the reward and to please you, when she subsequently feels angry with you or if the rewards cease, not using the toilet may become a means for her to express anger or to negotiate for goodies. If you can avoid trying to accelerate your child's toilet choosing by offering rewards when your child decides to use the toilet, she will feel an unconflicted sense of mastery and control over her life, and you will have avoided the dreaded "toilet wars" altogether.

PUBLIC TOILETS TERRIFY A TODDLER

A two-and-a-half-year-old was comfortable choosing to use the toilet at home, but he was terrified of public bathrooms. His parents noticed that when he seemed to be enjoying himself on an outing, he would frequently become very anxious and say he wanted to go home. The moment he entered their apartment, he would run for the bathroom. The parents tried everything to convince him that public toilets were no different from the ones at home—they even toted along a child's potty seat to put on the big toilet, but he remained unwilling to try. A friend suggested to them that if they arranged things so that they *couldn't* return home when their son began to feel the need to urinate, he would probably choose to use the public toilet rather than wet his pants, and then he would see that public toilets are OK.

Although the boy's parents were eager for him to begin using public toilets, they consulted us because they were uncomfortable with their friend's advice. We explained that many children go through a phase in which they are comfortable using a potty at home or even in someone else's house but are frightened to use public toilets, which may be very loud. We advised that these parents try telling the child that they would wait to flush the toilet until after he was out of the stall, or, alternatively, they could offer to let him wear diapers on outings. But when the child rejected these suggestions, we recommended that, rather than force their child to choose between wetting his pants or feeling terrified, the parents would gain everything by waiting this period out and trying not to take the child too far from home.

❧

Almost inevitably, children who have chosen to use the potty at home will feel brave enough to try a public toilet within three or four months if they are not pressured. At that point, they will be so flexible and adaptable that parents will be able to take them anywhere. On the other hand, children who are forced to use toilets that frighten them often become increasingly anxious. Sometimes these children will begin saying that they don't want to leave the house at all even for outings they have previously enjoyed, but they will deny that their reason for wanting to stay home is related to their fear of public toilets.

How Many Friends Does Your Toddler or Preschooler Need?

The accepted wisdom is that a young child needs plenty of time to play with other children so as to give him ample opportunity to develop social skills. We have found that there is no inherent value in arranging play dates for children under three years of age. Children under three want your love and attention, they want to own and rearrange every aspect of their environments, and, when their all-powerful self is in control, they want what they want when they want it. None of these desires is particularly conducive to civilized social relating, which demands a reliable quantity of deferred gratification and altruism.

Parents certainly enjoy socializing with other parents, and on occasion children under three can have a grand time together. It is fine to let your child inhabit the same space as other children of roughly the same age as long as he is having fun and all the parents present agree that children under three should not be expected to share, to ask another child politely to use her toy, to wait amiably for a turn, and so forth.

Parents frequently conclude that the grabby preschooler who refuses to share has a narcissistic, selfish personality that will continue into adulthood unless it is curbed decisively. Too often parents are advised that this is the right moment in their child's development to teach him that he must share and that he must wait. If children can't restrain themselves, parents are frequently told this is the moment for lectures, warnings ("I'm going to count to three now"), a time-out, or some other restriction or punishment.

But lecturing children about the golden rule ("How would you feel if no one shared with you?") or threatening them with sanctions ("If you don't give that truck back, you will have a time-out," "If you can't learn to share toys, we can't visit Teddy anymore") simply adds unnecessarily to their misery. *Children who are not prematurely forced to share will identify with their parents' generosity toward them and will eventually become generous themselves out of love for their friends.*

We reiterate that your child's secondary happiness ceases to depend on the gratification of everyday desires (getting the doll, winning a game, getting an A) only through a long-term process that is guided by your loving attention. Lecturing or criticizing children or demanding unquestioning obedience from them actually retards the process by which their secondary happiness becomes independent of the ups and downs of daily life. This process does not culminate until the end of adolescence.

Sharing

When children are made to share and told not to grab before they are old enough to choose to be generous, they feel hurt by their parents' demands and disapproval. These children will become increasingly driven to soothe themselves with possessions, or they will become fearful about expressing their desires. In contrast, two-year-olds who are confident of their ability to cause their parents' unconditional loving responses and who are never made to give up a toy they don't want to share will become generous, caring friends sometime between the ages of three and four. By the time he is four, friendships with other children will be more important to your child than any particular possession. Your child will choose to share and not grab because he will emulate your kindness to him, and because he will increasingly realize that by being generous he will have more friends and more fun.

THE HOARDING HOST

A mother and her two-year-old, Joe, were visited by the mother's close friend and the friend's two-and-a-half-year-old daughter. When the little girl headed eagerly for Joe's favorite truck, he rushed over and grabbed it and refused to let her have it, or even to look at it. The little girl began to shriek hysterically. The girl's mother waited expectantly for Joe's mother to make her son act like a proper host and share his truck. Joe's mother made him do so, but he was devastated and cried inconsolably. His mother felt uncomfortable forcing him to share and making him so upset, and later on she gave us a call to ask what we thought she should have done.

We agreed that her discomfort was well founded, because in fact Joe's moral education would be slowed down, not sped up, by forcing him to share at this point. We suggested that next time she could explain to the little girl that her son didn't feel like sharing his truck right then, but that there was an entire roomful of other toys to choose from.

The mother asked what to do if the small guest continued to weep and ask for the truck. We suggested that the mother might try to think of a cooperative activity that would engage both children. For example, she could blow up a balloon and suggest that the children make "baskets" by batting the balloon into a wastebasket. We also recommended that the next time the little girl came to visit, she could put the truck away in advance. If Joe noticed its absence, however, it was important to give the truck back to him. The goal of putting it away was to minimize opportunities for conflict, not to deprive him as a punishment for not sharing.

If another child's parent becomes upset or angry because your child is not sharing, do your best to explain why you believe your child will be harmed if you force him to share prematurely. If that doesn't work, fall back on the argument that both you and the other parent should be free to choose different parenting philosophies. If the other parent continues to challenge you, you may temporarily have to find another playmate for your child and see your friend for dinner.

The issue of sharing and not grabbing is most problematic when necessity brings together children under three as siblings, or at family or social gatherings. If two or more children under the age of three are going to be spending time together, it is a good idea to provide multiples of the most coveted toys. If this is not practicable, it's better to identify the problem toys in advance and put them away than to have the children driven to endless squabbling and tears.

What to Do When Your Child Grabs Toys

If your two-year-old grabs another child's shovel in the sandbox, and the other child begins to shriek so loudly that all eyes turn first to your child and then to you in horror and disapproval, you may well feel pressure to take the toy from your child with a decisive "No grabbing!" and hand it back to the victim. Yet because your child's behavior is both temporary and also normal for his age, you should not respond negatively. Your first move is to find the most attractive sand toy in your possession and offer it to the crying child. If the child accepts the substitute, you can relax and watch both children play happily. If the shovel's owner refuses the substitution and remains upset, you can try to engage both children in a joint activity. For example, you could fill a pail with water and suggest that one child dig a hole and the other pour the water in, and it is possible that one of the two children may actually prefer pouring the water to digging with the shovel.

If all your creative efforts fail, and it is clear that the shovel must be returned to its rightful owner, break the news to your child as diplomatically as possible. "I'm sorry, sweetheart, but the little boy really needs his shovel back. Let's return it and I'll give you your nice red shovel. Then we can make a really big castle with it." If your child refuses to part with his new treasure, you may have to remove it gently and hand it over, but you can remain sympathetic to his distress and try your best to comfort him. Your positive attitude and suggestions of attractive alternatives will make clear that while you had to insist that he give up his prize, he can count on you to do everything you can to ease his unhappiness. Sooner or later, the suggestion of an alternative toy or activity in the context of your continued sympathetic attentions will soothe your child. In the process, your child will come to the all-important recognition that despite the unhappiness he feels with the loss of the toy, he never loses the pleasure of knowing you think the world of him and that you care enough to continue trying to make him happy. You will have helped him toward the developmental goal of realizing that he can continue to feel inner well-being even when he doesn't get what he wants.

If you arrive at the playground only to discover that you forgot to bring toys, and you are fairly certain that when your child gets to the sandbox he will grab other children's toys, we suggest that you spare your child the pain of going toyless by staying away from the sandbox and visiting the swings, slide, and so forth. Or this would be a good day to visit some other part of the park (throw bread crumbs for the ducks in the pond, blow on dandelions). One parent reported that when she gave back the toy her child had grabbed because the other child wouldn't accept a substitute, her child immediately grabbed the toy again. In this case, the best course is to gently take your child to another activity and away from temptation. *This is not a "time-out," because you are accompanying your child and trying to make him happy, and you are not isolating him from your supportive relationship.*

If your child is still playing with another child's toy when the other child has to leave, explain to your child that the toy has to go home with the other child. If your child still has trouble parting with the toy, offer a substitute and, if necessary, suggest another activity. If that doesn't work, gently remove the toy from your child's grip and return it to the other child. Then comfort your child.

If your child is the one whose toy is grabbed, the smart love principle remains the same. Because you know your child is too young to want to share, don't force him to give up the toy. You and the parent of the grabbing child can try to find an acceptable substitute for the snatched toy or you can try to engage the children in a joint activity, but if your child remains upset, the toy should be returned to him.

Your Steady Caring Is the Best Way to Help Your Child Cope with Loss

Some parents respond to these smart love guidelines by asking, "You mean I just give my child everything he wants?" The answer is, "No, not everything." He can't always have the *things* he wants, but he can always have a positive, loving response from you. You can give him your approval instead of disapproval, thereby demonstrating that the relationship is the most important thing of all. Your child can count on your understanding and support even when he has to return the other child's shovel.

To parents who worry, "My child has to learn to live in the real world—he is not always going to have us to rearrange things for him, and a few tears and frustrations are just part of life," we respond, "Your child will not be under the age of three for long, and when he is older he won't need the world rearranged because he will want to play and share with other children." When you rearrange your two-year-old's world to make his day go more smoothly, you are protecting him from the consequences of his immaturity, just as surely as when you keep him away from the street.

There is all the difference in the world between the kind of inevitable unhappiness that comes to all children (for example, the misery of a bad cold) and the unhappiness that parents cause through responding to their child with disapproval and disciplinary measures. At this young age, your child's belief in himself as a worthwhile, competent individual depends both on your loving availability and also on getting what he wants when he wants it. You will help your child most if you are able to remain understanding and affectionate when your child reacts unhappily to having his wishes go unfulfilled. As your child matures, his inner well-being will detach from his success at getting what he wants when he wants it, and he will respond to frustration with resilience. Finding ways to allow your toddler or preschooler to have his way whenever you can will make it possible for him to grow into a sharing, caring adult.

Teaching and Learning with Smart Love

When you make the process of teaching your child as unpressured and enjoyable as possible, you will help her to reach her full learning potential because she will approach the role of learner and student with openness and optimism. *Young children derive more enjoyment from learning and learn more effectively when you simply offer information and avoid confronting them with gaps in their knowledge.* You can offer information gently by using phrases like "Oh, you chose the red crayon." "Oh, you have two pretzels. Would you like one more so you can have three?" "Look, there is an H. That's the letter your name begins with."

Parents are always invested in their children's progress. Often they will test children in the process of teaching them ("What is this color?" "How many dogs are in this picture?" "What letter does your name begin with?"). Some parents regularly insist that children learn specific facts or concepts, and then they test the children to see if they are progressing. At times children will not want to answer or will not know the answer. They will feel that they have disappointed their parents, and may lose confidence in their ability to engage their parents' love. As a result of this inner uncertainty, these children are more likely to approach learning situations with difficulties that include a fear of failure, trouble asking for help, inhibitions that culminate in a lack of curiosity, or desperate and unregulated demands for attention.

Children who are not pressured to show what they have learned will freely demonstrate their new knowledge to parents who are willing to wait until it crops up in conversation ("No, Daddy, I want more grapes—give me four!" "I want the green marker; you can have the red one." "Don't go! That sign says 'STOP'"). If you can refrain from showing close friends and relatives how much your child knows, you will help your child to develop a sense of pride in her learning for its own sake.

Smart Loving the Toddler or Preschooler Who Suffers from Inner Unhappiness

As we have already explained, when children's emotional needs regularly go unmet, children react by believing that their unhappy or alienated feelings are intended and approved of by their parents. Out of love for their parents, and in an attempt to care for themselves exactly as their beloved parents have cared for them, these children unknowingly develop the desire to cause themselves exactly the same discomfort they believe their parents want for them.

Unhappy toddlers' or preschoolers' unperceived needs to make themselves miserable can make them very difficult to live with. These children may provoke the anger of siblings, peers, and adults; court danger; respond to every disappointment with a temper tantrum; or be excessively shy and inhibited. Moreover, they may react negatively when things go well. For example, they reject gifts they said they wanted, refuse to participate in activities they really enjoy, and throw tantrums over something small when their parents have done something very nice for them (such as take them to a movie they have really wanted to see).

How to Help the Toddler or Preschooler Who Reacts Aversively to Pleasure

Parents understandably feel very irritated and frustrated when they make a huge effort to make their child happy and the child reacts by finding a reason to feel put out or otherwise unhappy. But when parents recognize that their child has acquired inner unhappiness and thus will react negatively to the pleasure of getting what he wants, they will be less likely to become angry or punitive, and they will be more willing to respond with growth-promoting affection and understanding.

On the other hand, parents who don't understand why their child becomes grouchy or complaining immediately after they have given him what he wished for often become angry at their child's "ingratitude." They may conclude that their child is "spoiled" and needs to experience a little deprivation in order to appreciate the efforts his parents make on his behalf. Anger and deprivation strengthen a child's conviction that his parents want him to feel miserable, and increase his need to cause himself unhappiness. Because these responses do not assure the child of his parents' loving support, they do not help him learn to manage his aversive reactions to having his wishes come true.

A CHILD KICKS HIS DOG

Two-and-a-half-year-old Mike, who had acquired inner unhappiness, woke to a chorus of "Happy Birthday" from his parents and to a new fire truck with sirens and ladders that went up and down. He was thrilled. A moment later, when the family dog came over to investigate the wrapping paper, the boy gave the pet a kick in the ribs.

Mike's parents had been working with us to help curb Mike's need to react negatively to positive experiences. They told Mike firmly that he needed to treat the dog well, and they insisted that he give the dog a pat and an apology. They did not become outraged, punish their son, or make any statements expressing regret that they had given him such a nice gift. Mike, who really loved the dog, told the dog he was "very sorry" and gave him a big hug. Then he asked his parents to join him in playing with the new fire truck. His parents readily agreed, and the rest of the morning was peaceful and happy.

If his parents had expressed outrage, sent him to his room, or taken the new toy away, Mike's needs to make himself unhappy would have been gratified and strengthened, and the cycle would have simply repeated itself. By using loving regulation and avoiding disapproval and disciplinary measures in response to Mike's mistreatment of the dog, these parents avoided fueling Mike's need to make himself unhappy in reaction to experiencing the pleasure of getting a new truck. They gave Mike the space to perceive that giving in to the desire to make his dog and himself unhappy was not nearly as enjoyable as preserving the affection he felt for his pet. Over time, with his parents' understanding responses, Mike's aversive reactions to pleasure decreased in severity.

∿

When parents realize that the child with inner unhappiness will react negatively when things go well, they will be able to make sense of behavior that otherwise appears incomprehensible. Although the child certainly can kick, bite, or throw things out of frustration, he may also become out of control in reaction to a positive experience that has happened seconds earlier. Parents can guide their child to make the connection between his negative response and the positive experience. In the example just discussed, the parents might have said, "Maybe you kicked your puppy because you felt uncomfortable getting something you liked so much."

How to Talk to Your Toddler or Preschooler About His Feelings

If you are not familiar with the experience of talking to your child about the causes and effects of his feelings, you may initially feel uneasy helping him to understand that he may have the need to make himself unhappy. We have had considerable experience talking with children who have developed inner unhappiness and helping their parents to communicate with them. Based on our experience, if adults take a friendly, positive, and nonjudgmental approach to helping their children explore their conflicting feelings, children will feel cared for, understood, and relieved. Our approach to helping children understand their feelings is entirely different from "psychoanalysis" because we never tell children things about themselves that would be alien to children and, therefore, alienate them (for example, we would not tell them that they have motives to hurt a parent or a sibling). Instead we help children make positive sense of behavior and feelings that are already upsetting them. We teach parents smart love responses that further the closeness of the parent-child relationship and provide children with the tools they need to engage in a healthy type of introspection that will enhance their abilities to lead happy and fulfilled lives.

How to Help Children Who Have Temper Tantrums

Temper tantrums are popularly considered an inevitable part of childhood, but children who are certain that their parents understand them and want to make them happy find the isolated fury and misery of temper tantrums unappealing. Tantrums interfere with the superior pleasure children can provide for themselves by engaging their parents' concerned and sympathetic ear when the children feel angry or unhappy. It is possible for children to grow up without having a single temper tantrum. Certainly all children get cranky and willful at times. All children will cry and become angry when they really want something they cannot have. But not all children will fling themselves to the floor howling and shrieking, hold their breath, break things, or hurt others.

Temper tantrums are acts of desperation. They are not calculated efforts at manipulation. *If your child is having temper tantrums, try to make yourself more available, not less available.* Unfortunately, parents are usually given the opposite advice; namely, they are told to ignore the child while the tantrum is in progress, and, often, to physically isolate the child or themselves as well. Parents are often counseled to tell a child, "I can't hear you when you scream like that," or "I am going in the other room until you can talk instead of screaming," or "If you're going to scream and carry on like that when I won't give you more candy, you can't have candy at all."

It is a popular misconception that young children have temper tantrums because they lack the language skills to express themselves. The issue isn't your child's communication skills; children who are convinced that they can engage their parents' love and understanding will not have tantrums even when they haven't developed effective language skills. When they are frustrated and upset, they will cry and protest, but eventually they will accept a hug or try again to communicate their wishes. But if children go ballistic when their parents cannot understand them, somehow these children have come to experience that breakdown in communication as traumatic, rather than as a difficulty that could be lived with or overcome.

Since children have tantrums only because they feel their parents are angry, unresponsive, or otherwise unavailable, when your child's frustration boils over, try to react positively and emphasize your availability. Above all, try not to distance yourself from your shrieking child. You might say something like, "I am sorry you are so upset. I'm right here, and I want to help you in any way I can. Why don't we sit here until you feel better." Offer a hug. If the hug is rejected, you can try to present a constructive alternative to whatever unfulfilled wish brought on the tantrum ("You can't have more candy today, but would you like to help me make popcorn?"). Even when your child throws things or becomes destructive and you must restrain him, you can do your best to hold him gently, in a positive and loving manner, while you tell him that you cannot allow him to hurt himself or anyone or anything else, and that you will let go when he calms down.

The advantage of responding to your child's tantrums or other upsets with loving regulation can be illustrated by an analogy from adulthood. Imagine yourself dissolved in tears in reaction to a terrible and devastating loss. Your spouse or best friend reacts by saying, "I am going into the next room and read my book until you stop crying. You can join me when you regain control of yourself." Next, imagine your loved one saying, "I am so sorry you are unhappy. Let me give you a hug and help you feel better." Which response would you prefer? Your child would make the same choice if the choice were available to him.

Portable Comforts

Portable comforts, such as a pacifier or a favorite blanket, are frequently helpful to young children and are usually not a cause for concern. By the time your child is six months or older if he doesn't become upset if his blanket or pacifier remains at home when he goes on outings, it is preferable to leave the child free to explore the world with both hands.

Children who have developed inner unhappiness may find portable comforts indispensable. When blanket-clutching or pacifier-sucking interfere with the child's activities, parents are often tempted to confiscate the offending items. It is better not to withhold portable comforts from a child who becomes really upset at their absence, because the child will conclude that the unhappiness he feels is not only caused by you but desired by you as well. Because your child wants to treat himself exactly as you treat him, your taking portable comforts away from him when he really needs them could increase his needs to make himself unhappy. On the other hand, when you show your child that you recognize that for the time being he needs this kind of comforting, your child will feel cared about and understood. These positive feelings will, in turn, decrease his need to depend on portable comforts.

A child's thumb is certainly the most portable comfort of all, and one the child feels rightly possessive of and proprietary about. Unhappy children may use constant thumb-sucking to provide them with an inner equilibrium they don't feel they can get any other way. Thumb-sucking can misalign a child's teeth. If a child is over three and not too terribly attached to thumb-sucking as a source of well-being, explanations from the dentist about the effects of thumb-sucking on teeth can sometimes be persuasive and are worth a try. But if the child seems unable to give up thumb-sucking after hearing how it is affecting his bite, it is better not to attempt to force him to stop.

Children's teeth will usually readjust once the thumb-sucking ends. What are more difficult to repair are the effects on your child's emotional well-being of punishing, ridiculing, using negative conditioning by painting his thumb with a distasteful substance, or even using rewards in an attempt (usually fruitless) to stop him from thumb-sucking.

From the thumb-sucking child's point of view, the thumb is an important and indispensable source of well-being and equilibrium. As a result, the child is likely to feel perplexed, confused, and misunderstood when adults react negatively to his efforts to soothe himself. The child who is pressured to abandon thumb-sucking is likely to feel more in need of his thumb and to make the thumb-sucking process more elaborate. For instance, we know one little boy who used his other hand to hide the thumb, so that both hands were occupied by thumb-sucking. The child has no way to understand why the adults that he adores want him to give up something that gives him so much pleasure and security.

A THREE-YEAR-OLD IS TEASED FOR THUMB-SUCKING

A three-year-old named Stan who had acquired inner unhappiness sucked his thumb for a good part of the day. Other children and adults upset him greatly when they teased him and called him a "baby." Uncertain what to do, his parents consulted us.

We suggested that the parents identify areas of stress, tension, and discomfort in Stan's daily experience and consider how these could be reduced or eliminated. We also pointed out that it was important to try to increase periods in which their son could feel a nonpressured type of enjoyment. On reflection, the parents realized that Stan spent the most time sucking his thumb when they were paying attention to his baby brother. They tried to think of ways to play with Stan when they were caring for the baby (like singing songs during diaper changes). They also put out some special markers and colored paper for him to use during moments when they were unable to pay attention to him. Most important, the parents tried to make Stan's daily experiences as positive as possible. Predictably, over the next few months, Stan's thumb-sucking began to decrease.

When Children Have Recurring Nightmares

Children who have acquired inner unhappiness may experience recurring nightmares in which they unknowingly seek to re-create the discomfort they experienced when they were not responded to, when they felt intruded upon, when they were not helped to regulate their out-of-control behavior, or when they were subjected to disciplinary measures. These children can be the authors of very frightening dreams. Happily, parents can use smart love guidelines to eliminate children's need for nightmares.

THE MONSTER UNDER THE BED

The parents of three-year-old Nate had great difficulty controlling their anger at their son when he embarrassed them by having temper tantrums in public spaces. Frequently they would jerk him off the floor and give him a slap on the bottom. In response to his parents' harsh treatment, not only did Nate's tantrums increase in frequency, but he began waking his parents up in the middle of every night screaming in fear at a recurrent nightmare. Crying hysterically, he would report that there was a monster under his bed who was angry at him and who waited for him to fall asleep so that he could begin eating him. He said that the monster started by biting off his toes, worked his way up his body, and was about to chomp off his head and swallow him completely when he finally woke up. Nate's parents consulted us because they wanted to know how to stop the nightmares so they could get a decent night's rest.

We explained that Nate's nightmares were his sleeping mind's way of expressing the same unperceived needs for unhappiness that Nate's waking mind expressed through the temper tantrums. The parents' anger and spankings were the model for Nate's scary and painful relationship with the monster at night.

Eventually Nate's parents came to see that his temper tantrums were acts of desperation, not deliberate attempts to embarrass them. As a result they gained better control of their anger, and they began to think of positive ways to help Nate maintain his equilibrium. For example, they rearranged their son's day so as to give him increased possibilities for choice and fewer opportunities to get in trouble. When Nate did have a tantrum, they learned to overcome their shame, pick him up, and carry him to a private spot where they could sit with him until he recovered.

Over the next month, Nate's parents discovered with pleasure and relief that their son grew happier and more resilient, that the temper tantrums abated, and that family outings were becoming more enjoyable. The commitment and caring Nate experienced from his parents stimulated more positive feelings toward himself, and he no longer had the need to make himself so miserable in his sleep. The monster under the bed disappeared, never to return.

When toddlers and preschoolers turn three and are certain that they have the ability to elicit their parents' caring and commitment, they will be well prepared for the new opportunities and challenges that await them. Getting what they want when they want it will still be an important source of secondary happiness, but their stable primary happiness will make them increasingly willing to wait or to share. The toddler or preschooler who has unknowingly developed needs for inner unhappiness but whose parents have used smart love guidelines to strengthen his desires for constructive pleasure will face a widening world of school and friendships with renewed optimism and self-confidence.

Chapter Six

$\sim$

Ages Three to Six: Smart Loving Your Young Child

In the years from three to six, children continue on their course toward sustained inner happiness and broad competence as they start school, make friends, hone important skills, and make earthshaking discoveries about their place in the family constellation. The focus of your relationship with your child changes from helping her establish enduring primary happiness to setting her on the road to achieving an unshakable secondary happiness in the world of everyday successes and failures.

Starting School

One of the biggest events for this age group is starting school. Currently, there is a wide variation in the age at which children begin school, and this latitude presents different challenges to parents. If your child remains at home until she starts kindergarten, the challenge is to find ways to provide her with sufficient intellectual stimulation. And if there are younger siblings at home, there is the problem of keeping children of differing capabilities and interests occupied and happy. On the other hand, if your child starts school at two or three years of age, she will be vulnerable to problems with separating from you and socializing with others.

Your child is ready for preschool if she is comfortable separating from you for short periods of time (she is happy to go to a friend's house to play, she likes to go with her aunt to the playground); if she generally enjoys the company of other children; if she has chosen to use the toilet; if she can sit quietly and work on a project for twenty minutes at a time; and if she is usually willing to follow directions. If your child would chafe at any of these preconditions, there is every reason to wait a year until she is really ready. *When* your child starts school is much less important than *how* she feels when she is there. Because this will be your child's first introduction to school, try to do everything you can to ensure that she will enjoy it.

Regardless of the age at which your child begins school, it is a crucial moment in her development, and the experience initially can be stressful for both you and her. Children may bring home surprising language learned from schoolmates, may have their feelings hurt by the rough-and-tumble nature of peer relations, and may resist school rules and regulations.

Selecting a Preschool

The first thing to consider before choosing a preschool is the nature of the benefit you want your child to reap from attending school. The true object of preschool is not to teach your child specific facts (letters, numbers) but to teach her to like school and to feel happy and competent there. If this goal is met, your child will enter grammar school with optimism and self-confidence. On the other hand, if your child emerges from preschool disliking school and feeling uncertain about her abilities, she may have trouble with academic tasks later regardless of how much knowledge she brings to them.

Try to find a school whose teachers believe their mission is to introduce your child to school in a positive, nonpressured manner; who don't think three- and four-year-olds should have the manners and social graces of adults; who don't use disciplinary methods, such as time-outs, to regulate children's wayward behavior; who are willing to let you stay with your child until she feels comfortable separating; and who generally take a positive and developmental view of children's behaviors and motives.

How to Help Your Child Separate

Because separation from you is a central part of your child's introduction to school, this process needs to be handled with extreme delicacy and sensitivity. Some teachers will encourage parents to remain with their child until she feels comfortable letting them go, but other teachers continue to tell parents some version of "Just leave. She's carrying on because you're here. When you go, she'll stop crying right away." When parents come to pick up their child, they may well be told that the child stopped crying almost immediately and was "fine" for the rest of the morning. The flaw in this reasoning is that the child's behavior, rather than her feelings, is being used to measure success at separating. Since the goal is not to force your child into accepting separation but to help her develop a positive attitude toward school, leaving her before she feels ready to separate is counterproductive.

What matters is that your child have a positive inner nourishment to sustain her while she is at school. If your child is anxious about starting school but is forced to separate from you, she may well respond by turning to maladaptive forms of soothing, such as depression, disruptive behavior, hanging on to a blanket, or withdrawing. If you grant your child's request that you remain with her at school for a few hours or days, your child may be better able to soothe her anxiety by relying on your presence and the positive intimacy it brings. In addition, just the knowledge that you will not leave her before she feels ready will do wonders for your child's self-confidence. By the time she is willing to let you go, she will have created positive bridges into her new environment, such as budding friendships, interesting activities, and nurturing relationships with her teachers.

The smart love guideline is *parents should remain at school as long as their child feels she needs them to be there.* Parents sometimes ask, "But what if my child wants me to stay for a week or more?" Given that most children will have fifteen years of school before graduating from high school, a week or two is a small investment in getting a child off to a good start. If the school is resistant to your wishes to stay, it is important not to be intimidated. You are within your rights as a parent to insist, saying something along the lines of "All children are individuals. Some children may be willing to let their parents go immediately, but mine will make a better transition if I stay as long as she needs me." If the school still demands that you leave, we would recommend that you consider changing schools. Increasingly, educators are aware that parents should remain at school as long as their child needs them.

How to Help Your Child Adjust to School Rules

Once in school, your child's customary freedom of choice is suddenly reined in by demands that she walk in a line, wait to talk, take turns playing with the most desirable toys, forgo eating her snack until everyone else is served, and ask permission to use the bathroom. Because your preschooler views much of the world through the unrealistic lens of her all-powerful self, she may well experience the multitude of school rules and regulations as oppressive and, more significantly, as applying to other children but not to her.

If your child resists classroom socializing, this does not mean that you should have been tougher on her; this reaction serves to emphasize the importance of her years of relative freedom. If you have consistently encouraged and facilitated your child's wish to make choices for herself, she actually will adapt more easily to the school's imposition of structure, because she will not enter school with a broken spirit or locked in a chronic battle with authority. Your child will soon realize that a few irritating rules and regulations are a small price to pay for the opportunities to engage in the exciting activities and satisfying social relationships that school can offer.

You can facilitate your child's transition to school in a number of ways:

- You can say something like "I know it's difficult not being able to eat anytime you want, the way you can at home, but, on the other hand, at school the paints are always out, and there are a water table and three hamsters!"
- When your child chafes at school rules, you can help by giving her as much latitude as possible after school. This is not the time to schedule ballet lessons or other structured activities.
- If your child is especially tired, grouchy, or fragile in the first weeks of school, try to remember that your child is experiencing emotional overload, and you may find it easier to be affectionate and understanding.

When School Talk Comes Home

You may be shocked when the child you have sheltered and protected brings home expressions she has heard from her classmates. Maybe you tell your child it is bedtime, and she responds with a scathing "I hate you, and I won't be your friend ever!" Or, perhaps you are a little slow managing the buttons on your child's shirt, and she comments scornfully, "You're really stupid." This is a challenging moment for even the most dedicated parent. It will help to remember that your child is unaware that you find her language outrageous. She is merely imitating people she admires—her new friends. Imitating you has been an indispensable tool in her successful development, and this process of imitation carries over to school and enhances her sense of belonging.

You can help your child distinguish between school and home by saying something along the lines of "I know this is how your friends talk at school, and they may be used to those words and not take them seriously, but people outside of school get their feelings hurt by that kind of language." We also suggest that you make clear to your child that she has greater freedom to express herself with you than with other adults.

When you grasp the benign cause of your child's rude speech, you will be better able to respond reflectively. Anger, disapproval, and sanctions will only confuse and alienate your child, who knows that this kind of language is regular currency among her friends.

When Schoolmates Hurt Your Child's Feelings

Unless your child has already encountered rebuffs from older siblings or neighbors, in the beginning she may return from school with her feelings bruised by the rough-and-tumble of peer relations. The child who knows that you love her and love being with her may be amazed and upset when other children exclude her or become angry with her. Because the child's all-powerful self believes it has the power to control other people, a child of this age feels especially wounded by a friend's refusal to play. You will feel for your child when she says plaintively, "Jenny didn't want to play with me today. She said she will never play with me again." Yet these moments provide golden opportunities to help your child to draw on the reservoir of love and trust she has accumulated with you to supply herself with secondary happiness in the face of the disappointments that result from others' conflicting motives.

You can sometimes help your child by emphasizing the difference between her relationship with you and her friendships. You might say, "It may feel confusing and hurtful because we always like to play with you and here's someone saying she doesn't want to. But sometimes other children don't do what you want. When that happens, it's better to try to find a friend who feels like playing. I am sure that there is someone in your class who would be delighted to play with you. I remember you said you had fun with Samantha." Over time, with your help and caring, your child will come to derive greater secondary happiness from the fun of playing than from the illusion that she can convince each and every child to play with her at all times.

Occasionally children will report that classmates have made cruel remarks to them. We know one little boy who reported to his mother that there was a girl he liked at school, and he had told her he wanted to marry her. She replied, "I can never marry you, your skin is too dark." Parents should acknowledge that the cutting remark must have really hurt. They can also emphasize that the other child was mistaken, saying, for example, "I know what she said hurt your feelings. But what she said is wrong; no skin color is better than any other, and people can marry whomever they please." *Parents' opinions are more important than peers' judgments at this age. If you emphatically disagree with the other child's put-down, your child will listen.*

It is sometimes difficult to know whether to take action outside the family when your child has been insulted. In general, most insults, such as comments about your child's clothes, weight, or glasses, are best dealt with at home. But if there is a pattern of racial, religious, or ethnic slurs, or your child is being teased because she has a significant disability, you might suggest to the teacher that a classroom discussion of differences in skin color or religious and cultural practices, or of the feelings of people with disabilities, might be in order.

"George Hit Me!"

Another delicate moment in your child's initiation into the school culture occurs when she tells you, "George hit me today!" Try to discover what happened and ask your child how she responded without imposing your own value judgments. Your child may have chosen one of a variety of legitimate responses (for example, telling the teacher, pushing the other child away, moving to a different activity). If your child successfully handles the aggression, and if you are certain she didn't provoke it, you have the opportunity to emphasize that if George is feeling grouchy these days, there are probably other children who would be fun to play with until George feels better. You need to be concerned only if your child takes no steps to stop the abuse or seems to incite more of it.

Obviously, we are not referring to situations in which other children put your child in real danger. For instance, your child says, "Bobby brought a knife to school and said he would cut me with it." These situations demand your immediate intervention. The responsibility for handling them remains with you (for example, calling the principal) and cannot be left to your child, who needs to feel you will do everything necessary to ensure her safety.

School Reports

Most teachers are well trained, well intentioned, and dedicated, and they can be very informative about all aspects of your child's experience at school. Your child's teacher can provide you with valuable information about your child. For example, the teacher may have noticed that your child becomes emotionally fragile toward the middle of the morning. This information may alert you to the fact that your child, who has been used to nibbling whenever she feels hungry, may not be eating enough breakfast to sustain her until snack time.

It is also important to keep in mind that even the most competent teacher has many children to care for and may misunderstand your child. If the teacher describes behavior that you have never observed in your child, or discusses your child in very negative terms, evaluate the teacher's conclusions carefully before you accept them.

How your child's teacher describes challenges your child is experiencing at school will tell you a lot about whether that teacher will offer your child constructive help. Consider these statements made by two different teachers:

- "Donald insists on running in class, and we can't allow that. If every child ran around when the class is supposed to be seated, we would have chaos."

- "It is obviously hard for Donald to get used to sitting for more than a few minutes. We are working hard to find an activity that will really engage him."

The first teacher is focused on the need for class order and Donald's disruptive effect on the other students. The second teacher is trying to understand Donald in order to help him feel more comfortable in school. Clearly, Donald will be happier and more successful in the second teacher's class.

If Your Child Is Unhappy at Preschool

Most children have days when they don't feel like going to school, but if your child regularly complains about going, feels sick before school but not after school, continues to have great difficulty separating from you, or begins to have regular nightmares or trouble sleeping, you need to give serious thought to whether she is with the right teacher, is in the right school, or should be in school at all.

The first thing to do is to spend a day or two observing your child's class. If the teacher seems harsh or has taken a dislike to your child, see if it is possible to change teachers. Check to see if there is another teacher who takes a more positive approach to regulating her students, and try to switch your child to his or her classroom. But if your child's teacher seems warm and positive toward her, yet your child shows the signs of unhappiness we have described, maybe she isn't ready for school and would benefit by waiting another year. Be sure to take the responsibility for this decision on yourself, and do not burden your child with it. You could tell her, "We made a mistake in starting you in school this year. We think by next year, you will like it much better. It's good you were able to let us know you aren't ready yet." While you may have to scramble to find alternative child care, your efforts will be well spent if you can spare your child from concluding that school is a place that makes her feel miserable.

What to Do When Your Child Bends the Truth

All children between the ages of three and six bend the truth a little now and then. When this occurs, many parents feel that their child is not being moral, and they react with disapproval, lectures, or punishments.

At this age, children's secondary happiness can still be shaken if they don't get what they want. So children may distort reality in an effort to ward off an unwanted turn of events or as a way of feeling in control of themselves and the world. In either case, if you adopt the smart love perspective that making up stories is normal behavior that will be outgrown if you respond appropriately, you will not feel obliged to react with sanctions, disapproval, or argument. Instead you can relax and help your child understand his wish to rewrite reality.

"I FLEW UP TO THE TOP OF THE TREE"

A four-year-old we know was being read a story in which a ball became lodged in a tree and no one could get it. The child thought for a moment and announced, "I flew up to the top of the tree and got the ball."

In response, parents who think their child might develop a permanent propensity to lie will be likely to say something like, "You know you can't fly," or "You mustn't make up stories. Look what happened to Pinocchio." A more positive response comes from understanding that bending the truth is appropriate to the child's age. You might say something like, "You really would like to help solve that problem."

∾

"I BLEW UP THE SCHOOL"

One five-year-old announced to his parents, who were about to leave for a parent-teacher conference, "You can't go because I blew up the school." His parents, who were consulting us, were aware that there was no need to comment on the untruth of their child's statement. They perceived that their son, who loved school, was feeling disappointed at being left behind.

They responded, "You really don't like it that we get to go and you don't." The child nodded his head vigorously, asked them to be sure to say hello to his teacher, and said no more about having destroyed the school.

∾

"I ONLY TOOK TWO PIECES"

One evening parents we know told five-year-old Kevin that he could go into the kitchen and choose two pieces of candy for dessert. When his parents came into his room to say good-night, they saw five candy wrappers and asked what had happened. Kevin said, "I only took two pieces. The other wrappers were from yesterday." His parents, knowing that there had been no old wrappers lying around, said affectionately, "Maybe it was too difficult for you to stop at two pieces when the candy looked so yummy." Kevin smiled and said, "It was!" His parents remained positive and made no further comment, but silently they concluded that Kevin was not old enough to regulate his candy intake all by himself. The next time there was candy for dessert, they simply handed him two pieces.

If your child bends the truth with another adult, and that person then complains to you and expects you to discipline your child, you can explain that you consider lying to be behavior that your child will outgrow. If the other adult continues to demand that you reprimand your child, you will have to insist gently, but firmly, that you will continue to be guided by your view that your child's behavior is normal and appropriate for his age.

How to Choose Books, Movies, and TV Shows That Are Appropriate for Your Child's Age

It is unfortunate that many of the adults who write and review children's literature and motion pictures do not have a better understanding of children's developmental needs. They mistakenly believe that if books and shows that raise troubling issues and portray upsetting situations have happy endings, children will enjoy the dramatic tension as much as the reviewer does. Parents rarely get the guidance they need to choose books and movies that are truly appropriate for their children. Children under eight or nine years of age do not shake off the death of Bambi's mother or the Lion King's father just because Bambi and the Lion King are happy at the end of the story. Children are very confused when their parents take them to a movie or read them a book that upsets and frightens them. Children with stable inner happiness will not enjoy these experiences. Children who have developed an inner unhappiness may experience their parents as wanting them to feel frightened and upset and will have their needs for unpleasant experiences strengthened. You cannot rely on your child's wishes when it comes to choosing a book or a movie, any more than you can let your young child have all the candy she wants. Your child may well say she wants to see a scary movie because her best friend has seen it or because she has seen an enticing commercial on TV. The rule of thumb is, *to the extent possible, shield your young child from upsetting and scary experiences of all kinds.* When your child sees that you want to protect her from unnecessary unhappiness, her inner well-being will be enhanced, and she will actually be better prepared to confront real-life trauma later in life.

"I DIDN'T MIND THAT THE LION KING'S FATHER WAS KILLED"

A four-year-old we know named Seth went to a friend's house after school. The friend's mother put *The Lion King* in the VCR. When Seth got home, the first thing he said was, "Dad, I got to watch *The Lion King*." His father, who did his best to protect his son from books and movies that contained upsetting material, asked, "And how did you like it?" Seth replied, "I liked it OK." The father said, "What about the part where the Lion King's father is killed by his uncle?" "I didn't mind," replied Seth. His father responded gently, "I was wondering, because many children find that part pretty scary." Seth looked down at his shoes and said, "Well, I did, too." He paused. "Why would Lion King's uncle do that?" he asked. "Why was he so mean? He made Lion King feel so sad!" His father replied, "Sometimes people (and animals acting like people) do terrible things to each other, and we don't know exactly why." Seth nodded and hesitated. "Next time I go to Bert's house, can you tell Bert's Mom that I don't want to watch it?" he asked. His father said he would.

When Your Child Reacts Angrily to Frustration

Because his secondary happiness is to a large extent still tied to his success at getting what he wants, when the child between the ages of three and six feels frustrated, his reactions can be very explosive. He may try to kick or hit his parents, teachers, or other children who seem to stand between him and what he feels he must have. Although these outbursts can be very intense, they are fleeting, and therefore they are easily distinguished from the blind, sustained fury that characterizes temper tantrums.

THE BOY WHO COULDN'T WAIT TO PAINT

A four-year-old we know named Richard invited a friend to come and play, but Richard became upset when he felt the little girl was taking too long a turn at the easel. When his guest continued to paint and did not show signs of giving up her place, Richard shoved her out of the way. Richard's mother helped the little girl up and put her back at the easel. The mother then sat down with her son and explained that she knew it was hard to wait, but that pushing was not OK. She asked Richard if there was something else he would like to do while he was waiting for the easel; for example, would he like to cut out a mask and decorate it. This activity appealed to him, and he worked energetically until it was his turn at the easel. Using loving regulation this mother stopped her son's aggressive behavior while simultaneously offering him uninterrupted closeness and affection.

Unlike toddlers and preschoolers, four-year-olds can be enlisted to wait their turn because, by four, relationships are beginning to be more important than things. Nonetheless, episodic aggression born of frustration is normal at this age. When a young child loses patience, it is crucial to respond with loving regulation. Your warmth and love will shore up his inner well-being when it starts to crumble because he can't have what he wants. The result will be that having what he wants will seem less crucial. For this reason, *the way to provide your child with the moral education that will help him become an adult who can tolerate frustration and consistently respect the rights of others is never to isolate the child or withhold your love and affection.*

How to Motivate Your Young Child to Help Out

Because your toddler or preschooler adores you, she loves to help you. At the same time, because her all-powerful self is still dominant, she generally resists being told either what to do or how to do it. Therefore, if you want your toddler or preschooler to begin to do chores, make the work fun and cooperative, and do not expect her to take responsibility for doing jobs by herself. Try to choose jobs that involve water, mixing, pets, or pounding, or tools that are small versions of grownups' tools, such as small brooms or pails. Your child would probably be delighted to use her pounding hammer to pound on a piece of meat that needs tenderizing, and she would love to help bathe the dog or wash the car.

Your goal is to teach your child that helping out can be fun and rewarding, not to get her to do any particular chore. Therefore, if she dislikes making her bed or can't concentrate on putting her books back in the bookshelf, do those jobs for her and find something else she will be happy to work at. Try to avoid using rewards to get your child to do a job she would otherwise resist, because you may soon find that the child also expects rewards for jobs she previously enjoyed.

When children resist chores, sometimes parents feel driven to make remarks such as "Life cannot always be fun," "Everyone has to do things they don't like," or "This is nothing compared to what I had to do at your age." But the child who is lectured at and forced to comply does not absorb moral precepts; she simply feels her parents are making arbitrary demands and involving her in a power struggle she doesn't want to lose. When a child is treated this way she may react to her parents' domination by developing a general dislike of authority or by adopting rigid compliance (becoming overly neat), but she won't learn to enjoy cooperating and accomplishing shared goals.

Developmental Milestone: The Romantic Child

Beginning around two-and-a-half years of age, children gradually become aware of the gender difference between mothers and fathers. From ages three to six, children are in what we call the romantic phase.

THE BEAR FAMILY

We know a child who had two identical bears, which he treated interchangeably until he approached his third birthday. At that point, he began to call them Mommy Bear and Daddy Bear, confidently and consistently distinguished them by mysterious characteristics, and related to each one quite differently.

ᖰᕽ

The notion that children go through a developmental phase characterized by the child's discovery of and attempt to control the romantic desires of the opposite-sex parent may be new to some parents. But it is crucial that parents understand the dynamics of this phase.

The **romantic phase** is about children's diffuse wishes to have the opposite-sex parent prefer them as romantic companions and about children's reactive fears that the same-sex parent will be angry with them for wanting to take the same-sex parent's place. These wishes are central at this age, and they explain a lot of puzzling behavior, such as ongoing, intense competitiveness; moodiness; extreme sensitivity to "slights"; and assertions of superhuman powers and perfect knowledge. Parents who aren't expecting the romantic phase will find much of their three- to six-year-old's behavior incomprehensible or, worse, blameworthy. While the existence of the child's romantic competitiveness has been recognized, we offer a new and different understanding of the nature and significance of this developmental milestone and offer new guidelines for helping the child surmount the phase successfully.

The Child Becomes Aware of Her Parents' Romantic Relationship

Between the ages of three and six, children become hyperaware of the personal aspects of their parents' lives. In particular, they begin to recognize their parents' friendship and romantic attentions toward each other. Children see no reason why they shouldn't be included in what they have newly discovered to be a source of enjoyment for their parents. At this point children focus in particular on the opposite-sex parent as a source of social as well as care-getting gratification. Children begin to want to control the opposite-sex parent's personal motives just as they have always been able to cause the opposite-sex parent to give them focused caregiving ("Mommy," says the little boy, "I'll be the daddy, and we'll go out to dinner together").

When children are pursuing the opposite-sex parent as a companion, their own sense of competence is enhanced. Children in this stage will often offer to care for the opposite-sex parent in imitation of what they observe the same-sex parent to do. One little boy began to hold the door for his mother. A little girl whose father had foot surgery vied with her mother for the privilege of helping him on with his orthopedic shoe.

Children at this age seek to spend time with the opposite-sex parent as a companion as well as a caregiver. The opposite-sex parent is usually very pleased about the child's attentions. One mother found that she could always count on her son to accompany her with enthusiasm on the most tedious errands.

Of course children at this age are not pursuing an adult relationship with the opposite-sex parent; they are imitating the relationship they perceive their parents to have. Children have a very nonspecific idea of their parents' romantic relationship, a diffuse notion that includes elements of romantic possessiveness, affection, and exclusivity. Tragically, sex offenders grossly misinterpret children's behavior as being romantic in an adult sense, and the abusers will sometimes try to argue that their child victims seduced them.

The Child's Point of View: I'm the Best at Everything

The child in the romantic phase wishes to be recognized by the opposite-sex parent as a more appealing companion than the same-sex parent. When one father complimented his wife on her attire, their three-year-old stepped between her parents, twirled vigorously, and exclaimed eagerly, "But look at *my* dress! It has stripes!"

During this phase, romantic competitiveness may influence any aspect of the child's experience. A child who, for instance, shows intense, seemingly irrational needs to be admired for his ability to draw may be expressing his wishes to receive the kind of admiration he sees the same-sex parent receive from the opposite-sex parent. A child's conviction that he is a viable competitor for the opposite-sex parent's romantic attentions is supported by the fact that his all-powerful self has a completely unrealistic body image. This more than counterbalances the undeniable differences in physical size and power between children and same-sex parents. Children between three and six years of age routinely announce that they are stronger, faster, taller, more dexterous, more knowledgeable, and more capable than their parents. *Since the romantic child's overvaluation of his capabilities is both temporary and also appropriate for his age, confronting him with the fallacy in his thinking will only hurt his feelings. It will not advance his development.*

Young children show that they feel all-powerful in many ways. For example, you are watching a football game on television with your four-year-old when he announces, "I can throw the ball farther than the quarterback, and I can push that other team out of the way with one hand." Since your four-year-old will outgrow his unrealistic body image on his own, you need say no more than an accepting "Oh!" Attempts to puncture the boy's illusion by laughing, teasing, explaining, disagreeing, or criticizing him will only make him defensively cling to his belief in his prowess and will retard, not hasten, the process by which he develops a more realistic self-image.

Romantic Competition

Children's all-powerful selves, the source of the type of secondary happiness that is based on the illusion that children can have and do anything, experience a crucial disappointment in this period. This loss is developmentally significant, because it causes children to question their inborn belief in the mightiness of their all-powerful selves and, in turn, to begin to understand that secondary happiness does not have to rest on getting what they want. This loss occurs when children realize that a mutual, special admiration exists between their parents, and that they themselves are not the center of the universe with regard to their parents' wishes for personal pleasure, even though as children they are the center of their parents' universe with regard to caregiving attention.

At first, when children learn that they cannot control the manner in which their parents gratify their personal desires, they react by renewing their efforts to attract the attentions of the opposite-sex parent and to interfere with their parents' relationship. Every time one mother and father became involved in a discussion with each other, their child would announce that they had to be quiet because they were bothering her dolls. Another child reacted to his parents' animated conversation by announcing loudly that they were "talking nonsense and boring everyone in the whole wide world."

During this phase, children demonstrate a need for increased attention, and when they see their parents are working or playing together, children may manifest seemingly irrational bouts of crying, anger, whining, or general unhappiness. You will find it easier to be more accepting of your child's bossiness and irritability when you identify this behavior as appropriate to his age and not as a sign that your child has taken an antisocial turn and needs decisive correction. Your child is experiencing intense feelings, and he needs help with his dawning awareness that the mutual involvement his parents have with each other can enhance rather than diminish the pleasure available to him in the parent-child relationship. For instance, if your son refuses to go out bike-riding unless his father stays home, you could say, "No, we're not going to leave Daddy home alone, but you will have both of us to go bike-riding with you." In this way, you can encourage your child to see that three can be a party rather than a crowd.

"ONLY MOMMY CAN READ TO ME!"

One four-year-old we know reacted to the romantic phase by telling his father that he didn't want him to read a good-night story anymore ("Only Mommy can read to me!"). His father accepted this rejection with good grace and said that he looked forward to a time when his son might want him to read again. At bedtime a month later, the boy announced enthusiastically, "I have a good idea. You can each read me a story, and I will sit in the middle." His parents agreed. The boy was well on his way to recognizing that he would have more fun including both his parents in parent-child activities. But he was not quite comfortable with the idea that his parents might like to sit next to each other.

Your Child's Point of View: Rivalry and Retaliation

During the romantic phase your child's belief that he has the power to regulate your personal desires gains credibility because he sees his spectacular success at eliciting your focused caring. Because you have been so attentive to his needs and also because in his earliest years your child's attention has been focused on your caregiving behavior, your child has rarely been aware of your personal desires. He enters the romantic phase unaware that he cannot control the nature and means by which you gratify these desires as well. One three-year-old could not understand why, when she could easily get her father to play checkers, she could not also convince him to take her instead of her mom to a party on Saturday night.

Children's all-powerful selves actually believe that they are viable competitors for the opposite-sex parent's romantic interest. Children resist the painful realization that the opposite-sex parent feels romantic love only for the same-sex parent. They jump to the conclusion that the opposite-sex parent's refusal to pay romantic attention to them must be owing to the interference of the same-sex parent. They come to feel angry with the same-sex parent, and the strength of children's rivalrous and angry feelings toward the same-sex parent leads them to believe that this parent means to retaliate against them. We call the fear engendered by this conviction **retaliation anxiety**. We prefer the phrase **retaliation anxiety** to the psychoanalytic term *castration anxiety* because it is important to emphasize that both girls and boys fear the same-sex parent, and also that children's fantasies about the nature of the harm that will befall them when the same-sex parent retaliates are more diffuse than the term *castration anxiety* implies.

There are many ways for the same-sex parent to reassure a child during this phase. Most important, the same-sex parent should try not to take the child's unprovoked anger and rejection personally. A parent who does not understand why a child is being so hostile may feel hurt and unappreciated. If the child rejects the parent's offer to play a game, the parent may lash out with a statement such as, "Well, that's fine with me. I certainly have a lot of other things to do besides play with you." Angry responses will intensify the child's retaliation anxiety, thereby retarding her ability to resolve this phase successfully.

Same-sex parents can help their children the most by showing them that they remain just as loving and available as they were before the children became periodically hostile and rejecting. A parent whose child has refused to play could say something like, "OK, I know you don't always feel like playing with me. I'll sit here and read the paper. If you change your mind, let me know and I would be delighted to play then." Same-sex parents can also help their children through this developmental phase by reassuring them when they become anxious and fearful after having had a pleasurable time with the opposite-sex parent.

A FATHER'S SMART LOVE REASSURES HIS SON

On returning from an enjoyable time playing catch with his mother, a four-year-old said to his father, "Why do you look so mean?" The father, who was familiar with the dynamics of the romantic phase, responded, "Maybe you are afraid I'm angry that you had so much fun with Mom, but I think it's great she's teaching you to play baseball. You know I love you, sweetheart!" Upon hearing this, the little boy gave his father an enthusiastic and very relieved hug.

The Romantic Phase Strengthens the Competent Self

In the romantic phase, the hollowness of the all-powerful self's claims to be able to control the world is exposed. Try as they might, children can neither take center stage as the focus of the opposite-sex parent's social and romantic attentions nor convince the same-sex parent to abandon romantic interest in the opposite-sex parent. At this point the competent self comes to the fore.

The esteem of the child's competent self is not based on the illusion that the child can get whatever his heart desires, so the child learns to accept and appreciate that the opposite-sex parent has refused to allow the child to regulate her personal choices. Retaliation anxiety eventually dissipates in the face of the same-sex parent's unfailing kindness. Over time, the child comes to realize that a relationship that includes respect for his parents' personal motives is far superior to his own attempts to coerce his parents to abandon their personal wishes.

Children Come to Accept Their Parents' Love for Each Other

As they mature, children recognize that the disappointment they experience in the romantic phase is not owing to their own short-comings but to the presence of motives parents have that do not include children, such as parents' love for each other. In this way, children learn the powerful and undeniable lesson that their all-powerful selves are unable to gratify each and every desire. It's important to understand that the process by which children come to acknowledge their true place in the family constellation never proceeds in a straightforward manner. Children who are beginning to realize that they are not going to succeed in interfering with their parents' romance can still be temporarily blinded by their all-powerful self's claims of superior power and attractiveness.

"MOMMY CAN BE THE CAT!"

One four-year-old we know was well on her way to accepting the inevitability of her parents' romantic relationship. One afternoon she spent the good part of an hour making two crowns and decorating them elaborately. She proudly gave a crown to each parent, saying enthusiastically, "Daddy is the king, Mommy is the queen, and I am the princess." When the girl's all-powerful self felt diminished by her acceptance of the child's role in the family, the girl responded by snatching the crown back from her mother, placing it on her own head, and announcing, "Actually, there's no queen in this story. Daddy is the king, I'm the princess, and Mommy can be the cat!"

In the process of becoming aware that he cannot regulate the romantic attentions of the opposite-sex parent, a child needs to feel positive about his future ability to participate in a satisfying romantic relationship. Although the opposite-sex parent must frustrate the child's belief that his wishes for the opposite-sex parent's romantic attention will be gratified, the opposite-sex parent has to be sensitive to the fact that the child needs to hear that he will someday be a desirable romantic partner to an appropriate peer. When a child asks the opposite-sex parent whether he can marry her when he grows up, it is important that the parent respond respectfully and seriously with statements like, "No, you won't be able to marry me when you grow up, because I am your Mommy and I will always be married to Daddy, but I know you will marry someone just as nice."

The Resolution of the Romantic Phase

The romantic phase is resolved when the child truly knows both that he is unable to control the romantic interest of the opposite-sex parent, and also that he is uncomfortable feeling alienated from the same-sex parent. By the end of the romantic phase, children whose emotional needs have been adequately satisfied deliberately choose the warmth of the parent-child relationship over the competitive romantic scenario that has been pursued by their all-powerful selves. They resolve the tensions they feel in the romantic phase by choosing the pleasure of feeling close to both parents.

Children become increasingly realistic about the true scope of their powers when they finally accept that although they can reliably cause their parents to respond to their developmental needs, they cannot govern how their parents gratify their personal aims. As this phase draws to a close, children gradually perceive both that they will never get the romantic attention of the opposite-sex parent, and also that they are still able to cause their parents to want to give them parenting attention—they can usually get their parents to read a book or go for a walk. A child at this stage has a wealth of experience that tells him that his greatest happiness will arise from endorsing his parents' decisions about his welfare. When he actively chooses to pursue the special closeness of the parent-child relationship over the less satisfying attempt to control his parents' personal lives, he gains a new sense of stability and security. This is a major developmental achievement.

Developmental Milestone: The Relationship Ideal

The child's growing appreciation of her parents' steadfast discrimination between their personal and parenting commitments leads her to make an identification we call the **relationship ideal.** An **identification** is simply an effort to be like those who are important to us. When children's developmental needs have been adequately satisfied, their identifications are always positive, because these children will choose to copy only aspects of others' behavior that promise to provide them with constructive pleasure.

The relationship ideal consists of ideals of intimacy and commitment in all types of relationships, including romantic love, friendship, and the parent-child relationship. Children's intense interest in their parents' personal lives, and especially in their romantic lives, stimulates them to identify with the way they see their parents relate to each other as well as with the way their parents treat them.

The child whose relationship ideal is shaped by her parents' abilities to regulate their own behavior effectively and with a healthy regard for their own needs grows up to possess a durable morality. This child's relationship ideal reflects her parents' abilities to offer genuine love and to nurture her even when she has made demands that could not be satisfied and then felt angry. She develops an abiding respect for the rights and needs of others as a result. This child's relationship ideal is the blueprint that allows her to mature into an adult who can acknowledge others' desires and respond appropriately. As she matures, she will lose interest in wishes for a competitive type of intimacy, and she will become permanently attracted to personal and caregiving relationships that are characterized by steady availability, involvement, and mutual respect.

Smart Loving the Three- to Six-Year-Old Who Suffers from Inner Unhappiness

Between the ages of three and six, nearly every child who suffers from inner unhappiness reacts dramatically to frustration. The young child whose developmental needs have been met has a secure primary happiness that provides him with a reservoir of optimism and goodwill, but the young child who has acquired inner unhappiness has an inner sense of well-being tied to external gratifications. When things do not go as he wishes, this child is thrown for a loop, with the result that he is likely to blow up or to sulk for long periods of time. In addition, this child has acquired needs for discord, which may lead him to create slights where none exist and then cling to his feelings of being victimized. Parents who recognize the special vulnerability that accompanies inner unhappiness can respond in ways that soothe rather than exacerbate the child's raw feelings.

"I GOT THE LEAST ICE CREAM!"

The parents of a five-and-a-half-year-old who had acquired an inner unhappiness were utterly perplexed by what they called their son's "excessive sensitivity." Arnold constantly felt slighted and believed that his sisters were always getting the better deal or the bigger share. One night, convinced that he had gotten the smallest portion of ice cream, Arnold rushed away from the table in tears and threw himself on his bed, where he cried miserably. His parents were at a loss to understand this "babyish" behavior and asked us for some advice.

We told them we believed that, deep inside himself, Arnold was always in danger of feeling utterly devastated. The parents had been told by others that he was spoiled, but they soon saw that the reason their son could not tolerate any sort of frustration was that his developmental needs had not been met sufficiently, rather than that his needs had been satisfied too easily. Arnold was not trying to manipulate his parents; he truly felt shattered when things did not go as he wished.

At first these parents felt sadness at having inadvertently caused their son's unhappiness, but they were also relieved to hear that they could help Arnold develop a greater resilience. They stopped responding to his hysterical outbursts with disapproval and sanctions, as others had advised them to do. Once they understood what was behind Arnold's reactions, they found it easier to respond with patience and kindness, and the boy increasingly turned to them for soothing. As he began to realize that he could always count on his parents' support, Arnold became less and less vulnerable to experiencing storms of emotion at times when things went wrong.

A few months after his parents began to implement smart love guidelines, Arnold once again concluded that his sisters had received larger portions of a favorite dessert. But this time he was able to stay at the table and complain to his parents that he felt deprived. His parents told him how pleased they were that he was communicating his upset feelings to them in words. They emphasized that there was enough dessert for him to have "seconds" if he wanted. The boy was reassured by their positive response, ate two servings, and continued to talk about the day he had had at school.

Parents can most effectively help the young child with inner unhappiness when they remember that this child maintains his inner equilibrium through a combination of constructive pleasure, destructive pleasure, and unhappiness. It is possible to significantly increase a child's well-being and level of functioning if you maximize the child's opportunities to experience constructive pleasure and minimize the child's opportunities to satisfy his needs for destructive pleasure or unhappiness.

AN OUT-OF-CONTROL FOUR-YEAR-OLD IS HELPED TO GO ON OUTINGS

The parents of an unhappy four-year-old were troubled and embarrassed by his wild behavior outside the house. Bringing him to stores and restaurants was always a nightmarish experience. Reggie spilled things, stood on chairs, and, in general, he was unable to sit still. Outings that were intended to be fun for him would soon degenerate into scenes of conflict and unhappiness. When his parents followed advice to respond to Reggie's problematic behavior by imposing time-outs and restricting his favorite activities, his behavior worsened and he seemed to become more alienated.

We explained to Reggie's parents that he needed their help to forgo his acquired appetite for discord. Because these parents were so concerned about spoiling their son, they had begun to demand a level of maturity that was not appropriate for a child Reggie's age. As a result, they were frequently disapproving of his behavior, and Reggie often experienced his relationship with them as a source of conflict and unhappiness. Like all young children, Reggie assumed that his parents were perfect caregivers, and when they were consistently critical of his behavior he unknowingly developed needs to elicit the disapproval and anger he misidentified as ideal parental love. Every time his parents became angry or imposed consequences intended to show him that he must learn to behave in the real world, they were actually fostering his learned needs to experience unpleasantness with them.

To help reverse this pattern, we worked with the parents to design outings that limited Reggie's need to cause conflict in order to make himself miserable. For example, they stopped taking their son to stores and restaurants; instead they brought him to outdoor playgrounds where the boy could run and climb to his heart's content. They would take a picnic lunch so that he could eat in any way he pleased. On cold days, they took him to children's museums, which were effectively childproof.

After Reggie's parents strengthened his wishes to experience constructive pleasure with them by arranging outings that were designed to be peaceful, enjoyable, positive experiences, his inborn desire for good relationships and positive experiences gradually became more appealing to him than his acquired need to cause himself unhappiness. At this point, Reggie's parents gradually introduced him to more structured situations, such as a half-hour gymnastics class that allowed him ample scope for running and jumping but that also imposed some rules and restrictions.

To their great relief and satisfaction, Reggie's parents discovered that his desires for constructive pleasure had strengthened enough for him to be able to accept some basic rules (taking turns, not jumping on the trampoline unattended) in order to have the fun of learning gymnastics. In another month Reggie's parents began taking him to restaurants that were popular with children and on short trips to stores. They found that as long as they remembered to bring one of Reggie's toys for him to play with, he was able to wait quietly for his food and to put up with brief bouts of shopping. Most important, his par-

ents were thrilled to see their son take steps that put him back on course toward a life of happiness and accomplishment.

Bedwetting, Shyness, Phobias, and Other Involuntary Symptoms

All expressions of inner unhappiness are involuntary in the sense that every child consciously wishes to feel happy and to create pleasurable experiences for himself. But some children develop symptoms of inner unhappiness that are involuntary in the sense that the child experiences the symptoms as alien and unwanted. This type of symptom of inner unhappiness can appear at any age, but it is especially likely to appear in children ages three to six. Examples are bedwetting, stuttering, nervous tics, excessive shyness, and phobias. Unfortunately, the most popular remedies commonly recommended to parents focus almost entirely on correcting the unwanted behavior without addressing the underlying cause. The smart love approach focuses on helping the unhappy child to feel happier, more competent, and more in control.

THE SMART LOVE APPROACH TO BEDWETTING

The parents of a six-year-old named Carl took him to the pediatrician because the child was wetting the bed, but the doctor could find no physiological reason for the problem. The doctor advised the parents to reward their son for each night that he kept his bed dry. When rewards proved ineffective, it was suggested that they withhold liquid from Carl after six in the evening even if he was thirsty, and also that they rig his bed to trigger an alarm when he wet the bed. When neither measure worked, the parents were given a specially designed apparatus that would deliver a mild electric shock when Carl urinated in bed.

Carl continued to wet his bed nightly, but he also became more withdrawn and less affectionate with his parents. In addition, his schoolwork, which had always been excellent, began to suffer. At their wits' end, the parents consulted us. We told them that we believed Carl's alienation and general feeling of helplessness were rooted in his belief that his parents were punishing him for behavior he couldn't control. Because he saw his parents as taking steps to make him more unhappy, his inner needs to make himself unhappy (for example, by doing poorly in school) were strengthened. His ability to base his inner well-being on constructive pleasure, such as doing well in school, was being significantly diminished.

We suggested that the parents' most important task was to show their son that they knew he could not help the bedwetting and also that their love and admiration for him was constant. If he continued to wet the bed, we recommended that they simply protect his mattress with a rubber cover and wash his sheets without comment.

When these parents realized that Carl's bedwetting was a symptom of inner unhappiness and not a manifestation of willfulness or hostility, their irritation was replaced by compassion. From that point on, when their son became upset because he wet the bed, they simply said, "We know you don't want to wet the bed. Someday you will be able to stay dry all night."

As Carl gradually noticed that his parents' positive feelings about him were unaffected by his bedwetting, he began to feel optimistic and confident even when he woke up to find he had wet his bed. In the course of the next year, the bedwetting gradually stopped.

Other common involuntary symptoms of inner unhappiness in children are excessive shyness and nervous tics. Parents of children who are suffering from involuntary symptoms should try to remove all pressure from their children. If the shy child hides behind you at the sight of friends, relatives, or strangers, protect him from feeling that he has to be conversational.

THE CHILD WHO REFUSED TO TALK IN ELEVATORS

A mother consulted us because she felt enormously upset with her three-year-old, Scott, for not being more "polite" to the people riding the elevator in their high-rise. The moment an adult tried to speak to him, Scott would bury himself in his mother's clothes. When his mother admonished him, "Don't you recognize Mrs. Adler? She's our neighbor, and she's trying to be nice. Can't you just say hello?" her son would try even harder to disappear.

When the mother understood that Scott was not trying to disappoint her and he was not choosing to be rude but was feeling utterly overwhelmed, she realized that she was adding to the problem by pressuring him. She started to take another tack. When he buried his head in her clothes, she would stroke his hair affectionately and say to the adult making the overture, "He's just feeling a bit shy today. Maybe he'll talk to you another day." She was surprised to find that when she deflected pressures for him to be sociable, Scott would often volunteer a "bye" to the other passengers as he left the elevator. Within a month he would say "hi" as well.

～

Eating Problems

The years between three and six are a time when eating problems are likely to appear in children who have developed inner unhappiness. The smart love approach is *neither to reward nor to punish the child who eats too much or too little*. Like all symptoms of inner unhappiness, eating problems are best solved with a relaxed approach to the problem and by a concerted effort to strengthen the child's desires for constructive pleasure.

SMART LOVE HELPS A YOUNG PROBLEM EATER

Six-year-old Ashley was a poor eater who was chronically underweight. To no avail her parents cajoled her and offered her special favors and treats for eating. They then consulted an expert on eating disorders, who cautioned them that Ashley was using her refusal to eat as a way of manipulating them. The consultant told the parents that they should ask their daughter what she wished to eat, and then put the food in front of her. After twenty minutes they should remove the food. If Ashley hadn't eaten enough, they should make her wait until the next mealtime to have more food. Her parents implemented these suggestions, with the result that they spent much of the day locked in battle with Ashley over whether she had had enough to eat. Meanwhile, the little girl ate less and less and grew thinner than ever.

Finally, Ashley's pediatrician referred her parents to us. We pointed out that their ongoing conflict with Ashley was actually strengthening Ashley's needs to make herself unhappy. The parents were relieved to hear that the daily food wars, which were making everyone miserable, were actually counterproductive. Our first step was to make it possible for Ashley to see that she could count on the stability of her parents' wishes to respond to her in a positive, loving, and growth-promoting manner.

A few days after they met with us, the family went to a local restaurant. Ashley ordered a chicken sandwich. After the order was well on its way to being ready, she announced, "I changed my mind: I want a piece of pizza." Her parents remembered that their new objective was to avoid conflict and to encourage Ashley's wish to eat whenever possible. They restrained their impulse to tell her that she had to eat what she had ordered, and instead they responded, "OK, we'll take the chicken sandwich home and someone will eat it later. You can have the pizza." Ashley's eyes widened with amazement, but she made no comment. When the pizza came, she ate most of it. Most important, her mood brightened, and she uncharacteristically held her mother's hand as they left the restaurant.

Understandably, her parents worried that their daughter would use their flexibility as a license to become impossibly demanding. They were happily surprised to find that over the next few months she rarely asked to change an order. The parents worked hard to create a positive and unpressured atmosphere in which Ashley could eat what she wanted. Their efforts paid off. Their daughter's eating improved, and she gained weight. Most important, she blossomed at school and was increasingly relaxed and affectionate at home. Her parents were thrilled when they began to experience an enjoyable, growth-promoting relationship with their daughter for the very first time.

～

Selecting a School for the Unhappy Child

Many parents respond that although they can tailor much of the day to meet the needs of their unhappy three- to six-year-old, they do not know how to select a school that will foster their child's desire for constructive sources of pleasure. The parents of children who chafe at restrictions are often advised to choose schools and teachers that will provide their children with "maximum structure." But this kind of advice is analogous to having someone who knows you hate Brussels sprouts tell you that, for that reason, they are sending you to a camp that serves only Brussels sprouts at every meal. You may eventually reach the point where you are so hungry you will eat them, but you will feel coerced and misunderstood.

Parents of the child who resists rules should try to select a school that provides the greatest possible choice and freedom of movement. Their child will thrive in a school that offers a wide variety of activities and imposes few limitations on how materials can be used (for example, the teacher is comfortable if the child uses the shape sorter as a mailbox). In addition, parents can try to make after-school time as relaxed and undemanding as possible. They might take their child somewhere he can roam and run, and they would delay signing up their child for rule-governed activities like ballet, piano lessons, or learning a foreign language.

Trouble in the Romantic Phase

Children between the ages of three to six who have not developed stable inner happiness are likely to have difficulty navigating the romantic phase. When children's emotional needs have not been adequately met, they naturally lack confidence in their parents' commitment to help them become happy and competent. As a result, their fear of retaliation by the same-sex parent can assume a truly frightening dimension that is not easily dispelled.

"MOMMY STOLE MY DOLL!"

We began seeing four-year-old Helen because she had acquired inner unhappiness, and at this stage of her life it was being expressed as an overwhelming retaliation anxiety (see page 164). Helen fought with her mother constantly, but underneath she was terrified that her mother was angry at her because of her romantic wishes toward her father. One day Helen discovered that her favorite doll was missing. She bitterly accused her mother of stealing and hiding her doll. She was unconvinced by her mother's assurances that she had not seen the doll. Repeatedly and angrily Helen demanded to know why her mother would not give the doll back, but she was unable to turn to her mother for help with her fears. Therefore she continued to believe in and to be plagued by suspicions that her mother was retaliating against her—and she persisted in this belief even after her mother searched the house and found her doll.

In working with us, Helen at first assumed that we, too, had wishes to make her miserable. Over time she began to realize that she was imposing these fears on our relationship with her, and that these fears were getting in the way of the fun she could be having with us. As she became more able to trust her relationship with us, her wishes for constructive pleasure in all areas of her life were strengthened. She was increasingly able to give her mother the benefit of the doubt when things went wrong. On one occasion when she discovered that the pieces to a game she wanted to play were missing, Helen did not accuse her mother. Instead she sought out her mother and asked if she would help her find them.

Children who suffer from inner unhappiness are dependent on their success at getting what they want to supply themselves with inner well-being. As a result, they are likely to cling to the belief that they can win the opposite-sex parent away from the same-sex parent. To the degree that these children acknowledge that their romantic competitiveness is not succeding, they tend to blame their disappoint-ment on differences in body size. The little girl will think, "Daddy loves Mommy more because she is bigger and has breasts. When I'm bigger and have breasts, then Daddy will love me more." In general, children with inner unhappiness may persevere indefinitely in intense forms of competitive behavior with their same-sex parent, may gen-erate conflicts with those closest to them, or may cover up competi-tive feelings completely.

Children who don't have the inner freedom to recognize that they will never have the romantic attention of the opposite-sex parent are ill prepared for future relationships. They continue to be influenced by their all-powerful self's belief that winning is everything, winner takes all, and might makes right. This creates a relationship ideal that involves using rather than respecting others. Moreover, because they feel threatened when others have wishes that conflict with their own, these children find it hard to tolerate the differences of opionion that occur in every friendship. When they grow up, these children may destroy potentially rewarding friendships and love relationships by reacting with unregulated competitiveness (the other person's success is experienced as threatening their own emotional equilibrium rather than as a cause for rejoicing), or by engaging in endless squabbles over minor but entrenched differences (they love golf, and the other per-son hates it; they think it is important to plan ahead, and the other person is more comfortable with last-minute decisions).

The best way to help your child seek positive, balanced, caring relationships and to avoid relationships characterized by power strug-gles and acrimony is to remember that you are the most important model for your child's relationship ideal. If you show your child love, respect her feelings and wishes, use loving regulation rather than dis-cipline, and show consideration for the needs and wishes of your partner and other adults, your child will strive to emulate you. Most important, it is never too late to change. At any age, your child will appreciate your efforts to create a more enjoyable relationship with her. Even though she will have occasional aversive reactions that may cause her to become irritable with you or to isolate herself from you, you will find that most of the time your child will be delighted at the opportunity to get closer to you. You will also find that her other relationships will improve as well because her relationship ideal will embody the increased caring and compassion you show her.

School, friendships, and extracurricular activities will take center stage in the next phase of your child's development. Whether your child enters her seventh year with a secure inner well-being or with acquired needs for experiencing inner unhappiness, with the aid of smart love guidelines you can respond positively and constructively to the challenges she will encounter.

Chapter Seven

Ages Six to Twelve: Smart Loving Your Older Child

In the years from six to twelve, children are expected to develop important new intellectual, social, and physical capabilities, including the ability to establish close, satisfying peer relationships; the capacity for complex thinking and grasping sophisticated ideas; and increased skill in extracurricular activities such as sports, music, or other art forms. As is true in all phases of your child's life, you want to offer the six- to twelve-year-old maximum opportunities to exercise choice while you keep in mind his need for guidance and protection.

We advise that you try to offer your six- to twelve-year-old more latitude for making choices than is typically recommended, and that you simultaneously offer an unstinting love and support that your child can turn to and lean on whenever he wants. In this way, you will help your child to accomplish his most important task in this stage, which is increasingly to derive his secondary happiness—the well-being that comes from engaging in everyday activities—from the reliable pleasure produced by making good choices and pursuing them well. As your child matures he will rely less on the satisfaction he derives from the illusion that he has the power to gratify each and every wish. In other words, your child will come to realize that the solid pleasure generated by his own creativity, diligence, and competence is superior to the undependable pleasure arising from his all-powerful self's unrealistic claims to control the world.

Although you remain indispensable in this stage of your child's development, you are no longer the direct focus of your child's most intensely felt needs. Rather, you serve as an available and appreciative audience and to facilitate your child's pursuit of extrafamilial activities. When reality proves frustrating, your child will need you to help him respond constructively.

School Days

Children whose developmental needs have been adequately satisfied will experience the increasing rigor of grades one through seven as a positive and exciting challenge. Because they have acquired an unshakable primary happiness—the inner well-being that stems from their certain knowledge that they are causing their parents to respond lovingly to their needs—and because their secondary happiness is increasingly independent of everyday successes or failures, their learning will be generally pleasurable and stimulating rather than painful and stressful. For example, when as first graders these children encounter new words they don't know, they will be willing to try to sound them out and, if unsuccessful, will be able to ask for help without feeling any loss of face.

People who misunderstand our emphasis on nurturing children's inner happiness may conclude that happy children will be complacent, unmotivated children. Nothing could be further from the truth. Because they have minds of their own in the sense that they can make good choices and pursue those choices without conflict, truly happy children are resilient self-starters. They are naturally curious, undeterred by setbacks, and they will reach their full potential. This does not mean that they will be radiantly happy or content all the time. Inner happiness is not synonymous with a good mood. *Stable inner happiness refers both to children's unshakable primary happiness and, in turn, to a reliable secondary happiness.*

When parents satisfy their child's developmental needs, she will like school and be a competent and enthusiastic student. Most of the time, her secondary happiness will be neither dependent on success nor vulnerable to failure, so she will rarely be thrown into disequilibrium by a poor grade or by making mistakes as she learns. For her, the process of gaining academic competence will be enjoyable in its own right.

Unhappy children, on the other hand, often become anxious or paralyzed when faced with a learning task, because they can be tormented by self-doubt or develop such a desperate need to succeed that they are prevented from thinking clearly.

How to Help Your Child with Homework

In trying to help your child with homework, use the same approach as when you taught her to tie her shoes or to ride a bike. Foster your child's efforts by making concrete assistance available in a relaxed way and with ongoing love and affection. Parents often worry about the extent to which they should supervise and assist their children with homework. Fortunately, the child who possesses a durable inner happiness will most likely resolve this dilemma for you. Because she enjoys using her own mind, your child will neither hesitate to ask for help when she needs it, nor seek help when she doesn't. Still, in the earlier grades children may need an occasional reminder to get to their homework.

The most effective assistance you can offer your child with her homework assignments is to establish a daily work time before or after dinner. You can use this time to sit down and read, knit, do crossword puzzles, pay bills, write letters, or do other desk work. Your child will feel proud and grown-up to be doing her work right alongside Mom, Dad, big sister, or big brother. Try to avoid pursuing distracting activities, such as watching TV or playing video games, during prime homework times.

It is crucial that you view your efforts to help your child with her homework as purely facilitative. Your aim is to advance your child's abilities to derive secondary happiness from making constructive choices and becoming proficient in her efforts (for example, to help her to learn how to organize, schedule, and complete homework), rather than to make certain that any particular homework assignment gets done or is done to some established level.

If a child asks for help with a homework problem or project, feel free to offer it, secure in the knowledge that the child wants to feel and to be competent. The more you can respond positively ("I'd be delighted to help you; let's try this problem together") and show the child how to think through and analyze a question, the more effectively the child will navigate the important balance between sticking with a difficult task and appropriately asking for help when she needs it.

Children will occasionally fall prey to the unrealistic goals proposed by their all-powerful selves, based on the illusion of invincibility and omniscience. They may become convinced that they can work on their homework late in the evening, when they will be too tired to concentrate, or that they can finish in only five minutes, when half an hour is more realistic. When these miscalculations occur, try not to react by using them as the basis of an object lesson. Don't say, "We hope you at least learned that if you don't get your homework in on time, there are consequences—like this time, when your work was marked down." Rather, show your child that a misstep does not affect your confidence that she wants to make good choices and that she can learn. You might say, "You're just learning to figure out how long things will take. As time goes on, you will judge more accurately." This comment helps the child who has made an error in planning to maintain her feelings of being worthwhile as well as her optimism about her eventual ability to make good decisions and to pursue them vigorously and well.

How to Help Your Child with Other School Responsibilities

You can take a similar approach to other school-related responsibilities, such as getting ready for school and keeping track of library books and lunch money. Children will occasionally be led astray when their all-powerful selves talk them into believing they can get dressed and eat breakfast in five minutes, or make them think they can remember the due dates of library books without checking. You can build on the fact that the experience of rushing or being late will feel less satisfactory to children than getting to school in an unpressured way. You can offer to help your child get her school things organized the night before, or you may want to suggest that there will be more time to be together if she can get ready before it is time to leave.

If your child forgets her lunch or her homework, bring it to school if at all possible. Allowing children to experience the "natural consequences" of their actions is really a form of punishment, and children will feel doubly wounded when they forget something of importance and you could help them out but refuse to do so. *The only lesson parents teach their child when they force her to suffer the consequences of her mistakes is to be unforgiving toward herself.*

How to Choose Rules and Regulations That Are Appropriate for the Six- to Twelve-Year-Old

The smart love perspective is that the degree to which children are willing to cooperate with rules and regulations depends not only on the rules in question, but also on the developmental stage the children have reached. We believe that with the exception of health and safety issues, few rules are so important that they must be obeyed in an unquestioning manner. *Your primary goal is not to get your child to obey, but to allow your child the freedom to discover that he prefers to be guided by sensible rules because he feels happier that way.* When your child makes the inevitable slip, try to avoid giving him the message that you must control his behavior because he is untrustworthy, lacks good intentions, or is incapable of governing himself.

Parents are sometimes advised to approach children between the ages of six and twelve as though each rule, regulation, or request presents a crucial test of parents' authority and the child's virtue. But children at these ages are still vulnerable to the heady, if unrealistic, belief that they need not do anything they don't want to do. By the time he turns twelve, your child will be much less invested in believing that he is too powerful to be interfered with.

Children whose developmental needs are met will gradually find that they feel happier when they follow rules and honor requests. Try not to short-circuit the way your child arrives at this awareness. Don't demand instant and rigid compliance for every rule. Clearly, not every rule or request can be the subject of endless discussion, and not every rule, regulation, or request is equally important. Most are negotiable; some are not.

SOME DEADLINES ARE NEGOTIABLE

When an eight-year-old we know was told he needed to write thank-you letters for the birthday presents he received, he said he wanted to wait until the following weekend when he would have more time. His parents easily agreed. When they reminded him the next weekend, he remembered the deal he had made with his parents and honored it, although he grumbled a bit at having to postpone work on his new train set.

Rules and regulations that relate to health and safety issues, such as wearing a seat belt, are not negotiable. Your child must follow them, no matter how outraged his all-powerful self becomes. Other nonnegotiable rules and regulations arise out of the need to respect the rights and wishes of other family members

Responsibility for Chores

One of the thorniest issues you will confront in this stage of your child's life is the extent to which you can reasonably expect your child to help out around the house (or farm, or business). Obviously, more can be expected of an older child. A six-year-old should be expected to assume less of the responsibility for the chores that are necessary to keep the household functioning, such as taking out garbage, making beds, and vacuuming, than a twelve-year-old. Parents are commonly told that these are the years when habits of discipline and responsibility should be laid down, and, therefore, that they need to communicate clear expectations to their children and enforce these responsibilities by imposing sanctions, such as the limiting of privileges, if necessary.

We recommend that you try to adapt your expectations to your child's readiness to help, and that you try to respond with loving regulation when chores go undone. At six, a child is too young to remember every chore, to do every chore on your timetable, or even to want to do chores consistently. By the time your child turns twelve, she will be much more likely to remember chores and to want to do them well and on time.

Initially, you can build on your child's positive relationship with you by suggesting that you do chores together, and the more fun, the better. One father opened the clothes hamper and suggested that his seven-year-old try to shoot "baskets" with the dirty clothes that were scattered around the room.

Children are so in love with their parents that most of the time they will be eager to help. Again, the six-year-old is best approached with joint projects that have some intrinsic appeal. Children will usually be happy to assist with cooking projects involving snapping beans or stirring cookie dough; household jobs involving water, such as washing the floor or the tiles in the bathroom; or taking care of animals—for example, feeding and brushing the dog.

Since your primary object is to show your child that working together can be fun, and only secondarily to accomplish any specific chore, there is no need for you to ask your child to help with chores he really dislikes. If your six-year-old hates to make his bed, but is happy straightening up his toys, there is no reason why you shouldn't make the bed while your child puts his toys away. If he has an off day and refuses to help, it is not necessary to view your child's refusal as an insurrection that must be squelched decisively. Often if you simply start the chore, your child will join in. And if he misses a day of picking up his toys, you won't have violated any health or safety principles, and no ground really will be lost. In order to sympathize with their children, it sometimes helps for parents to ask themselves how often they put off "until tomorrow" things they don't feel like doing at the moment.

Your child continues to imitate you as he grows older. If you like things neat and keep your possessions orderly, your child will be inclined to enjoy picking up his things, as long as he is not reminded too insistently. On the other hand, if you are comfortable with disorder, your child may not see anything wrong with it either. Your habits will set an example.

Although children need to be guided by reasonable expectations and requests appropriate to their age, they also feel it is very unfair if the standards they are held to are more exacting than the standards their parents live by. They have a point. A good example is foul language. Parents who constantly use profanity may want to suggest that their children confine their swearing to the house, but it is probably futile to forbid the child to use words the parents commonly use.

Handling Hygiene

Like chores, learning appropriate personal hygiene should be viewed as a developmental process and not as a test of your child's ability to obey. Certainly children between the ages of six and twelve need to brush their teeth and hair and take baths, but they will come to no great harm if they miss a day or two. The smart love guideline is *avoid unnecessary confrontations with children about behavior for which they will eventually assume responsibility.*

THE BOY WHO WOULDN'T BATHE

We know a seven-year-old who was otherwise quite reasonable but who resisted mightily each evening when his parents told him he needed a bath. He said baths were a "big bother." He was very agreeable about washing his face and hands when necessary. His parents tried every creative solution they could think of, including showers, tub toys, bath crayons, and squirt guns, but the child's dislike of bathing remained undiminished. The pediatrician said that one bath a week would suffice to ward off skin diseases. The boy accepted the prescription for one bath a week, which was all the bathing he did until he turned eleven and began going to "boy-girl parties." At that point he began showering every day.

We cannot overemphasize that *the most important determinant of whether or not your child will grow up to take responsibility for his body and his possessions is your assumptions about his motives.* When you view your child as disposed to take responsibility in a manner that is appropriate for his age, you will find it easier to approach him with relaxed affection and focus on accomplishments instead of deficits. For example, just before you give your child a kiss good-night, you can say affectionately, "Did you remember to brush your teeth, sweetheart?" If your child says she forgot, you need not admonish, lecture, or threaten her. You might simply reply, "Oh, OK, can you do it now?" If your child says, "I'm just too tired tonight," you might respond, "All right, but it's probably not good to go too much time without brushing. Let's agree that you will definitely brush in the morning."

Parents who approach their child with a suspicious or critical attitude ("Are you telling the truth? Did you really brush? You have got to start remembering things!") are actually interfering with the child's natural wish to be like his parents and take care of himself and his things. Fostering that wish will help the child continue to take care of himself when he is living on his own. Parents might bear in mind that when their child grows up and moves out, he may either choose never again to brush his teeth, make his bed, or pick up his things, or conversely, he may continue to care for himself with the same pleasure he felt at home.

Encouraging Personal Choice

Try to endorse your child's developing need to govern his own life when appropriate and to the extent possible. This guideline is especially important because your child spends so much of his weekdays following school rules. Obviously there are health and safety restrictions (for example, a child cannot swim in the lake alone, or go to a party when he is running a high fever), and children may have to yield to the needs and wishes of other family members (for example, when a boy is asked to forgo pizza with his friends in order to attend his sister's piano recital). Nevertheless, it is important to allow children at this age to experience broad freedom of choice in the many areas that do not affect their health, interfere with the legitimate interests of others, or conflict with an external authority, such as school.

One area of your child's life where your child is entitled to exercise choice is in his appearance. By and large, your child has the same right to choose his clothes and hair style as you do. No matter how much your taste is offended by clashing color combinations or apparel that looks decrepit or three sizes too big, it is important to try to hold your tongue and let your child design an appearance that he feels represents him. One father found it difficult to compliment his daughter on her appearance when she wore jeans with holes in the knees. A mother was uncomfortable when her son wore the same sweatshirt for three days in a row. Just as you baby-proofed the house to allow your toddler maximum scope for choice, try to facilitate your older child's personal choices whenever possible.

Keeping the Work Out of Play

There is a crucial distinction between the worlds of work and recreation. Your child *must* go to school, turn in homework, take tests, and obey school rules about conduct. Your child *need not* engage in or excel at any particular extracurricular activity.

Allowing children maximum free choice enhances their sense of purpose, and this is central to their development of lasting inner happiness and competence. It is essential to allow your child both to choose forms of recreation that appeal to him and also to determine the level of commitment and accomplishment he wishes to attain. Like adults, children need to have some part of their daily lives that is just for fun. Within health, safety, and developmentally appropriate guidelines, your child has as much right to decide how to spend his leisure time as you yourself do. This principle is hardest to follow when children are quite accomplished at an activity and decide they are no longer interested, or they stop practicing wholeheartedly.

The child whose emotional needs have been satisfied will tend to ride out disappointments and persevere at activities he enjoys. But any child can decide at any time that an activity is no longer fun or rewarding. Needless to say, this decision can be trying to adults. Understandably, parents who have spent countless hours chauffeuring their child and lots of money on equipment and lessons may feel personally disappointed by their child's decision. There is every reason to try to talk to your child about the benefits of continuing with a skill that he has worked so hard to develop. But if the child still insists on abandoning the activity, you will give your child a true gift if you avoid burdening him with your frustration and accept this decision as gracefully as possible. In this way, you will have the satisfaction of meeting your child's developmental need to choose how he spends his free time.

Winning and Losing

Like other recreational activities, games are primarily meant to be fun. They should not be used to teach lessons about life and how to live it. Your child will be able to enjoy playing different kinds of games depending on his age and how he feels on any given day.

Six-year-olds will like winning. They will probably not have much fun if they lose. Because much of their esteem still depends on their winning rather than their playing well, to them games do not feel very different from real life. It's not surprising, then, that six-year-olds are likely to arrange the game to ensure that they will win. They will turn the die over if it is not to their liking, ignore penalty cards and draw again, and take as many turns in a row as are necessary to get ahead.

If you adopt the smart love principle that games are only for fun and are not proving grounds for establishing your child's moral character, you will be more comfortable with your child's creative rule bending. If your child wants to play with friends or older siblings, you may suggest that she follow the rules so as to prevent the other children from becoming angry at her. But you can also convey that if adhering to the rules does not seem enjoyable, your child can always wait until she is older to play with the other children.

When children's developmental needs are met, as they mature they will increasingly derive their secondary happiness from the satisfaction of making a good effort rather than from the pleasure of winning. As a result, they will want to play by the rules, because they will be bored rather than reassured by the knowledge that they can control the game's outcome. Not knowing who will win will be more interesting and enjoyable.

Friendship

You can play an important role in helping your child to navigate the occasionally stormy seas of peer relations. The experience of having friends is of major emotional importance to children between the ages of six and twelve. They pair off with best friends and tell each other their deepest secrets.

The child whose parents have responded appropriately to his developmental needs will ride out the bumps in peer relationships with relatively minor discomfort. His primary happiness will have become unshakable, and his secondary happiness—the well-being that derives from everyday activities—will be increasingly separated from his success at getting what he wants, including the approval of peers. Although he may feel hurt and disappointed if he is excluded or teased by his friends, he will not be devastated because he will be able to turn to other friends or to alternative sources of satisfaction. He will not be inclined to engage in power struggles with his friends over whose wishes should prevail. And he will have no motive to cause himself unhappiness: He will not provoke fights or focus on slights, nor will he be attracted to self-destructive activities (for example, substance abuse) because everyone is doing it.

The relationship of trust and closeness you have developed with your child will invite him to turn to you for assistance when friends bruise his feelings. When plans with friends fall through, you can help by providing a sympathetic ear and serving as a backup.

～

HELPING THE CHILD WHO IS NOT INVITED TO THE PARTY

One nine-year-old girl we know returned from school with a downcast look. In response to her mother's inquiry, she said that a girl she thought of as a friend had not invited her to her skating party. Her parents listened attentively and then said, "It's hard to be left out, especially when you thought you would be included, but it's also her loss because she won't have the pleasure of having you there. Would there be something you would like us to do with you that night, like going to a movie?" The child responded, "Yeah, that's a good idea. Let's go out that night."

Children's all-powerful selves often convince them that they can make difficult friendships run smoothly. Parents may need to help their child realize that there is little he can do to change a friend's personality.

A FRIEND WHO COULDN'T TOLERATE CLOSENESS

Eight-year-old Mary was constantly having her feelings hurt by a particular friend, Eleanor. The girls would get along well for a few days, and then Eleanor would make cutting remarks about Mary's intelligence or appearance. Mary was convinced by her all-powerful self that she had the power to inspire Eleanor to remain positive about her. As a result, Mary gave Eleanor many new chances, and she felt slighted and hurt when Eleanor insulted her yet again. Her parents explained that there was probably nothing Mary could do to change this pattern in the way Eleanor related to her. After Eleanor had cut her down two more times, Mary was able to recognize the truth in her parents' assessment and to turn to friendships with children who were able to offer a more reliable and pleasant type of relationship.

Children will relate to their peers based on the standards of their own relationship ideals. As we described in Chapter 6, a child's relationship ideal arises from the way his parents treat each other and him. A person carries this internal model of relating into all kinds of relationships that occur throughout life. The relationship ideals of a child whose developmental needs have been met will include a respect for other people's motives even when they are incompatible with his own, the ability to care deeply and appropriately for significant others, and the capacity to resist attempts by others to derail his own healthy intentions.

When a young child has a best friend, his all-powerful self may tell him that if he sees his best friend laughing with other friends, he himself is being deprived or somehow diminished. As a result, he may feel hurt and angry. But over time, he will come to see this type of discomfort as unnecessary, as he realizes that the fun his best friend has with others in no way diminishes the good times he and his friend can have together.

The child between six and twelve whose emotional needs have been adequately responded to will seek appropriate and realistic relationships with his peers and will not allow them to lead him into activities that are not good for him. Two obvious examples are drugs and premature sexual activity. This child will not be swayed by arguments that he should experiment with sex because everyone else is doing it.

THE UNCHAPERONED PARTY

Eleven-year-old Molly was invited to a party by a good friend. Because Molly had been to this particular friend's house for parties many times before, her parents did not think it necessary to check with the friend's parents. It turned out that unbeknownst to Molly, her friend's parents were out of town. Liquor was made available to the guests. Molly herself did not drink. When she became bored with the effort of talking to friends who were not making much sense, she called her parents to take her home. She told her parents what had happened, and she concluded that in the future she would make sure to avoid unchaperoned parties. She was very matter-of-fact about her experience, and she was happy to see her friends at school the next day. When they asked her why she had left, she simply said she had wanted to go home. She managed to take good care of herself without alienating her friends because she viewed her actions as reflecting a personal choice, and not as being a sign of moral superiority.

～

Puberty

Children's all-powerful selves regain credibility as children's bodies take on adult form and as boy-girl relations heat up. The loving closeness children experience with parents who are able to respond positively to their developmental needs will play an important role in helping children avoid the unrealistic temptations of their all-powerful selves, and in steering them toward a reliance on the constructive and reliable pleasure of which their competent selves are capable. The inner well-being of the competent self is not outcome-dependent; rather, it arises from the experience of making constructive choices and pursuing them effectively.

Many children develop secondary sex characteristics (an increase in breast tissue, pubic hair, changed male voices, and so forth), and many girls have menstrual periods before they become teenagers. Preteen parties may include sexually stimulating games like spin the bottle, as well as alcohol and drugs. Children who consistently have received positive, caring responses from their parents even at times when these children were upset or angry will feel comfortable turning to their parents to discuss their changing bodies and to get the information they need to handle puberty comfortably. They will not be convinced by their peers to participate in unsafe or unsavory activities. Having successfully come to terms with the desires and disappointments of the romantic phase, they will not be influenced by peer pressure to become sexually active prematurely. Most important, these children will remain aware of and appreciative of the help and support available to them in the relationship with their parents.

THE BOY WHO DIDN'T PRACTICE FREE THROWS

We know a basketball star named Tim who responded to his growth spurt, lowered voice, and sprouting whiskers by feeling he was so grown up that he could slack off on the half hour a night of free throws his coach had prescribed. In other words, Tim's all-powerful self temporarily overrode his competent self. As a result, his free throw average suffered, and in an important game he found himself benched in the fourth quarter. He sought out his parents after the game and told them how angry he felt about having been removed from the game at a decisive moment. He was convinced that the coach was playing favorites and had sidelined him unjustly. His parents commented sympatheti-cally on how frustrating it must have felt to have to watch from the sidelines. They gently suggested that there was another way to look at the reason for his being benched: Maybe the coach really admired Tim and thought he had tremendous talent, but he might have felt unable to keep Tim in the game because his free throw skills were rusty.

Because his parents' manner was affectionate and nonjudgmental, Tim was disposed to turn to them for help. He was relieved to be offered an expla-nation that dispelled the pain of feeling persecuted and that made clear that he had the power to change this unpleasant situation. He chose to resume his practicing and was rewarded for his efforts with increased accuracy and more game time. With this accomplishment the trustworthiness of his all-powerful self was diminished, because he recognized that that part of himself had con-vinced him to let up on practice and had affected his skill for the worse. Tim's competent self gained standing when Tim saw that the process of practicing and improving was gratifying in and of itself.

Children who have not acquired needs to make themselves unhappy will enter the middle years of childhood with an uncon-flicted happiness and enthusiasm that they will export to the world of school, friendships, and recreational activities. They will consistently enjoy school and learning, be resilient in the face of the ups and downs of peer relationships, and pursue outside activities with enthu-siasm. These children will move on to adolescence well prepared for the transition into adulthood. Although they will not be spared frus-tration and disappointment, they will encounter these with an unfail-ing primary happiness and an increasingly stable secondary happiness based on the knowledge that they can make good choices and pursue them well. Because they will be comfortable with success, and because they will be fair and caring in their dealings with their friends, most of their days will be filled with accomplishment and enjoyment.

Smart Loving the Six- to Twelve-Year-Old Who Suffers from Inner Unhappiness

Because six- to twelve-year-olds have the latitude to make momen-tous choices for themselves, there are correspondingly more ways in which children at these ages can express inner unhappiness. For example, they can ignore rules, skip homework assignments, choose friends that make them miserable, and provoke anyone who tries to help them. They can also get into serious trouble through such illegal actions as vandalizing property, stealing, or using controlled substances.

As with other ages, the smart love guideline for helping the unhappy older child is *keep in mind that no matter how self-destructive or aggressive his behavior, he retains his inborn wish to lead a life of happiness, fulfillment, and close relationships.* You will be much more effective in helping the unhappy older child if you avoid punishments, anger, and disapproval, all of which will only strengthen his needs for creating unhappiness. Try to respond with understanding and support, thereby strengthening his motives for seeking constructive pleasure.

"I NEED MY BLANKET!"

An eight-year-old we were treating was unable to leave home without bringing his special blanket in his backpack. When Noah arrived at school one day, he realized that he had left his blanket at home. He became so hysterical that his teacher called his father, who left work to bring the blanket to Noah.

Fortunately, the father had come to realize that his son depended on the presence of his blanket to maintain his inner equilibrium. The father didn't judge Noah's panic as manipulative or babyish. He knew that he was helping his son to mature, not holding him back, by showing him that he understood that for the time being Noah needed his blanket to feel calm enough to remain at school. Over time, Noah used his parents' understanding of his need for his blanket, in combination with his work with us, as a source of feeling cared for, with the result that having his blanket with him at every moment came to seem less urgent.

No material thing can ever substitute for the type of parenting that children with inner unhappiness have missed out on. Even the gratification of these children's most ardently desired wish will not bring with it the inner well-being they are expecting. On the other hand, when parents respond with understanding and compassion to their child's expressions of disappointment, he will come to see that a truly satisfying type of well-being is available in the relationship with his parents.

WHEN CHILDREN GET WHAT THEY WANT AND THEN FEEL DISAPPOINTED

Heather, an eight-year-old girl we know, begged her parents to buy her an expensive doll she coveted intensely. When she received the doll for her birthday she felt vaguely disappointed in her choice and did not really enjoy playing with it. Her parents believed she was exhibiting signs of being spoiled, so they reacted by scolding her for being "ungrateful." They said they would not buy her any more toys until she learned to be appreciative. The girl learned to hide her feelings of disappointment from her parents, but she felt no less sour the next time she received a gift.

Nathaniel's parents responded differently in a similar situation. Their eight-year-old reacted negatively when he was given the miniature racecars he had been urgently requesting. Although his parents had not been able to give their son the emotional support he needed from the time he was born, they had begun to consult with us after Nathaniel turned two and began exhibiting signs of unhappiness. With the miniature racecars, his parents correctly anticipated that the gift could never live up to Nathaniel's unrecognized expectation that the racecars would alter his frame of mind and make him happy forever. Instead of becoming angry when Nathaniel morosely recited all the shortcomings he found in the racecars, his parents gave him a hug and said it was too bad that he was feeling discontented with a gift he had wanted so badly. Then they tried to help Nathaniel consider the possibility that the cars were not responsible for his bad feelings; the racecars were probably making him as happy as racecars could. They said to him, "We know they're not perfect, but no racecar will have every feature you want, and we bet you can have fun with the things they can do. Can you show us how they can race each other across the floor?" Nathaniel was relieved that his parents were understanding of rather than angry at him for the discontent he had been feeling. Warmed by the closeness he felt to them, he found that he no longer felt so keenly disappointed and that he could enjoy demonstrating and then playing with his new racecars.

Problems in School

Children who have developed inner unhappiness often have trouble learning and even participating appropriately in classroom activities. Parents can work with their child to stimulate his appetite for learning.

Building on Your Child's Interests and Strengths

The smart love guideline is *build on your child's interests and strengths rather than focus on the academic subjects in which your child is weakest*. If a child who is doing poorly in every subject shows the most interest in English, parents might begin by working with him on his English homework. As he begins to experience small successes in English, the child will begin to see that school can be a source of constructive pleasure. Parents who anticipate that their child will react aversively to success will feel less discouraged at those times when their child's test scores take an occasional dive. They will see the reason to avoid making negative remarks such as, "I know you understood the material because we went over it together. You must not have concentrated on the test." Instead, parents might say, "You did such a good job of studying for that test. It's too bad you weren't able to show what you learned. But the important thing is you really know it. You will get another chance to let the teacher see that."

When parents find that, for whatever reason, their attempts to teach their child consistently make their child angrier and more distant, they may want to call in other family members (for example, an aunt, or a grandfather) to help with homework. Or there may be a caring older child or retiree in the neighborhood who would welcome the opportunity to earn extra income tutoring.

Fear of School

When children are abruptly frightened of or unwilling to go to school, they are experiencing a genuine emotional crisis. It is crucial that parents respond with loving regulation rather than with anger, threats, or disciplinary measures. First, it is important to ascertain whether the problem lies with the philosophy of the child's school: Are students expected to adhere to rules or meet expectations that are too exacting for their age? Or is there something about the personality of a particular teacher: Does the teacher, for example, prefer studious girls and you have a boisterous boy? Is your child having difficulties with peers: Is the school bully threatening your child? Once you have identified the source of the problem, try to improve the school environment for your child. You may need to change schools or classrooms or talk to the principal about the bully.

If the school is not the problem, consider whether your child is worried about something at home. One girl whose parents were thinking about divorcing believed that if she stayed home she could help her parents reconcile. A boy who overheard his father say that his elderly dog was "on his last legs" became hysterical when it was time for school. With gentle questions his parents discovered that he was afraid his dog would die while he was away.

Even if you are mystified by your child's fear of school, try to convey your awareness that he is not behaving capriciously; instead let him know you realize that school really feels frightening or unpleasant to him. In keeping with the principles of loving regulation, show your child that although you must insist that he attend school, you are standing by available to help him get there. You might offer to drive or walk your child to school instead of sending him on the bus. Or you could get up half an hour earlier to spend some time with your child before it is time to leave for school.

Inner Unhappiness Can Create Obstacles for the Elementary Schoolchild

Elementary schoolchildren who are burdened with inner unhappiness may be driven to deny their need for help, because they feel shame when they don't know everything. They may also pretend to know unfamiliar words, may convince themselves that reading is stupid and they don't want to try, may develop emotionally caused stomachaches or headaches that prevent them from trying, or may feel victimized by their teachers and accuse them of asking them to do assignments that are too difficult. Alternatively, these children may be so frightened by the experience of not knowing how to complete an assignment that they may cling to their teachers and beg for attention and help constantly.

School-age children who lack stable inner happiness pose a considerable challenge for parents and teachers. For reasons we have previously described, these children may actually seek out unpleasant consequences by doing badly in school or being late, and, in addition, they may be reluctant to ask for help (see Chapter 9 for further discussion of problems with learning and school).

A GIRL ANSWERS THE WRONG QUESTION

An eleven-year-old named Justine had great difficulty following directions. She spent many hours on a school report, only to discover that the assigned question differed in significant ways from the question she had answered. When her work was marked down, Justine became furious with the teacher, accusing the teacher of having changed her mind about what she wanted.

Justine's parents had been consulting us about their daughter's school difficulties. We had observed that Justine had acquired needs to make herself unhappy, and that was why she was unknowingly sabotaging her hard work. We suggested that, rather than reprimand her for misunderstanding the assignment, her parents might try to help Justine to become aware of her conflicting motives.

The next time Justine answered the wrong question, her parents commented sympathetically, "We know how hard you worked. But sometimes people can be uncomfortable when their hard work is rewarded. They can undermine their good effort without realizing what they're doing. Maybe there is a part of you that didn't get the question straight as a way to make sure your work didn't get the credit it deserved. "

Justine initially continued to insist that the teacher was at fault, but then she volunteered that everyone else in the class had answered the correct question. The next time a report was assigned she double-checked her transcription of the assignment. Because she answered the correct question, Justine received a grade that reflected her effort. Most important, she made it a practice from then on to check the accuracy of her understanding of assignments.

How to Help Children When They React Aversively to Success

Parents who know that their child finds it difficult to enjoy life will find it easier to help the child who explodes or sabotages himself in reaction to getting what he wants. Without this understanding, the child's behavior may seem willful and outrageous.

AN ATTACK OF THE GROUCHIES

We worked with a ten-year-old boy whose inner unhappiness was often expressed through difficulty getting along with his peers. Ron irritated his friends by violating confidences and spreading unfounded rumors. One day he received an invitation to a birthday party given by a boy he admired. He was quite delighted and told his parents that he couldn't believe his good fortune at being included in the "party of the year." As the day approached, however, Ron became more and more difficult and irritable. He tormented his younger sister, and when his father told him he must leave her in peace, Ron burst into tears and said, "Everyone hates me!"

Ron had no idea why he was so irritable or why he suddenly felt convinced that no one liked him. His parents were fairly sure that he needed to react negatively to the pleasure of being included in the birthday party, so they remarked to Ron that maybe he was feeling angry and unloved because he was uncomfortable with the good feelings stimulated by the invitation to the party.

A BOY RUINS A PLAY DATE

A child named Norman invited a cherished friend to come over after school. Then he reacted to the pleasure of having his friend over by starting an argument over how to divide up the cars they were going to race. The argument escalated, and the boys seemed doomed to spend the afternoon angry and miserable.

Norman's father, who had been consulting us about his son's difficulties, realized that Norman's need to pick a fight was his way of reacting to the pleasure of having his friend come to his house. He reminded Norman of how much he had been looking forward to having his friend over, and he suggested that Norman might feel sad later if the afternoon didn't work out well. He added that maybe Norman would be happier if he either let his friend use whatever cars he wanted or if he put the cars away and found a game they could both enjoy playing.

In offering this advice, the father was neither disapproving nor angry. The warmth and affection in his father's response convinced Norman that his father was on his side and was trying to help him have what he really wanted—a good time with his friend. With his father's help Norman was able to cooperate with his friend in building a garage for the cars, which he was then able to share. Soon the boys were totally absorbed in enthusiastic and harmonious play.

Losing Is Especially Painful for the Unhappy Child

Although all six- to twelve-year-olds occasionally feel upset when they lose a game, unhappy children may feel utterly devastated and behave explosively. The smart love guideline is that *the least helpful reaction to the child who can't tolerate losing is to react with lectures, punishments, or disapproval.* When parents or other adults respond negatively, the child feels bad about losing and he also feels hurt and misunderstood. When parents, teachers, or coaches demonstrate that they know how terrible the child feels about losing, the closeness the child will feel to these important adults makes the experience of losing less traumatic.

THE SMART LOVE RESPONSE TO A BAD SPORT

Ten-year-old Ken habitually became very upset when he lost. One day when his brother beat him at chess, Ken threw the board and all the pieces across the room. His parents reacted by telling Ken he could not have access to any of his board games until he could act his age and be a good sport. Ken ran to his room and slammed the door, shouting, "I don't care. I never want to play that stupid game again anyway." At school, he continued to get in trouble for reacting to defeat in unacceptable ways such as kicking the ball out of the field when the other team scored, or refusing to shake hands with the other side after a closely contested match.

When teachers and coaches repeatedly demanded that his parents do something about Ken's "bad attitude," the parents consulted us. We suggested that they take another approach based on the premise that when he lost a game their son was not *choosing* to become irritable and to break the code of good sportsmanship. He really could not tolerate losing because his inner well-being was dependent on successful outcomes. Losing threw him into emotional disequilibrium, which, in turn, made him angry. We counseled the parents to respond to Ken with a calm understanding of how raw he felt when he lost. In that way they could help their son build an inner equilibrium that would not be shaken by storms of anger over losing.

The next time that Ken threw a game to the ground when it did not turn out as he wished, instead of sending him to his room, his father said, "I can see how bad you feel when you lose. Why don't we do something else together." Ken was startled both by his father's lack of criticism and also by his father's willingness to stay with him and do something else. After reflecting for a moment, Ken asked if his father would like to help him make an airplane model. His father said he would be delighted.

Supported by his parents' new understanding, Ken chose to avoid playing games at home that entailed winners and losers. Instead, he consistently opted for cooperative projects. In school, he started to show more self-control when his team lost. His parents' sympathetic responses to his upset feelings at home helped Ken establish a new equilibrium that carried over to school.

Your smart love will help you and your six- to twelve-year-old successfully and enjoyably navigate this challenging and exciting period. Even if your child enters this phase of his life with needs to cause himself unhappiness, if you respond to his out-of-control behavior with loving regulation and give him the broadest possible scope for making choices every day, you will help him want to choose experiences that will bring him constructive pleasure. This positive orientation will be invaluable as he embarks on the demanding and transformational years of adolescence.

Chapter Eight

∼

Smart Loving Your Adolescent

Contrary to popular opinion, the period in which children make the transition to adulthood can be largely trouble free if children enter adolescence in possession of enduring primary happiness forged in the relationship with their parents. We have defined *primary happiness* as the inner well-being that originally stems from children's conviction that they are causing their parents' unconditional wish to pay loving attention to their developmental needs. With the help of smart love guidelines, parents can nurture children who possess a reliable primary happiness so that they blossom into enthusiastic, thoughtful, affectionate, and usually agreeable teenagers.

Equally important, if you have an adolescent who is difficult and unhappy, you can use smart love principles to increase her appetite for experiences of constructive pleasure, thereby helping her become much happier and much more functional.

The Goal of Adolescence Is Stable Secondary Happiness

In our society, adolescence is a fairly prolonged phase and always includes (1) the final stages of intellectual and musculoskeletal development and the completion of puberty, (2) dramatically heightened social and academic demands and expectations, and (3) increased opportunities for the exercise of initiative and creativity.

Most important, in the course of their adolescence children whose emotional needs have been adequately satisfied will succeed in completely insulating their secondary happiness—the pleasure generated by everyday activities—from experiences of success or failure.

They come to obtain their secondary happiness entirely from their competent self, which always has access to the pleasure of making good choices and pursuing them well.

An adolescent becomes truly adult when she permanently loses interest in the unrealistic claims of her all-powerful self to be able always to get what it wants, and when she approaches the world with the ideals and values of her competent self, which will enable her to enjoy activities and relationships for their own sake. *A child will have achieved the true goal of childhood development when her inner well-being becomes entirely independent of experiences of success or failure and is sustained by the reservoir of loving closeness with her parents and by the pleasure of making good choices and pursuing them well and without conflict.* When this developmental milestone is reached, the adolescent will not react to disappointments with withdrawal, depression, self-criticism, or rage at others. While all people are likely to feel sad when they encounter everyday disappointments that occur in spite of their best efforts, adults whose developmental needs have been adequately satisfied will not feel that they are bad, will not become irrationally angry, and will not lose the inner happiness of feeling complete, lovable, and loved.

FEELING SAD, BUT NOT BAD

A high school senior we know practiced diligently with her school orchestra and was thrilled when the orchestra advanced to the state finals. When a fellow musician failed to practice regularly and made a conspicuous mistake that cost her school the victory, the teen felt keenly disappointed, but she also felt good about how hard she had worked and about her participation. The unshakable inner happiness her parents had helped her develop shielded her from dwelling on the disappointment, becoming depressed, angrily confronting the girl who hadn't practiced, or feeling angry at herself for "wasting" her time. She continued her own practicing and looked forward to trying out for a college symphony in the fall.

As in middle childhood, your adolescent's all-powerful self is stimulated each time she experiences new intellectual, physical, and social desires and capabilities (for example, the ability to learn to drive and get a driver's license, to vote, to outrun you, to develop an adult level of expertise). If you respond sensitively to your teenager, this resurgence of needing to feel in control in order to feel happy will be short-lived. These reemerging desires will eventually meet with frustration, and this frustration exposes the shaky ground that under-lies the all-powerful self's claims of control. In the process of navigat-ing adolescence, reality strikes even the most confident and accomplished teenagers. The illusion of invincibility can be punctured by a low grade, a missed field goal, or rejection by a romantic inter-est. At the same time, your adolescent's developing competent self derives pleasure from making constructive choices and pursuing them well; it is not outcome-dependent. Because it never falters, it eventu-ally wins out over the all-powerful self.

You play the crucial role of helping your teenager to weather dis-appointments by encouraging and facilitating her ability to take plea-sure in sustained and proficient effort. By following smart love guidelines, you will make it possible for her to make the transition from a secondary happiness that is based on the illusion that she can gratify every wish to a secondary happiness that is nourished by the competent self's ability to make good choices and pursue them well. Even if you did not start out following smart love principles in rais-ing your child, it is never too late to adopt them to help ensure that your child develops stable secondary happiness.

THE HISTORY AWARD GOES TO SOMEONE ELSE

An adolescent named Carl worked diligently and enthusiastically in his history class. He felt sorely disappointed when he failed to win the school award for the best history student. After the award ceremony, he found his parents and shared his bruised feelings. His parents gave him a sympathetic hug and said they could understand his disappointment because he had done such good work. They emphasized that the lack of an award did not diminish the quality of his accomplishment. Carl nodded and replied that it still would have been nice to get the award. His parents agreed. It was obvious that Carl felt soothed by his parents' warmth, understanding, and admiration, and within a few min-utes he was engaged with his friends, although he still seemed a bit subdued.

Carl needed his parents to help him with the unhappiness generated when his all-powerful self convinced him that good effort would inevitably result in a reciprocal social recognition. He felt relieved when his parents, whom he respected and adored, made clear that, although they shared his disappointment, they did not blame him, as he blamed himself, for not getting the award. They were just as admiring and positive about the work he had done as if he had actually received the award. As a result, Carl was helped to maintain a genuine pride in himself and his accomplishments, and the pain of the disappointment did not torment him and ruin his day.

THE GYMNAST WHO GREW TOO TALL

A girl we know named Sandra excelled at gymnastics and hoped to become a national competitor. In the year after she turned thirteen, however, she experienced a growth spurt and became too tall to compete successfully at the highest level. She was devastated. She felt that all the sacrifice and hard work she had put into her training were totally wasted. Her parents acknowledged that she had suffered a genuine disappointment. Then they helped her think of other ways in which she could apply her talents. At their suggestion, Sandra used her finely honed skills to teach gymnastics to younger children, and she also joined the modern dance club at school and became its star. Although Sandra still felt disappointed that her gymnastics career had ended, she no longer believed that the effort she had expended had been for nothing, and she genuinely enjoyed the related activities her parents had helped her to pursue.

How to Help Your Adolescent Attain Genuine Independence

The popular belief is that adolescence is about achieving independence from parents, and that adolescents must go through periods of rejecting their parents in order to become free of them. In this view, it is normal and even growth promoting for teens to look down on their parents' politics, intelligence, and values; to be embarrassed at being seen with members of their family; and to embrace wholesale the taste and opinions of their peers. We would argue that adolescents who behave this way are suffering from a preventable and correctable inner unhappiness; they need to deny their parents' importance in order to feel independent of them.

Because true independence is achieved when a child's inner well-being becomes permanently independent from the ups and downs of everyday life, teens cannot achieve true autonomy by rejecting their parents. To the contrary, adolescents who achieve true independence carry the feelings of closeness and love they share with their parents into the wider world of school, friendships, and recreational activities. *Teens need not jump, and should not be pushed, out of the parental nest.* Your teenager's awareness that his parents remain available and committed to him is actually the most important ingredient in his evolving conviction that he can regulate his own life so as to make himself happy and to bring happiness to others.

Adolescents are not ready to stand alone. If you refuse to let your adolescent lean on you whenever he wishes, you induce him to rely on less constructive forms of soothing himself (sleeping twelve hours a day, staying out past curfew with friends, overinvesting in a relationship with a boyfriend or girlfriend). Allow your teen both to turn to you and to try his wings without you.

If your teen wants to spend his free time with you, make him feel welcome. Don't say or imply that he is too old to want your companionship, or that he should be engaged in more "appropriate" activities, like going out with friends. Conversely, if your adolescent goes through a period of constructive socializing that keeps him out of the house much of the time, try to make clear that this is OK, too.

Teens who can count on parents to be responsive to their developmental needs are not attracted by self-destructive or antisocial sources of enjoyment. The boy whose friends spent Saturday nights entertaining themselves by courting trouble found it easy to avoid this temptation because he could always get his parents to rent a movie and watch it with him or take him to play miniature golf. And because his parents were happy to have him include a few of his friends, he did not have to forgo socializing with his peers.

Parents who say their adolescents never want to spend time with them commonly make some of the following mistakes:

- They try to force their adolescents to go places they don't like (typically to visit parents' friends and relatives).
- They impose their own ideas of how much time adolescents should spend with them and are wounded or critical if these quotas are not met.

- They unintentionally create a negative atmosphere by nagging or criticizing their adolescents about their manners, appearance, opinions, or language.

If you let your teen decide when and how he will spend time with you, and you adopt an accepting attitude toward his dress and speech, you will find that you will actually see a lot of your adolescent and that, when you do, your encounters will be generally enjoyable.

WHEN YOUR ADOLESCENT CALLS, DON'T HESITATE TO RESPOND

A seventeen-year-old named Larry took a job as a counselor at an overnight camp that had engaged us as consultants. Larry called his parents frequently to say hello and to ask advice about how to handle difficult campers. In addition, he inquired whether his parents would be willing to come and visit him on one of his days off. Because his parents were aware of and comfortable with their son's need for their positive involvement, they responded to his requests generously and affectionately. As a result, Larry had a successful and happy summer.

There was another seventeen-year-old counselor named Jim whose parents consistently misidentified their son's needs to lean on them as an unhealthy dependence. When Jim expressed the wish to call home frequently, his parents reacted by teasing him, with the result that he felt embarrassed about his desire to be close to them. When he felt lonely at camp, Jim was ashamed to tell his parents. Instead, he turned to other counselors for consolation. They were in the habit of drinking after hours in their cabins, and soon Jim was joining them, although he had never touched alcohol previously.

You may dread the coming of adolescence because you have been warned that the teenage years are the ultimate test of parental patience and goodwill. *But children who have acquired an unshakable inner happiness will not experience an adolescence that is troubled, turbulent, and characterized by protracted conflict with parents.* Even children who have developed inner unhappiness can experience a relatively calm adolescence if their parents pay attention to their developmental needs and follow the smart love guidelines.

How to Respond to the Teen Who "Knows Everything"

Nearly all of the transient problems and stresses that affect adolescents whose parents have met their developmental needs result from the influence exerted by the all-powerful self, which makes adolescents vulnerable to excesses of sensitivity and determination. For example, the adolescent's temporary but appealing belief that he can do and have anything may make him especially susceptible to reacting strongly at moments when his parents need to give him guidance.

If you try to keep in mind that your adolescent is not a finished product, you may be less likely to feel upset when your teen's behavior shows the unmistakable influence of his all-powerful self. For instance, many parents overreact when their adolescent asserts that he knows more than they do. Most parents are only too keenly aware both of their own hard-won knowledge and also of their adolescent's naiveté, so it is not surprising that they might catch themselves responding to their adolescent's claims to superior wisdom by pointing out the disparity in their accumulated experience. For instance, a parent might say, "I was holding down jobs before you were born, and I know what employers expect from their employees." If you keep in mind that your adolescent's overestimation of his knowledge is both temporary and also appropriate for his age, you will find it easier to respond with the same relaxed affection that you felt when your adolescent was a toddler and announced that he was bigger and stronger than you.

THE TEEN WHO KNEW EVERYTHING ABOUT RUST

A teen we know named Karen worked diligently to earn the money to buy a first-class bike. One day as she was riding home from school she got caught in a rainstorm. When her father saw her walking away from her bike without drying it, he suggested that she might want to wipe the water off to prevent rust. Karen replied that she didn't need to dry off the bike because it was rustproof. She dismissed her father's attempt to explain that in fact some parts of the bike would rust. Her father understood that Karen was not trying to be impertinent. She was temporarily blinded by her need to feel that she knew everything about bikes and rust. He felt neither personally affronted nor impelled to let the child find out "the hard way" that she was in error. He said affectionately, "Well, you may be right, but nothing will be lost if it's wiped off. If you don't want to, I would be happy to." His daughter rolled her eyes and said, "Oh, OK, I'll do it, but it's not necessary, you know." We emphasize that if this father had simply bowed out of the discussion with the words, "Well, I guess you know best," and the bike had rusted, his daughter (understandably) would have felt betrayed.

Don't Stand By and Watch Teens Fail

Many experts recommend that parents let their children and adolescents experience the "natural consequences" of their immaturity or willfulness. The smart love perspective is that *when you stand by and let bad things happen, your child experiences the twin disappointments that something went wrong and that you did not seem to care enough about her to lift a finger to help prevent the mishap.* The "natural consequences" approach is really a form of punishment. Children are never fooled into thinking that you had nothing to do with the unpleasant outcome.

A common situation in which parents might be advised to let "natural consequences" teach teens a lesson involves teenagers' difficulties getting out of bed on school days. Parents are often told to let their adolescent experience the results of her tardiness, such as detention, a lowered grade, or extra work. What they don't realize is that their child will believe that her parents are letting her down out of indifference or anger. A more effective approach is to have a discussion with your teen the night before about the difficulty of waking her up. You can ask your adolescent to suggest effective methods to help her get going. One teen we know decided that the only arrangement certain to arouse her would be a cold washcloth placed on her face, and, in fact, this proved an effective wake-up call. If, despite your best efforts, you cannot wake your child, you can at least spare her the disappointment that you knowingly let her harm herself.

Parents sometimes say, "But she is practically an adult. If I keep performing these basic functions for her, how will she ever learn to take care of herself?" The smart love response is that, just as she needed you to get milk for her when she was a hungry six-month-old, she needs you now. We cannot overemphasize that adolescence is a developmental phase. Your adolescent still requires your responsive love and affection, and she will not be helped to grow up by your "tough love" or disapproval.

HELPING A TEEN BALANCE SOCIALIZING AND SCHOOL

There will be times when a telephone conversation with a friend will be so engrossing that teens will start their homework late or be unable to complete it with their usual thoroughness. An adolescent named Pat seemed constantly glued to the phone. Her parents, who had been consulting with us about Pat's problems at school, would remind her in a friendly manner that it was getting late. But they neither set arbitrary limits on her telephone time nor punished her for staying on the phone too long. In spite of her parents' gentle reminders, Pat turned her homework in late and received a disappointing grade.

Her parents gave Pat the space to admit to herself that she had fallen victim to the unrealistic belief that she could talk on the phone practically all evening and still manage to do a good job on her homework. She realized that her parents had tried to help her make a better choice, and she was able to share with them her disappointment in the poor grade and to ask their help in planning her evenings. The next time she felt tempted to continue on the phone when she had a major homework assignment due the next day, she was able to tell her friend she would call her back after she finished her work.

We emphasize that Pat did not change her behavior because her parents let her experience the "natural consequences" of her actions. Without punishing her or disapproving of her, they had made every effort to help her by alerting her to the fact that she was making a decision that would have consequences she would not like.

∽

Adolescents will learn to make constructive choices and to pursue their choices in an effective manner only when you facilitate their desire to take care of themselves without demanding obedience. With smart love guidelines, you can show your adolescent that you want to help her to live a rewarding life. In other words, she will not see you as standing aside while she comes to harm or as being intrusive and overcontrolling.

How to Choose Appropriate Rules and Regulations
for Adolescents

Try not to impose too many rules and regulations on your adolescent. Limit the nonnegotiable matters to those relating to health and safety issues. If you make rules about how your adolescent should dress, what he should eat, and so on, you and your adolescent will likely become locked in a power struggle over just about everything. Your teen is more likely to see the sense of rules designed to keep him safe and healthy—such as being home by a certain time, not getting in the car with a friend who has been drinking, and avoiding controlled substances—because your teen will see the caring and logic in these limits, and will feel relieved to have protective boundaries, even if he grumbles a bit. Moreover, your rules will go over better if you try to involve your teen in the process of setting limits. It never hurts to ask a teen what time he thinks he should come in on a weeknight. Many teens will respond with reasonable curfews, and if they participate in establishing the rules, they will be happier following them.

If a teen breaks the health and safety rules you have established together, begin by asking him what course he thinks would be most constructive. Teens are developing the ability to think abstractly about issues, and they may surprise you by coming up with a solution you can accept. For example, one teen we know missed a curfew by an hour and did not call to tell his parents he would be late. When asked what he thought he could do in the future, he suggested that the next time he went out he would like to call home an hour or so before curfew as a way of reminding himself that the end of the evening was approaching.

Avoid Both Rewards and Punishments

Although you need to protect your adolescent from the consequences of his immaturity, try to avoid the pitfall of using either rewards or punishments to force your adolescent to make good choices. Children whose developmental needs are adequately satisfied already have an appetite for positive experiences and will not have self-destructive desires (although the exaggerated claims of their all-powerful selves can get them into trouble), so they do not need to be rewarded for behavior that is in their interest, or disciplined for behavior that they already know will make them unhappy. You can help the child who has acquired inner unhappiness by applying smart love principles, which will motivate him to make constructive choices. Attempting to control adolescents, or children of any age, with rewards or punishments actually interferes with the crucial process by which they establish stable secondary happiness and learn to regulate themselves effectively.

If your adolescent violates an important rule or regulation, try to restrict your response to establishing limits that will keep him safe and healthy. Try to avoid imposing punishments or restrictions that are unrelated to the lapse. For example, if your adolescent came in after curfew, don't deprive him of phone privileges. You'll only cast yourself as his adversary—as someone whose role is arbitrarily depriving him of things he likes. If he continues to have a hard time getting home on time, consider going yourself to pick him up. *As in his earlier years, your object is not to punish him for doing the wrong thing but to help him develop into the type of person who will be able to take good care of himself when you are not around.* He will be much more likely to attain this goal if he experiences you as an ally in his wish to make good decisions.

When adolescents make decisions based on getting rewards or avoiding punishments, they are trying to please (or not to disappoint or displease) you, but they are not listening to themselves. Like punishments, rewards are damaging because they do not promote the adolescent's budding recognition that the most satisfying secondary happiness is the product of making constructive choices and pursuing them well.

IF YOU PRACTICE THE PIANO, YOU CAN USE THE CAR

One father had always regretted that he had never had the opportunity to become proficient at a musical instrument. Therefore, when his daughter Beth's piano practicing became erratic after years of lessons, the father felt keenly disappointed. He hated to see Beth lose a skill she had worked so hard to develop. He made every effort to show her that there were good reasons to resume her previous level of practicing. But when Beth still did not practice consistently, her father tried to sustain her interest and progress by promising rewards. He offered her the use of the family car every Saturday night if she practiced every day of the week.

Beth really wanted the car on weekends, so she put in the practice time, but she began to experience music as the key to getting the car, rather than as an enjoyable activity in and of itself. She started to practice mechanically with an eye on the clock, and her playing lost its spontaneity and subtlety. The father's ear for music told him that his reward strategy was not working, so he consulted us. We agreed with his conclusion that rewarding Beth for practicing was counterproductive. We suggested that the father sit down with his daughter and acknowledge that the reward had not been a good idea because it was inducing her to practice when she didn't want to. We also recommended that he say that although he believed that studying piano was a wonderful opportunity, it was optional, and he wanted her to feel free to tell him if she wanted to stop her lessons.

Beth responded that actually she still enjoyed playing, but that there were now so many demands on her time that she found it hard to practice every day. She said she would like to continue her lessons, but she wondered if she could schedule a lesson every other week so that she could practice a little less often and still be prepared. With our encouragement, the father agreed to this arrangement. Beth continued to play and to make good progress. Her music remained an ongoing source of pleasure both for her and also for her family and friends.

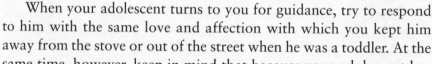

When your adolescent turns to you for guidance, try to respond to him with the same love and affection with which you kept him away from the stove or out of the street when he was a toddler. At the same time, however, keep in mind that because your adolescent has more opportunities to make decisions in your absence, there are more ways for him to make mistakes. Try to leave no room for your child to be swayed by his all-powerful self's message that he is immune to harm.

HELPING THE TEEN WHO WANTS TO BECOME SEXUALLY ACTIVE

A high school student named Tim told his parents that he had met a wonderful girl and thought he was falling in love. Over the next few months, he continued to share his feelings of floating on air. One evening he sat down with his parents and asked them their opinions about premarital sex. His parents had expected this and had called us to ask what to do. They asked him whether this was something he was thinking about, and he nodded. The parents explained why, in general, they thought it was better that people his age wait to have sex until they were older, but they added that they realized that sometimes teens felt very strongly that they didn't want to wait. Their son said that he probably belonged in the latter category.

His parents told him they were glad he was confiding in them, and that if he really was unwilling to wait, it was crucial that he always use a condom. They talked about the importance of preventing pregnancy. They reminded Tim about the realities of sexually transmitted diseases: There was always the chance that his girlfriend could be infected and not even know it; studies have shown that people do not always tell the truth when they know they are infected; and also blood tests, while worthwhile, are not always accurate.

Tim listened attentively. He agreed with his parents that an unwanted pregnancy and the potential threat of sexually transmitted disease were unacceptable risks. He concluded that he and his girlfriend should both get tested and then retested for sexually transmitted diseases, especially H.I.V., and, even if both tests were negative, that he would always use a condom. His parents said that sounded like a sensible decision.

Clearly, if the child has been in a setting where premarital sex was considered sinful or otherwise absolutely prohibited, the boy's parents would have responded differently. They would have made every effort to convince their son to adhere to the family's values.

Teens whose developmental needs have been adequately satisfied will take a cautious approach to other typical dangers that confront adolescents. Their all-powerful selves may tell them that no harm can befall them if they experiment with "harmless" drugs, but they will still want to discuss this assumption with their parents and will feel a superior type of pleasure when they allow themselves to be guided by their parents' experience and wisdom. If your adolescent has not regularly turned to you for this kind of guidance before, you can rewrite your relationship by consistently letting him know that you are willing to discuss issues with him in a nonjudgmental way.

Chores

The issue of which chores an adolescent should do, and when, is often at the center of parent-adolescent conflicts. Try to remember that even though your adolescent may be taller and stronger than you are, he is still in the process of growing up. His all-powerful self can sometimes convince him that he can do what he wants when he wants. This normal developmental trait means that you need to have realistic expectations about what is appropriate for your child's age. You also need to present the topic of chores diplomatically.

Certainly, it is reasonable to expect an adolescent to help out around the house, farm, or business. But given that there is always a lot of work to be done, try to go under the radar of your child's all-powerful self by asking him to select the chores he prefers. Just as some adults prefer cooking and others would rather do dishes, your adolescent has developed his own predilections, and there is every reason not to force him to do chores he really hates.

In addition, because adolescents can be unfocused and forgetful, help him succeed at getting chores done, and avoid creating situations in which he is likely to fail.

SMART LOVE CHANGES A FAMILY'S APPROACH TO CHORES

Every Sunday night Ned's parents posted the chores they expected the adolescent to do during the week, because they believed that teenagers should have an adult sense of responsibility. One of the chores was cleaning the basement. When one Friday came and went, and the basement remained filled with clutter, Ned's father said, "When are you going to clean the basement? It's Friday already!" Ned, who was heading out to a party, said, "I'll do it, don't worry." His father replied, "Well, if the basement isn't clean by tomorrow night at this time, you can't go out with your friends." Ned exploded and went out slamming the door. He spent the next day in a foul mood and worked on the basement angrily just before it was time to leave to meet his friends.

Concerned by the ongoing strife with their son, Ned's parents consulted us. As they became aware that Ned was in some ways still a child, even though he looked so adult, they changed their approach. Every Sunday they asked him which of a number of family chores he would like to do that coming week. The first week he chose mowing the lawn. When Friday came, and the lawn was still not mowed, his father said, "I see you haven't had time for the lawn yet. I have to pull some weeds out there tomorrow afternoon. How about keeping me company and mowing the lawn then?" Ned replied, "I really want to watch our team play baseball tomorrow afternoon. How about in the morning?" His father said that would be fine. The two spent a companionable morning working in the yard and concluded their efforts by going out for lunch.

Your Child: A Friend for Life

In the course of your child's adolescence, you undergo a developmental process of your own. Whereas for two decades you have had the pleasure of parenting your child, now for increasing periods your child can take care of herself. In the place of parenting pleasure, you increasingly experience the satisfaction of having a warm, loyal, enjoyable, and appealing friend. In addition, you have an ongoing sense of fulfillment because you have given your child the gift of a life of lasting inner happiness, which will endure regardless of the trials and tribulations she subsequently encounters. In that sense, your parenting satisfaction is as ongoing as your child's inner happiness.

Although your child may well turn to you for guidance after the adolescent years, it will be as a special friend and wise confidant. And you will increasingly find that you can rely on your child for friendship and advice.

We have emphasized that every parent is born with the potential to meet children's developmental needs, and every child is born ready and expecting to receive this special love. If you give your child the gift of a love guided by smart love principles, you will make a lifelong friend in the process. Your child will receive the supreme gift of enduring inner happiness and gain the additional blessing of having parents who become admiring and utterly devoted companions.

Smart Loving the Adolescent Who Suffers from Inner Unhappiness

The adolescent who has developed inner unhappiness will find it much more difficult to turn to his parents for advice or to accept the advice once it is given. He will not have grown up feeling the closeness to his parents that occurs when children can count on their parents to understand their point of view and meet their developmental needs. He also will have unknowingly developed needs to cause himself unhappiness and, as a result, he may welcome or even court danger.

Self-Destructive Behavior

Self-destructive behavior in teens—for example, dangerous risk-taking, substance abuse, eating disorders, failure at school, provoking other children's scorn or aggression—is often very perplexing to parents, who find it difficult to understand why their child, whom they have tried so hard to make happy, seems intent on harming himself. When parents can see that their child unknowingly needs self-destructive experiences to maintain his inner equilibrium, they can better comprehend why the child cannot simply stop his self-destructive behavior, and why punitive responses, such as restricting the child's privileges, will only make their child more, rather than less, likely to harm himself.

Parents who react to their child's self-destructive behavior by causing him further unhappiness (for example, by prohibiting the teen who crashed his new bike from playing after-school soccer), are mirroring the child's own needs to make himself unhappy. Parents who employ the principles of loving regulation demonstrate to their child both that they will do everything they can to keep him from harm, and also that they will never punish the child or withhold their love in the process of trying to protect him.

HELPING A RECKLESS FOURTEEN-YEAR-OLD STAY SAFE

The parents of fourteen-year-old Kelsey came to see us because their son was given to reckless behavior and had in the past broken bones biking and rollerblading. They were especially concerned because Kelsey had announced that he planned to take up skiing.

We helped his parents see that Kelsey's interest in skiing represented a combination of desires for constructive pleasure (the joy of being outside and exercising) and desires for unpleasant experiences (the unperceived wish to hurt himself). Kelsey's parents told him of their concern that his recklessness might get the upper hand when he was skiing and lead him to have a bad accident. They made an agreement with their son that they would take him to a nearby ski area on weekends if he would join a ski class. The ski class would serve the functions of helping him to improve his technique and of guaranteeing that he was guided by an expert's judgment about how fast and on what terrain he should be skiing. Kelsey agreed, and he managed to learn to ski without injuring himself.

PARENTS' SMART LOVE MAKES AN ENJOYABLE SUMMER POSSIBLE

Kim's parents consulted us because they became worried after they saw that she intended to spend her summer with friends who amused themselves by getting into trouble. Because Kim really enjoyed drawing, we suggested that the parents investigate summer art classes, collect brochures, and give them to their daughter with the comment that if she were interested, they would be delighted to help her enroll in the program of her choice.

At first Kim expressed no interest in any class. Subsequently, she showed some curiosity about a drawing class, but she made no move to follow through on signing up for the class. Her mother asked her daughter if she would like her to turn in the application the next day. Kim assented. The mother also offered to drop her daughter off at the art class on her way to work each morning. Kim had a busy and productive summer and improved her art skills so much that she attracted a lot of positive recognition from her classmates and teachers during the following school year. In addition, she made a new set of friends who shared her love of art.

Because her parents understood that Kim was unknowingly attracted to the destructive pleasure of spending time with out-of-control friends, they were undeterred by her initial reluctance to pursue the art class. Nor did they become angry with her or lecture her about the need to take responsibility for herself when she had difficulty following through and signing up for a class. Without pushing her so that she felt robbed of initiative, they gently directed her toward a summer organized by constructive rather than destructive pleasure.

Tough Love Harms the Unhappy Child

The most perplexing and distressing problems for parents are posed by adolescents who chronically and defiantly engage in delinquent behavior, such as drinking to excess, taking drugs, staying out all night, or skipping class. Although parents are often advised to turn to "tough love" to help their troubled teen, tough love only makes teens more unhappy and difficult.[6] The smart love principle of loving regulation will help keep your adolescent safe and also increase his desires for constructive pleasure.

The prescription for reforming difficult children known as *tough love* is an outgrowth of the popular view that treating these children too nicely will make them worse rather than better. According to this mode of caretaking, parents should refuse to help children extricate themselves from a predicament (for example, the advice would be, don't bail your teen out of jail). If the teen's antisocial behavior continues, parents are counseled to force their child out of the house until he reforms.

Those who advocate tough love measures tell the parents of troubled children (children who take drugs, skip school, steal, "talk back," are violent, or are just generally difficult to live with) to set forth strict, unconditional rules of acceptable behavior. If the child does not adhere to these demands, the parents are to mete out stern responses that range from withholding privileges to actually changing the locks in order to bar the child from entering the house. The notion behind the tough love approach is that parents who truly love their child should be uncompromising about refusing to be "manipulated" by him; the message is that it is preferable to lose the adolescent than to collude in his misbehavior by allowing him to continue to enjoy the security and comfort of home.

The tough love approach, in our view, is thoroughly wrongheaded and based on a faulty and pessimistic understanding of human nature. In practice, it has caused grievous unnecessary suffering to both teens and their parents. Tough love advocates assume that, by their nature, all children are driven to manipulate their parents in order to gratify forbidden desires, and that parents must be ever vigilant in order to deflect and defeat this manipulation. Thus parents are encouraged to be skeptical about the quality of their children's motives, even those motives that appear to be most positive and benign. Advocates of tough love argue that parents who permit refractory teens to enjoy the privileges of home are "enabling" teens to act out, and that when parents cease their "enabling" behavior and force teens to choose between antisocial behavior and their families, salvageable teens will ultimately choose their families. We have seen no evidence to support this conclusion. Children whose parents practice tough love experience their parents as negative, critical, and suspicious. Ironically, parents' suspicious, disapproving attitudes foster the very type of behavior they are trying to stamp out, because such parents are encouraging their children's needs to use unpleasant experiences to supply themselves with inner well-being.

Tough love is based on an extremely negative view of children's natural inclinations. When parents buy into this concept they become persuaded that in order to save their children from themselves, they must be prepared to sacrifice them. Advocates of tough love will tell parents that this willingness to sacrifice children in the service of reclaiming them is the embodiment of the highest and most selfless parental love.

Even when teens do not change in response to their parents' demands and the teens become lost to their families, tough love advocates believe that the parents have behaved appropriately. The tough love view is that the loss of their children only illustrates that parents had been "in denial" of the severity of their teens' problems and their own powerlessness to affect them.

THE TOUGH LOVE STANCE: WE ARE WILLING TO LET KEVIN KILL HIMSELF

A representative illustration of the harshness of tough love is the stance taken by the mother of a marijuana-smoking teen. She reported that by following the principles of tough love she was able to feel "acceptance" of the intractable nature of her son's difficulties and, as she put it, to "remind myself that I was powerless to stop my children from doping or smoking cigarettes or making bad grades." She told her son, "I'm going to give you a choice, and I'm doing it because I love you. Either be drug-free or get out of the house." In appraising this ultimatum, she concluded, "We had no guarantee that Kevin would ever want to get straight again. We had to be willing to let him kill himself with dope if he wanted to do that."[7]

Our argument is that the most serious drawback to the tough love approach is that it simply does not work. Externally imposed behavioral sanctions are no better at changing teens than they are at controlling the minds of citizens of repressive governments. At best, sanctions produce a fragile truce in the form of shallow cooperation or a smoldering, dissembling compliance; at worst, they result in open rebellion and defiance. External sanctions encourage teens to turn to unpleasant experiences and discourage them from basing their well-being on constructive pleasure. In contrast, the smart love principle is that *meaningful change occurs only when a child or adolescent actively and freely chooses constructive pleasure as representing the most desirable type of happiness.*

Why Smart Love Is More Effective Than Tough Love

Both smart love and tough love are based on the premise that parents must unequivocally avoid encouraging teenagers' delinquent behavior. According to tough love, any parental involvement with unreformed teens represents enabling behavior, and parents should be suspicious about their own tender feelings toward and wishes for closeness with their children. The smart love perspective is that when teens engage in self-destructive or antisocial behavior, these behaviors represent neither the sum total of the teens' only functional desires, nor even the wishes the teens intrinsically find most appealing. Therefore, we reject the tough love principle that the only way to change delinquent behavior is by using severe sanctions to force teens to comply with parents' directives. When parents withhold their love and support, they strengthen their adolescents' most self-destructive wishes.

The smart love view is that no matter how thoroughgoing teens' wishes for delinquent and self-destructive behavior appear to be, these needs *always* coexist with wishes for inner well-being based on constructive pleasure. These more constructive desires can be strengthened through positive experiences with parents (and, if clinically indicated, with a psychotherapist).

Given the popularity of the punitive approach to children captured in the old adage "Spare the rod and spoil the child," it is important to emphasize that smart love does not encourage irresponsible indulgence or counsel parents to ignore the existence or strength of some unhappy teens' self-destructive and antisocial wishes. This approach helps parents acknowledge their adolescent's problems and shows them how to use loving regulation to safeguard their child, while at the same time maintaining a loving and stable relationship with that child.

If you adopt the use of loving regulation with a troubled adolescent, you can make concrete efforts to help your child by making yourself available for discussions, driving him to and from school, assisting with homework, and, if indicated and feasible, arranging for psychotherapeutic help. You should also be aware that your teen may have aversive reactions to pleasure that will necessarily make the process of turning away from self-destructive and antisocial behavior an uneven one. With this understanding you can respond to your adolescent's inevitable lapses with renewed commitment. Try to avoid feelings of self-criticism and the painful conclusion that your supportive efforts are "enabling" your teen's misbehavior. If you persevere, your adolescent will have the meaningful and growth-promoting experience that even though you are aware of the strength of his need for sustaining his inner equilibrium through unpleasant experiences, you are also prepared to go to any lengths to support his desire for creating a genuinely positive type of inner happiness.

Chapter Nine

———————————— ❧ ————————————

Special Circumstances

In this chapter we discuss issues that, while important, do not apply to every family. These issues would be best served by an extended discussion, but given space limitations, we are able to provide only general guidelines.

Smart Loving Your Adopted Child

The literature on adoption generally assumes that even children who are adopted as newborns will experience significant harm if they never know their birth parents. But this assertion rests on a misconception of the nature of parenting. Parenting is an ongoing caregiving experience, not a one-time procreational act. When adoptive parents meet their child's developmental needs with informed, responsive love, she will develop the same stable, completely satisfying inner happiness as do children who live with their birth parents and whose emotional needs are met. That is, your adopted child will feel complete and completely loved. Adopted children whose developmental needs have been adequately satisfied do not feel deprived of their natural parents. They may wish to meet their biological parents, but they won't feel driven to do so in order to feel whole.

When and How to Tell Your Child She Was Adopted

There is probably no aspect of adoption about which there is so much disagreement and confusion as the issue of when and how to tell a child that she is adopted. The smart love guideline is *allow your child's developmental needs to determine the timing of your revealing the circumstances of your child's birth and adoption.* Contrary to popular belief, no harm will come to your child if she passes through her infant, toddler, and preschool years without knowing she is adopted. In fact, there are real benefits to waiting until her primary happiness is securely established before introducing the existence of a man and woman who gave birth to her and then decided to give her away.

Most children who were adopted as infants do not ask questions about where they were before they were born until they turn three. On the other hand, a child may be told by an older sibling or relative, or special circumstances—such as when there are marked differences in the child's appearance as compared to the rest of the family, there is an open adoption arrangement, or her parents adopt a new sibling— may cause the child to want information at a younger age.

The smart love guideline is *wait to tell your child she is adopted until she shows she is ready to hear this information by asking a pertinent question.* At that point she is less likely to feel that the information you provide is being dumped on her. For instance, one day a child may say, "Did I kick you a lot when I was in your tummy?" or "Did I cry when I was born?" At that point, parents should try to limit their answers to a simple statement of fact. For example, the mother might reply, "Well you didn't kick me because you were inside another woman who wanted us to be your parents after you were born." Parents should then wait to see how the child reacts. Many children will then wait months before they have any desire to follow up on this amazing information, while other children will demand more information immediately.

Sometimes children will show you that they are not ready to assimilate this emotionally charged information by totally ignoring the new facts. The day after his mother told him he was adopted and carefully explained the meaning of the word, one little boy said, "I remember when I was in your tummy. It was very dark in there." Fortunately, his adoptive mother realized that he was neither deaf nor afflicted with memory loss; he was simply too overwhelmed to face what he had been told. She didn't contradict him but simply responded, "Uh-huh." It was months before this child wanted to hear anything more about his birth parents or the fact of his adoption.

Obviously, when children are involved in an open adoption, they will know about their birth parents from an early age. Again, however, it is important not to force them to face facts before they are ready. If they refer to visiting birth parents as "Aunt and Uncle" or don't seem to want to know what "birth parent" means, don't correct or instruct them.

If children are allowed to regulate the flow of information about their history, once they are really ready to learn about their adoption, they will develop feelings of ownership and pride in their adoptive status. One little boy who showed no interest in knowing about his origins until after he turned four amazed his parents by proudly telling everyone in his kindergarten class that he was "'dopted" and had "extra" parents.

Parenting the Child Who Is Adopted After Infancy

Unlike parents who adopt infants, parents who adopt older children face the difficult task of taking into their lives and their hearts a child whose heart already belongs to someone else. These children can be very difficult to parent. They miss their birth parents and may be homesick for their place of origin. In addition, they may have acquired needs to make themselves unhappy and thus may react negatively to their adoptive parents' most tender, committed efforts.

When parents who adopt an older child understand that no matter how perfect their parenting, their child will sometimes react to their gifts, hugs, and efforts with rejection, anger, and upset, the parents will find it easier to avoid blaming themselves or concluding that their child doesn't love them or is ungrateful or spoiled. They will be better able to respond to their child's negative behavior with kindness and to allow her the time she needs to grow to appreciate their loving commitment. If parents use the smart love principle of loving regulation to contain the out-of-control behavior of the older adopted child, and if they offer their love without expecting or demanding affection in return, they will find that, over time, their child will come to adore them and accept them as her true parents.

"YOU'RE NOT MY REAL MOMMY!"

Three-year-old Suzie was removed from a drug-abusing mother and adopted by infertile parents who were utterly thrilled to have a child of their own at last. But in spite of their best efforts to make the child feel welcome and cared for, Suzie remained resentful and withdrawn. If they were on an outing, and her parents introduced her as their daughter, Suzie would immediately scream at the top of her lungs, "I'm not yours—I have a mommy already!" Suzie also rejected her parents' affectionate hugs and kisses. Utterly at a loss, the parents consulted us.

We could certainly understand why these parents felt so upset. We explained that the best way to forge a close and loving relationship with their daughter would be to avoid triggering her feelings of disloyalty to her birth mother. While the adult world knew that her birth mother had been an inadequate parent, Suzie, like all children, adored the first mother she had met as an infant. We suggested to the parents that instead of introducing the child as "our daughter," they simply say, "We would like you to meet Suzie."

Further, we advised the parents to offer Suzie hugs and kisses, but not to insist that Suzie respond, and not to make her feel guilty, bad, or alienated if she wasn't able to return their affection. The parents followed these and similar guidelines, and over the next year or two they saw Suzie become more accepting of her situation. They were thrilled when as a five-year-old, Suzie said proudly to a friend she had invited home, "I want you to meet the best mom and dad in the world!"

Nontraditional Families and the Romantic Phase

Earlier we have described the developmental milestone we call the relationship ideal (see page 167), which is established at the end of the romantic phase (see Chapter 6). For the rest of their lives children will draw on their identification with the way their parents treated them and the way they experienced their parents' relationship with each other.

Since the romantic phase and the relationship ideal are fundamental developmental milestones, parents often ask how children in single-parent families or other nontraditional families such as those consisting of a homosexual couple cope with the romantic phase. The children who live in these arrangements may not have the opportunity to experience the romantic phase in the company of two parents of different genders who are in love with each other. Nonetheless, all parents can help their children profit in whatever family configuration they find themselves.

If her parents are homosexual, a child will often choose one parent to relate to as though the parent were an opposite-sex parent. The child will try to get that parent to shower attention on her and will experience retaliation anxiety toward the other parent. The child's most crucial accomplishment in this phase is gradual acceptance that while she can cause her parents to love caring for her, she cannot control the way in which her parents satisfy their personal desires. Homosexual parents can effectively help their child to reach this developmental milestone if they are comfortable and positive about the child's time-limited need to relate to them in very different ways.

If you are a single parent it is important to remember that, in her mind, your child will nonetheless experience herself relating to a parent of the opposite sex. Try to offer your children opportunities to spend generous amounts of time with caring, interested, opposite-sex friends or relatives. If opposite-sex friends or relatives are not available, children may attach themselves to adults who cross their paths or create romantic scenarios in their imagination. One fatherless girl announced that she was going to marry the policeman who directed traffic on her corner. She brought him cookies every day and spent as much time as possible talking to him. A little boy whose mother had died imagined that she returned every night to kiss him good-night and that she sat reading in his room until dawn.

When single parents understand the nature and intensity of their children's romantic wishes, they will be better able to help their children to navigate the increased turbulence of a romantic phase that occurs in the context of parental death, separation, or divorce.

"YOUR SNORING MADE MOMMY LEAVE!"

Five-year-old Clyde, who was living with his father after his parents divorced, accused his father of driving his mother away with his loud snoring and also of being "glad" she was gone. The father consulted us about the best way to help his son with his raw feelings about the divorce. This parent's newfound understanding of the romantic phase allowed him to respond to his son's outburst without becoming hurt or defensive.

He said to Clyde, "I know how much you miss Mom and how much you want us back together. And I can hear that you sometimes feel it was all my fault—that I made Mom leave and I didn't care whether the divorce would make you unhappy. Actually," the father continued, "Mom and I both need to live apart for reasons that have nothing to do with you, but both of us know how unhappy the divorce makes you, and we hope you will keep telling us how you feel about it."

Clyde said, "Well, I hate divorce!"

His father responded, "I know you do, and I would too if I were you. But Mom and I will do our best to show you that the divorce doesn't have to mean a break in your relationship with either your mom or me."

The father realized that his son was interpreting the divorce as the father's way of retaliating against him for his romantic desires for his mother. The father made clear that he was understanding of his son's desire that his mother remain, and that he knew Clyde was angry at him. He then helped Clyde to become aware that while he lacked the power to affect his father's personal decision to be divorced from his mother, he could engage his father's responsive caring and cause his father to listen with steady love and understanding to his hurt, anger, and frustration. Equally important, although this father was very angry at his ex-wife, he made every effort to accept his son's love for her and to avoid burdening Clyde with his own resentments.

Children are harmed, not helped, when parents try to maintain a hollow charade of a relationship in order to preserve a conventional family configuration. If parents really dislike each other, it is better that they separate. Parents who are homosexual should not take a heterosexual partner in order to give their children the experience of a heterosexual family. If single men or women want the pleasure of committing themselves to care for a child but they do not have a spouse, they need not marry just for form's sake.

It is much worse for children to be in a traditional family filled with acrimony, indifference, dislike, or unhappiness than in a harmonious alternative arrangement. Children in nontraditional families with highly responsive and capable parents will be happier and more functional than children in traditional families where the marital relationship is corrosive, or where one of the parents is consistently grouchy and negative. Therefore, status discrimination is never warranted. The parenting capability of the single parent or homosexual couple should never be assessed by criteria that are any different from those applied to parents in traditional family arrangements.

How to Help the Child Who Has Problems Learning

As a category, learning problems comprise a complex set of behaviors that may include disruptive behavior, difficulty concentrating, and problems mastering one or more academic subjects. If your pediatrician says your child is healthy but your child is having difficulty in school, the likelihood is that the cause is inner unhappiness. Nonetheless, have your child tested by a specialist to rule out a physiological problem in the central nervous system.

In our clinical experience, which is supported by the relevant scientific literature, we have found that the majority of learning disorders, including attention deficit hyperactivity disorder (ADHD), are the result of inner unhappiness. The intelligence of children with inner unhappiness is frequently subordinated to their unperceived needs for causing themselves discomfort. In the presence of inner unhappiness, a child's intelligence can remain virtually intact (a child with a paralyzing fear of the dark may be a brilliant student), or it can be significantly compromised (an unhappy child who is physiologically normal may have difficulty learning to read or to add). Between these extremes, children's abilities to develop and exercise their intelligence to its fullest potential are often hampered to some extent by the presence of inner unhappiness. Examples are the child who excelled at written reports but could not think clearly in a testing situation, and the child who read three grades ahead but was convinced that he could not do math.

Whatever the cause, when children are having difficulty learning, the most effective response on the part of both parents and teachers is the same—a positive, stable, unpressured helping relationship. This type of support can be difficult to give. Parents understandably become anxious when their child struggles to learn because they want her to get the best education possible. And teachers who have an entire class to move along often lack the time or resources to spend much extra time with a few slower learners.

Children who are having trouble learning do best when a parent, older sibling, relative, friend of the family, teacher, or tutor sits with them, watches them work, and offers assistance as needed. The smart love guideline is *don't offer help if the child is struggling but making an effort, but also don't make the child who is having difficulty learn-*

ing beg for answers. If you step in and offer help when the child is still trying, the child will feel you are impatient with her slow pace and she will become even more intolerant of her own limitations. On the other hand, if you withhold answers, saying something like, "Look at it a little longer. I'm sure you can get it," or "You got this right yesterday. I'm sure you can get it now if you try," the child may stop feeling she is involved in a cooperative effort, and she may begin to feel as if she is in a power struggle with you over whether answers will be forthcoming.

Also, children who have difficulty learning should not be forced into tutoring sessions they hate. If your child resists, accept the refusal with good grace and try to find another time of day, a different tutor, or another means of teaching the material. Your first priority is to maintain your child's curiosity and joy in learning. Teaching her specific content is always secondary.

Because children love their parents more than anything or anyone in the world, parents can do a lot to help them when they have difficulty learning—if the parents can remain kind and supportive. If you find it necessary to consult professionals, such as reading or speech specialists, or your child is in a special education class, you should monitor the teaching process enough so as to make sure that your child is being treated gently and patiently. The most important test is whether your child generally likes the professional or teacher and is usually happy to attend sessions. If your child consistently complains or refuses to go, take her response seriously and find someone with whom she will enjoy working.

The Importance of Avoiding Brain-Altering Medications

Unlike the category of clinical epilepsy, which has a clearly identifiable neurological cause and is directly and positively affected by medication, there is no scientific evidence to indicate that the vast majority of difficulties in learning, concentrating, or sitting quietly are caused by a specific, identifiable brain lesion.[8] Most children who disrupt classrooms or develop problems learning and concentrating suffer from inner unhappiness, and their problems are best treated with a helping relationship and not with medication.

Although the notion of solving a problem by taking a pill can be very appealing, giving brain-altering chemicals such as Ritalin to children who disrupt their classrooms and/or have problems learning and concentrating will actually increase these children's inner unhappiness and make them less able to develop autonomous learning skills. Treatment with brain-altering chemicals such as Ritalin further undermines children's already shaky confidence in their capacities by giving them the message that their parents and other knowledgeable adults have concluded that there is something wrong with their brains. Children who are given this negative message will feel less in charge of their own minds, and their unperceived needs to create unpleasant experiences for themselves will increase. At best, medications may produce a drugged compliance, but the children will be further removed from the true goal of discovering that learning can be a source of pleasure and competence.

There are many convincing reasons to avoid giving brain-altering chemicals to children who exhibit behavior or learning problems:

- There is no conclusive evidence that the cause of the learning problems for which medication is prescribed is a physiological defect. With rare exceptions, it has never been shown that children who disrupt classrooms and/or have problems learning do so because their brains are damaged or abnormal.

- While there is a class of brain-altering drugs that can override the brain's functioning and force anxious or boisterous children to become more tractable, there is no scientific evidence that these medications have any positive long-term effect whatsoever on learning problems or problems with social adaptation.[9]

- On the other hand, it has been demonstrated repeatedly that every category of brain-altering medications—including stimulants such as Ritalin and amphetamines, as well as tranquilizing and antidepressant medications—have significant, harmful side effects in children. There appears to be no dose so small as to be free of the risk of producing injurious side effects, which include irreversible damage such as retardation of normal growth and tardive dyskinesia, an irreversible syndrome of tongue and facial tics.

• Brain-altering chemicals intensify a child's negative feelings about learning by interfering with the child's belief in her ability to regulate her own behavior. Drugs can cement the child's feeling of helplessness with regard to her life. She may experience her parents and the specialists they engage as having determined that she cannot be helped to govern herself.

Parents should not allow brain-altering medications to be prescribed for disruptive behavior except as a last (*and temporary*) resort when there is no other way to maintain the safety of the child or of others with whom the child comes in contact. Equally important, when these drugs cannot be avoided, they should be used only in combination with relationship-based therapy aimed not at assessment or social control but at helping the child discover that learning and cooperating can be a source of real pleasure. The only time we have ever used brain-altering medications in our practices was on a temporary basis with teenagers in an inpatient setting who were both suicidal and homicidal. The drugs were used in conjunction with around-the-clock, one-to-one child care staff and were the only means to control destructive impulses long enough so that the adolescents had a chance to establish a life-saving therapeutic relationship with their child care workers and psychotherapists.[10]

There are solid scientific grounds for opposing the most common therapeutic rationales for prescribing brain-altering drugs: simply to make children more tractable, and to save money on more time-consuming and expensive professional interventions, such as learning specialists or psychotherapy.

In addition to the significant risk of producing serious side effects, brain-altering chemicals interfere with the search to find the true causes of children's unhappiness. We emphasize that even when brain-altering chemicals do help regulate children's disruptive behavior, behavioral restraint is the only benefit, and the child pays a high price for it. As we have said, children come to experience their minds as in need of external control. Drugs undermine the child's need to feel she herself has chosen to give up the problem behavior and take control of her life. There is all the difference in the world between a fidgety child who remains in her seat in the classroom because she is drugged into tranquillity and the child who remains in her seat because she has been helped to feel happier with herself and to derive more enjoyment from the learning process. In other words, brain-altering chemicals are harmful to children and adolescents even when the drugs seem to be working by causing them to appear markedly more compliant. A far more effective solution to learning and behavior problems is to offer children a helping relationship that will allow them to discover and pursue the pleasure of owning and using their own minds.

∾

We regret that not all specialized topics of interest to parents could be included in this chapter. Some of the topics we couldn't address because of space limitations are the sexually and physically abused child, the child with a severe speech disturbance, the retarded child, the accident-prone child, the overly aggressive child, the overly fearful child, the antisocial child, the child who hallucinates and is delusional, and the autistic child. The parents of these children can draw on the smart love guidelines described throughout this book. You will help these children most effectively if you satisfy their need for your love and admiration and foster their desire to feel in charge of themselves. Try not to focus exclusively or even primarily on changing their behavior. In other words, you will help these children fulfill their own inborn wishes for happiness and competence if you facilitate their constructive desires and respond with loving regulation to any destructive or dysfunctional behaviors.

Afterword

In most areas of our lives we make momentous decisions only after much deliberation, and even then we may experiment a bit to make sure we have chosen the correct path. Parents, however, are faced every day with a multitude of vital decisions that come thick and fast. Because parents can't see the final result of their choices until their children have reached adulthood, they find it difficult to evaluate the quality of their responses, and they worry about whether they are making the right choices. Some examples of the dilemmas parents face on a daily basis are: Do we feed our baby whenever she wants or put her on a schedule? Do we make our toddler share and stop her from grabbing, or do we let her outgrow these tendencies on her own? Do we discipline our child when she is disobedient or destructive, or is there a kinder method to guide her? Do we impose consequences on children who don't do their homework or pick up their room, or do we help them do chores and homework? Should we respond to the difficult adolescent with tough love or tender love?

We wrote *Smart Love* to help you with the thousand and one decisions you have to make as parents. Because smart love principles remain the same whether you are parenting a newborn or an adolescent, *Smart Love* can be your companion and helpmate at every step on your child's journey to adulthood.

The choices parents make are particularly tough at moments when their child is difficult or unhappy and, especially, if their child is chronically difficult or unhappy. If you have a problematic child of any age, we have also written this book for you. By following smart love principles you can help your child recapture her birthright of inner happiness.

By using the smart love guidelines you can provide your child with a reliable, enduring core happiness that is unwavering even in the face of life's unavoidable disappointments and misfortunes. We emphasize that this accomplishment is made possible by establishing a pleasurable relationship and not by frustrating your child's needs or depriving her of your attention. Your child's inner well-being rests on her certain knowledge that she has caused you to love caring for her. Of all the gifts you can give your child, this is the most important, because it is the foundation of all happiness and goodness and the shield against self-caused unhappiness.

If you choose to use the principles of smart love, you will have more confidence that you know what to do every day and every year to sustain and nurture your child's emotional well-being. One reason that you can rely on smart love to guide your daily decisions about your child is that smart love considers childhood from your child's point of view. In fact the entire smart love approach is built on this unique perspective. Smart love establishes a more realistic, less pressured timetable for your child's emotional development; introduces you to new developmental milestones and shows you how to help your child reach them; and offers you a way to shield your child from the consequences of her immaturity without resorting to permissiveness, disciplinary measures, or rewards—all of which are counterproductive. With the help of smart love guidelines, you can raise a successful, well-regulated, and, most important, a truly happy child while loving and enjoying her to your heart's content.

Notes

1. This new view of human nature is comprehensively presented in our academic book, *Intrapsychic Humanism: A Comprehensive Introduction to a New Psychology and Philosophy of Mind* (Chicago: Falcon II Press, 1990). We chose the name *Intrapsychic Humanism* because it embodies the two most fundamental principles that shape this new psychology: (1) the source of the only sustainable and truly fulfilling human happiness is *humanistic* in that it is entirely enfolded in human relationships, most especially, the parent-child relationship; and (2) this happiness originates in the child's empirical, demonstrable certainty (termed *intrapsychic pleasure* in our first book, and *primary happiness* in the present book) that she has the ability to elicit her parents' loving responses to her developmental needs. Intrapsychic humanism should not be confused with the humanistic psychology that has evolved in American academia, because we do not render human nature in terms of an assumed tendency toward self-actualization that does not depend on relationship experience (most important, the parent-child relationship).

2. We have changed the names and other identifying information of all individuals to protect their identities.

3. Mary Taylor Previte, "What Will They Say at My Funeral?," *The New York Times,* August 7, 1994, Section E, p. 17.

4. The study that is the basis for many claims for the existence of inborn personality, the Minnesota Twins Study (Bouchard et al., "Sources of Human Psychological Differences: The Minnesota Study of Twins Reared Apart" [*Science*, October 12, 1990, p. 223]), actually provides more evidence for the acquired nature of personality. In spite of the fact that the twins are described as "reared apart," the twins in the study had lived together for up to four years before they were separated (the mean length of time the twins were together was eight months). In addition, many of the twins were reunited before the testing took place (two of them lived apart for only six months). Many claims have been made for personality-determining genes, but so far all of the studies have fundamental problems and none of these findings have been borne out.

5. Arlene Eisenberg, Heidi Murkoff, and Sandee Hathaway, *What to*

Expect the First Year (New York: Workman Publishing, 1989), p. 275.

6. This critique of tough love is adapted from our article "It's Not Tough, It's Tender Love," *Chicago Medicine* 94, no. 7 (1991): pp. 10-16; reprinted in *Child Welfare* 71 (1992): pp 369-377.

7. Pauline Neff, *Tough Love: How Parents Can Deal with Drug Abuse* (Nashville: Abingdon Press, 1982), pp. 93, 98.

8. The fact remains that there is no established, testable, diagnosable syndrome for which Ritalin and other mind-altering drugs are indicated, which means that they are given symptomatically and anecdotally for a grab-bag of behaviors that may appear similar but have no demonstrated identity (see *The Physician's Desk Reference,* 1997 edition). Similarly, although these substances are often prescribed by doctors without psychiatric training, they are being prescribed for a psychosocial problem, which these doctors are not trained to diagnose or treat, and not for an established medical disorder. Also, the list of contraindications would rule out the vast majority of children for whom these drugs are prescribed. For Ritalin these contraindicated behaviors include anxiety, tension, tics, agitation, fatigue states, and emotional instability (*Physician's Desk Reference*). In addition, there is no recognized scientific trial that establishes Ritalin's therapeutic usefulness, so its many potential side effects are especially appalling. These include convulsions (in the presence of a normal EEG and a normal neurological history), insomnia, agitation, psychosis, and growth inhibition. Also, there is experimental evidence that Ritalin causes liver tumors in mice.

9. Larry S. Goldman et al., "Diagnosis and Treatment of Attention-Deficit/ Hyperactivity Disorder in Children and Adolescents," *JAMA* 279, no. 14, April 8, 1998, p. 1103.

10. Martha Heineman Pieper and William J. Pieper, "Treating Violent 'Untreatable' Adolescents: Applications of Intrapsychic Humanism in a State-Funded Demonstration Project," in Katherine Tyson, *New Foundations for Scientific Social and Behavioral Research* (Boston: Allyn and Bacon, 1995), pp. 455-473.

Glossary

All-powerful self   The all-powerful self is your child's temporary source of secondary happiness based on the illusion that the child can do and have everything. By the end of adolescence, the all-powerful self should be replaced by the competent self. Children who do not have the good fortune to have their developmental needs adequately satisfied never outgrow the all-powerful self.

Aversive reaction to pleasure   The reaction to and interference with moments of enjoyment caused by acquired (though unrecognized) desires for unpleasant experiences or destructive pleasure. Aversive reactions to pleasure can be mild or severe, but they occur only in individuals who have acquired needs to make themselves unhappy.

Caregiving lapse   Caregiving lapses are aberrations that occur when parents who are normally able to respond adequately and lovingly to their children's developmental needs pursue personal aims when their children need parenting attention. Because these parents do not have frequent caregiving lapses, these episodes do not interfere with children's emotional development.

Competent self   The source of secondary happiness based on the capacity to make constructive choices and pursue them well. It develops as a result of parents' smart love.

Discipline   An attempt to regulate unwanted behaviors by attaching unpleasant consequences to them, including not only punishments, but also natural consequences, lectures, disapproval, and time-outs and other ways of isolating children. Also see Loving regulation.

Encouragement   The encouragement of children's wishes for constructive pleasure is helpful. Unlike rewards, encouragement is not contingent on any particular outcome: The child gets the encouragement whether or not she attains or even tries for a given goal. Also see Rewards.

Identification   The conscious or unconscious attempt to become like parents or others who have emotional significance in the child's life. When children's developmental needs are adequately satisfied, their identifications are freely chosen; in children whose developmental needs go unmet, identifications are always involuntary.

Independence   True independence is freedom from the need to use everyday satisfactions as a source of inner happiness. Independence is not simply separation from parents. True independence is made possible only by parenting that adequately satisfies children's developmental needs.

Inner unhappiness   When children's developmental needs are not adequately met, their inner happiness is unstable. Unstable inner happiness is the same as inner unhappiness. Children's inner happiness becomes chronically unstable when it remains vulnerable to the ups and downs of everyday life and when children acquire unrecognized desires for a substandard type of inner happiness, which are equivalent to desires to cause themselves to feel unhappy.

Loving regulation   Loving regulation is the smart love approach to children's out-of-control behaviors. Loving regulation effectively contains children's out-of-control behaviors without coercing children with rewards or adding any type of unpleasantness. Loving regulation never interrupts children's experience of being loved, admired, and respected by their parents, and it is the only way to regulate children's immature behavior without diminishing their primary happiness. All disciplinary measures, including time-outs, disapproval, and restrictions and other punishments, are incompatible with loving regulation and are counterproductive and harmful to children. Loving regulation can be used by any adult who is responsible for children, for example, parents, teachers, coaches, pediatricians, and babysitters.

Normality   True normality is an attainable condition of enduring inner happiness that is not interrupted or threatened by the ups and downs of daily life. Normality is usually defined incorrectly in terms of typical self-experiences and behaviors, and, as a result, it often includes feelings and behaviors that are really signs of a preventable and treatable inner unhappiness.

Parenting desires   Parenting desires are aimed at helping children to acquire a lasting inner happiness and an abiding sense of competence.

Permissiveness   The failure to impose necessary regulations on children's behavior.

Personal desires   All motives parents have that are not in the service of responding to their child's developmental needs.

Personality   Personality is the collection of acquired, patterned ways of evaluating and responding to life experiences. The most important characteristic of the personality of the child whose developmental needs have been adequately met will be an acquired inner happiness that is separate from and impervious to life's ups and downs. Personality, in the sense of rigid, fixed response patterns, occurs only in children whose developmental needs have not been satisfied. In contrast to the popular view, personality traits are not inborn.

Primary happiness   The inner well-being produced by children's inborn convictions that they have the ability to cause their parents to love meeting their developmental needs.
    Unstable primary happiness   From birth to age three, primary happiness is unstable because it is conditional on parents' moment-to-moment ability to respond to children's needs for caregiving attention, or on substitute gratifications.
    Stable primary happiness   Stable primary happiness stems from children's deep and unshakable certainty that they have caused their parents' unconditional love of responding adequately and generously to their needs. Stable primary happiness is not dependent on children's moment-to-moment abilities to effect a given

parenting response. Primary happiness becomes stable when children are about three years of age.

Relationship ideal   Children's identifications with their parents' and other significant adults' ideals and commitments in all types of relationships, including romantic love, friendship, and parenting. These identifications will determine whether a child will grow up to have mutually enjoyable close relationships or conflictual, unrewarding relationships.

Retaliation anxiety   A fear of the same-sex parent that occurs in the romantic phase, between three to six years of age, and is caused by children's illusional conviction that they are competing with the same-sex parent for an exclusive relationship with the opposite-sex parent, and that the same-sex parent will retaliate against them.

Rewards   A technique for managing children's behaviors by granting privileges or items in exchange for some desirable behavior. Rewards interfere with rather than advance children's abilities to base their secondary happiness on the ability to make constructive choices and pursue them well. Also see Encouragement.

Romantic phase   Children between three and six years of age wish to have the same relationship with opposite-sex parents that they perceive their same-sex parents to have. The children's idea of their parents' relationship is very nonspecific. They imagine a relationship that includes elements of possessiveness, affection, and exclusivity.

Secondary happiness   Inner well-being that stems from everyday activities.
   Unstable secondary happiness   Secondary happiness that is outcome-dependent. Secondary happiness remains unstable to some degree until the end of adolescence. Also see All-powerful self.
   Stable secondary happiness   Stable secondary happiness results from satisfying children's developmental needs. Stable secondary happiness stems from making good choices and pursuing them well and is unaffected by the ups and downs of everyday life. Stable

secondary happiness is not securely established until the end of adolescence. Also see Competent self.

Separation anxiety   Separation anxiety is unhappiness that appears near the end of the first year when infants react to a parent's departure as though it signaled the end of all earthly security and contentment. Separation anxiety is a developmental achievement that results from the child's increasing recognition of the importance of the unique pleasure (primary happiness) she feels in her parents' presence.

Smart love   An approach to caring for children that has as its goal the establishment of a strong and stable inner happiness, which in turn will allow each child to reach his or her fullest potential. Parents who use smart love guidelines discover a warm and effective alternative to rewards and punishments for regulating a child's behavior and encouraging a child's emotional growth (see Loving regulation). Smart love encourages parents to view the world through the eyes of the child, and the smart love guidelines are tailored to each stage of the child's development.

Stranger anxiety   Although it is manifested as unhappiness, stranger anxiety is actually a developmental achievement that results from the infant's newfound capacity to recognize and prefer her parents' faces over all others. Whereas previously the infant was outgoing, relating well and happily to strangers, around the age of eight months, unfamiliar faces may make her lower lip begin to tremble, and she may actually burst into tears until a parent's beloved face reappears.

Symptoms   Symptoms are persistent unwanted, unregulated behaviors, thoughts, and feelings. Symptoms can be divided into two categories: unregulated behaviors, thoughts, and feelings that are typical, and those that are more severe than average. Typical symptoms of inner unhappiness are popularly considered normal expressions of human nature. Whether typical or severe, symptoms are indications of the presence of inner unhappiness, which occurs when children's developmental needs are not fully satisfied. Therefore, the misery caused by unwanted behaviors is both preventable and curable.

Index

Rage
distinguished from anger, 56
unhappiness-caused, 50, 56-57
Reactive identification, 60-61
Recklessness, 216-217
Relationship ideal, 167-168, 225
defined, 240
Relationships, inner unhappiness and,
48-49
Responsibility, distinguished from
cause, 42-43
Restrictions, counterproductiveness of,
9
Retaliation anxiety, 164
defined, 240
Returning to work, after childbirth,
86-93
Rewards
avoiding, 210-211
case example of, 211-212
coercive nature of, 71
defined, 240
Ritalin
contraindications to, 236
disadvantages of, 230-232
Romantic phase, 160
case examples of, 159, 161, 163,
164-165, 166
child's point of view in, 161-165
in children with inner unhappiness,
175-177
and competent self, 165
defined, 240
in nontraditional families, 225-227
resolution of, 165-167

Schizophrenia, 50
School
fear of, 195-196
hurt feelings from, 151-152
language at, 150-151
older children in, 179-181
older children's problems in,
195-197
reports from, 153-154
responsibilities at, 181
rules at, 150
socialization at, 150

starting, 147-148
for unhappy child, 174-175
Secondary happiness, 3, 179
in adolescents, 108, 201-204
defined, 240
development of, 107-112
sources of, 4-5
stable, 3, 201-204, 240-241
unstable, 240
Self
all-powerful, 4, 46, 109-113,
202-203, 207-208, 212, 237
competent, 4, 165, 203, 237
Self-awareness
development of, 57
types of lack of, 57-58
Self-discipline
absence in children, 6
fostering, 10
Self-esteem, 48
Separation, coping with, 148-149
Separation anxiety, 6, 7
case example of, 85
defined, 241
infantile, 84-85
Seuss, Dr., 29
Sexual activity, communicating about,
212-213
Sharing, 133-134
case example of, 134
toddlers' dislike for, 134-137
Shyness, 171
case example of, 171-172
unhappiness-caused, 24
Sleep
infant's inability to, 98-99
teaching infant to, 81-82
toddlers and, 126-128
Smart love
of adolescents, 201-221
of adopted child, 222-225
of baby, 74-100
caregiving lapses and, 27-28
case examples of, 64
and constructive pleasure, 62
defined, xv-xviii, 241
importance of, 1-2
of learning disabled, 228-229

About the Authors

Martha Heineman Pieper, Ph.D., is a psychotherapist who works with children and parents. A Phi Beta Kappa graduate of Radcliffe College, she earned her doctorate at the University of Chicago. William J. Pieper, M.D., is a child psychiatrist and psychoanalyst on the staff of Rush Presbyterian–St. Luke's Hospital in Chicago. His B.S. and M.D. degrees are from the University of Illinois. The Piepers' decades of experience as professionals and their pathbreaking research into the causes and effects of children's inner happiness form the foundation for this book. They are the experts on emotional well-being for the popular site www.babycenter.com. Parents of five, they live in Chicago, Illinois.